THE DREAM LIFE OF CITIZENS

THE DREAM LIFE OF CITIZENS

Late Victorian Novels and the Fantasy of the State

Zarena Aslami

Fordham University Press
New York   2012

Copyright © 2012 Fordham University Press

All rights reserved. No part of this publication may be reproduced, stored in a retrieval system, or transmitted in any form or by any means—electronic, mechanical, photocopy, recording, or any other—except for brief quotations in printed reviews, without the prior permission of the publisher.

Fordham University Press has no responsibility for the persistence or accuracy of URLs for external or third-party Internet websites referred to in this publication and does not guarantee that any content on such websites is, or will remain, accurate or appropriate.

Fordham University Press also publishes its books in a variety of electronic formats. Some content that appears in print may not be available in electronic books.

Library of Congress Cataloging-in-Publication Data

Aslami, Zarena.
   The dream life of citizens : late Victorian novels and the fantasy of the state / Zarena Aslami.
      p.   cm.
   Includes bibliographical references and index.
   ISBN 978-0-8232-4199-6 (cloth : alk. paper)
   1. Politics and literature—Great Britain—History—19th century. 2. English fiction—19th century—History and criticism. 3. Schreiner, Olive, 1855–1920. Story of an African farm. 4. Hardy, Thomas, 1840–1928. Woodlanders. 5. Gissing, George, 1857–1903. Odd women. 6. Grand, Sarah. Heavenly twins. 7. State, The, in literature. 8. Social problems in literature. 9. Afghanistan—In literature. I. Title. II. Title: Victorian novels and the fantasy of the state.
PR878.P6A85 2012
823'.8093581—dc23

2011040616

Printed in the United States of America
14 13 12 5 4 3 2 1
First edition

Contents

	Acknowledgments	vii
	Introduction: The Lyricism of the State	1
1.	An Imperial Origin Story: Aloof Rule in Schreiner's *The Story of an African Farm*	26
2.	"Rather a Geographical Expression Than a Country": State Fantasy and the Production of Victorian Afghanistan	45
3.	The Rise of the State as a Sympathetic Liberal Subject in Hardy's *The Woodlanders*	85
4.	The Space of Optimism: State Fantasy and the Case of Gissing's *The Odd Women*	109
5.	Hysterical Citizenship in Grand's *The Heavenly Twins*	131
	Coda	161
	Notes	163
	Bibliography	171
	Index	183

Acknowledgments

I have many people and institutions to thank for their support, inspiration, and generosity during the process of writing this book. First, my thanks go to Lauren Berlant, Elaine Hadley, and Elizabeth Helsinger for their advice and mentorship of this project in its dissertation stage and beyond. Hilary Strang has been an invaluable and untiring reader and interlocutor of this project in its many life forms. I am also grateful to Emily Barman, Jamie Franklin, Hana Layson, Mary Lass Stewart, and Carrie Yury for their encouragement and humor. At the University of Chicago, as a graduate student and later in the Society of Fellows, I benefited from the questions and comments of Samuel Baker, Katherine Biers, Homi Bhabha, Bill Brown, James Chandler, Virginia Chang, Andrew Hebard, Neville Hoad, Aeron Hunt, Benjamin Lazier, Saree Makdisi, Curtis Marez, Michael Milner, Michael Murrin, Steve Pincus, Lawrence Rothfield, Jonathan Sachs, Rebecca Zorach, and others to whom I apologize for not including them here.

I also wish to thank my Michigan State University colleagues and friends, Jennifer Fay, Ellen Pollak, and Judith Stoddart, without whose incisive comments and advice the book would not have taken its final form. The (Im)Morrill Writing Group, Eng-Beng Lim, Lloyd Pratt, Karl Schoonover, and Jennifer Williams, kept me going through the final stages. Stephen Arch, Ilana Blumberg, Salah Hassan, Scott Juengel, Ellen McCallum, Scott Michaelsen, Justus Nieland, Patrick O'Donnell, and Robin Silbergleid helped me in crucial ways to complete this project. For his advice and friendship, I am indebted to Aimé Ellis, whose memory I cherish. Nancy Armstrong, Brian Aslami, Lauren Goodlad, Daniel Hack, Mary-Catherine Harrison, Ivan Krielkamp, Sarah Winter, and the reviewers of the manuscript helped me turn a manuscript into a book and a much better one than it might have been. I also wish to thank Helen Tartar at Fordham University Press, along with Thomas Lay, Eric Newman, and others at the Press who contributed their time and expertise to this project.

I have presented earlier, partial versions of the book's chapters to the wonderfully helpful members of the Midwest Conference on British Studies, the National Conference on British Studies, the Midwest Victorian Studies Association, the North American Victorian Studies Association, and the Modern Language Association. Thanks go to the individuals in those audiences who asked me to clarify and refine my ideas. I also thank Derek Sayer and Yoke-Sum Wong for inviting me to the Oxford Discussion Group on the State. The International Studies & Programs, the College of Arts and Letters, and the Department of English at Michigan State funded my participation in that unique event.

Financial support for this project also came in the form of the Rosenthal Foundation Dissertation Fellowship (The University of Chicago) and government-sponsored student loans. As a Harper Postdoctorate Fellow in the Society of Fellows (The University of Chicago), I received a teaching leave that enabled me to keep writing. Likewise, generous support in the form of teaching leaves from the Department of English at Michigan State allowed me to complete the manuscript. The Department of English and the College of Arts and Letters at Michigan State also provided a subsidy that aided the publishing process.

Chapter 3 was previously published as "The Rise of the State as a Sympathetic Liberal Subject in Hardy's *The Woodlanders*," in *Novel*, Vol. 42, issue 1 (Spring 2009): 62–85. Copyright 2009, Novel, Inc. It is reprinted here by permission of the publisher, Duke University Press. An earlier version of Chapter 4 appeared in *Victorian Studies* vol. 47, issue 1 (Autumn 2004): 55–85. Full credit is given to Indiana University Press as publisher. Thank you to the editors of these journals for all their work in bringing my writing to print and to the presses for allowing the inclusion of the materials here.

Finally, I wish to thank Mark, Sadie, and Alexander. They know why. I dedicate this book to my parents, Janice and M. Azim Aslami, to whom, quite simply, I owe the greatest thanks.

Introduction

The Lyricism of the State

It has become commonplace to think of the nation in terms of fantasy, but what about its less glamorous, less sentimentally charged other: the state? Following Benedict Anderson, literary and cultural scholars have written extensively about the affective obligations of the nation form and the role that fantasy plays in citizenship. Anderson's crucial intervention, of course, was to encourage his readers to move away from dismissing nationalism as ideology. Used reductively, the concept of ideology can connote delusion and imply that an actual reality lurks behind its veiling effects. Instead, Anderson argued that nationalism be thought of as a cultural artifact that is neither true nor false, but which has a unique structure that rewards attentive analysis. More specifically, he proposed that the nation be thought of as a kind of community mediated through the imaginations of all of its members. In focusing on the imagination in this way, Anderson inspired studies of the nation to use the concepts of psychoanalysis to try to understand the psychic mechanisms that attend personal and collective processes of national identification. After Anderson, it now seems intuitive to claim that national belonging is an affective affair. But what about the state? Can we think of it as a subject of feeling, as well? This book argues that late Victorian realist novels certainly did. They often framed the state in affective terms, dramatizing the feelings and fantasies of a culture that was increasingly optimistic about the state's capacity to intervene on behalf of its citizens.

Aside from a few significant studies, the state has been more or less ignored as an object of psychoanalytic inquiry.[1] The state is instead most often folded into studies of the nation as the forlorn tag hanging on the back of the term "nation-state." When literary and cultural studies scholars do address the state as a separate formation, they frequently refer to it as the legal domain of citizenship, the material practices of administration, and the coercive apparatuses of the military and the police. In such works, one could say that the state seems to function as the infrastructure to the superstructure of the nation. It determines the nation in the last instance, but it is not itself invested with affect. Or, the state appears as the manifest content to the latent existence of the nation. Its operations and experiential effects on human subjects are all too coherent, physical, and unambiguous, while those of the nation are irrational, symbolic, and contradictory. In critical and common sense thinking, we could say that the nation runs warm, while the state runs cool. For those who are happily included, the nation feels personal and collective—internal and essential to one's sense of self, yet fundamentally connecting one to many unseen others. It provides recognition. In contrast, even for those included within the nation, the state can feel impersonal and isolating—external and at odds with one's sense of self. In its punitive mode, it cuts one off from others. In its regulatory mode, it denies individuality and lumps everyone into the same group, doling out serving after serving of painful misrecognition.

Perhaps the state is not the object of psychoanalytically informed critiques precisely because it seems so obviously fantasmatic in this Kafkaesque regulatory mode of primal horror. Consider Michel Foucault's critique of political science and state-focused Marxism in his 1978 lecture "Governmentality." Foucault argued that scholars in both camps tended either to cast the state as a kind of actor in a human tragedy, awash with affect and bristling with immediacy, creating what he pithily alluded to as the "lyricism of the *monstre froid*," or they pared its numerous practices down into a limited set of functions (1991, 103). Both of these tendencies posit the state as the origin of power and thus, for Marxists, the site of political contest. Foucault famously countered that the state is neither unified nor individual. Nor is it merely the amalgam of a certain set of functions. He ultimately suggested that the state was not even that important to a study of how power *really* works.

As these shifts from a Marxist focus on the state to a Foucauldian emphasis on the diffusion of power to an Andersonian view of nationalism as cultural artifact should make clear, the state goes in and out of style as an object of critical attention.[2] Taking inspiration from Foucault especially, Victorian studies scholars have examined nineteenth-century British culture in light of disciplinary and regulatory procedures that did not emanate from the state alone, such as those found in the domains of education, sanitation, and public health. For example, Mary Poovey's *Making a Social Body* shows how state and non-state institutions participated in constructing a new paradoxical theory of personhood that, borrowing from Foucault, she calls disciplinary individualism. Here power-bearing institutions shape individuals who assert their freedom by willfully submitting to a variety of external authorities. Lauren Goodlad's *Victorian Literature and the Victorian State* is an exception to the Foucauldian turn away from the state. Her study focuses on the complex and often incoherent practices and discourses of nineteenth-century liberal government. But, perhaps because of Foucault's injunction to look away from the state and his dismissal of people's cathexis to it, Victorian studies scholars have yet to analyze the idea of the state enacted by these nineteenth-century practices or the feelings such an idea incited. More specifically, they have yet to consider what kind of person came into being in late-nineteenth-century Britain not only because of disciplinary power and governmentality, but also by virtue of how that person imagined the state as a primary agent in specific scenarios. This oversight is striking because, as I argue in the following chapters, late Victorian writers were often extremely interested in, and usually anxious about, how people imagined the state and their relationship to it.

In this book, I make the case for thinking about the production of state fantasy. While the state and the nation are not equivalent forms and thus require different modes of critical approach, my inquiry is nevertheless informed by studies of national fantasy. It is also motivated by Foucault's provocative if undeveloped critique of the lyricism of the state. Rather than move away from instances where the state is personified, mythicized, or lyricized, I examine them and ask what appears to be at stake in writers' accounts of this phenomenon. By state fantasy, I mean a two-part psychic and linguistic process familiar to us today: the packaging of what are, in fact, contradictory and often incongruous practices, discourses, institutions, and administrators into a coherent, knowable entity, commonly referred to as "the State" with a big "S," and the simultaneous investment of this entity with person-like qualities. Political scientist Timothy Mitchell has noted that scholarly discourse, even the kind that is devoted to deconstructing the self-evidence of the state, tends to reproduce this self-evidence through the act of analysis and, I would add, the rhetorical performance of referring to "the state" (1999, 76). How then do we analyze state fantasy without reproducing one of its most effective means of power? My approach to literary texts in the following chapters suggests one possibility. My hope is that this book, taken as a whole, demonstrates the critical imperative to illuminate state fantasy, even if one's efforts to detach from it are only momentary and bound to fail. In fact, that we cannot fully escape state fantasy tells us how fundamental an idea of the state is to modern psychic lives.

The packaging and personifying of the state has specific meanings at specific times, which literature is especially adept at registering. In liberal cultures, how citizens fantasize about the state reveals the contours of historically possible subjectivities. After all, fantasies about state power lie at the foundation of classical liberal theory. For example, John Locke's *Two Treatises on Government* (1689) conceives the historically emergent bourgeois individual in relation to a proper state that does not appropriate his goods, but rather protects his ownership of them. We can find instances of modern state fantasy in literature, starring a person-like "State," as early as the mid-Victorian period. Skimpole in Charles Dickens's *Bleak House* (1853), for instance, engages in state fantasy when he explains to Esther why he accepted money from the police detective Bucket in exchange for Jo:

> If it is blameable in Skimpole to take the note, it is blameable in Bucket to offer the note—much more blameable in Bucket, because he is the knowing man. Now, Skimpole wishes to think well of Bucket; Skimpole deems it essential, in its little place, to the general cohesion of things, that he *should* think well of Bucket. The State expressly asks him to trust to Bucket. And he does. And that's all he does! (886)

In this passage, Dickens lampoons the unconscious bargaining and rationalizations that it takes for subjects of the liberal state to maintain their belief in it and, by extension, their own sense of self. What jumps out in a novel that otherwise depicts governmental power as an invasive fog (the Court of Chancery) is the introduction of "the State" as a concentrated character. Skimpole's self-exonerating speech activates the idea of the state as a person, *stately* and dignified, gravely leaning over him and, perhaps with a knowing, conspiratorial wink, asking him personally to trust his agent. Skimpole refers to himself in the third person, indicating a level of detachment from the complicated act of exchange he describes. He exalts his acceptance of the bribe as an act of citizenship, not an act of corruption. In his logic, to refuse the money would be to recognize its offer as a violation of the rules of the liberal state. Such an act would radically throw the legitimacy of a relatively new liberal government, nominally devoted to transparency and the promotion of the liberty of the unlanded (if not unpropertied), into doubt and would unravel the "general cohesion of things." By accepting the bribe, Skimpole explains to Esther, he makes the act acceptable. The exchange is no longer incongruous with, or threatening to, political authority because Skimpole has, in the fantasy that he describes to Esther, carried out the wishes of the state. By doing so, he has avoided a moment that might expose the illegitimacy of the state and thus lead to anarchy, a real concern in the years following the continental Revolutions of 1848. Of course, Skimpole receives Esther's and the novel's condemnation, but his explanation to Esther nevertheless sheds light on the ways that individuals use their creativity to maintain the power and legitimacy of a state that they have internalized as a person with whom they have a relationship. In the mid-Victorian period, following the reform measures of the 1830s, this person-like state appears as a surveying, paternalistic figure atop a thickening web of disciplinary procedures.

In the 1880s and 1890s in Britain, a striking, new version of state fantasy emerged, one that Dickens perhaps anticipated but might not have recognized. In this fantasy, the state was not only coherent, knowable, and personified, but also heroic and endowed with the capacity to transform people's lives. Political thinkers, politicians, and activists, such as the New Liberals D. G. Ritchie and L. T. Hobhouse and the Fabian Socialist Sidney Webb, were beginning to bestow the state with the ethical obligation to intervene in the brutalities of capitalism and the social injustices of gender inequality, thereby helping all of its citizens to achieve the good life. In late Victorian political writing and fiction, the state, often with a big "S," thus began to appear in the form of a meta-liberal individual among liberal individuals, who, through the transforming powers of the law, could grant to those who appealed to it the plenitude that liberal political philosophy and capitalist ideology promised and denied. The state was emerging as an agent of positive self- and social transformation, not oppression.

For example, in *Liberalism* (1911), Hobhouse, who helped to shape the policies of the Liberal government in the early decades of the twentieth century, described the proper role of the state in this way: "It is for the State to take care that the economic conditions are such that the normal man who is not defective in mind and body or will can by useful labour feed, house, and clothe himself and his family" (76). Along with J. A. Hobson and Ritchie, Hobhouse figured the state in his writings as a benevolent figure that would assist the development of human faculties. In this example, Hobhouse figures the state with a big "S" in the subject position. It is personified and coherent, something we can see in earlier decades, but it is now also an ethical being. Antonio Gramsci's model of the ethical state helps to describe the economic interests served by such a fantasy. In his writings, the ethical state works in conjunction with non-state institutions, such as philanthropic and religious organizations, to elevate the masses culturally and morally so as to meet the needs of production (Gramsci 259). It thus operates according to norms, judging its subjects in relation to how well they achieve them. For Hobhouse and other New Liberals at the turn of the century, the state should regulate the economy, but it should also regulate people, setting the standard for normalcy and utility. In the case of this statement, the state reinforces patriarchal relations, supporting the household that is headed by a male, biologically related, and financially solvent.

The circulation of the fantasy of the state as a hero generated both optimism that the government could enact change and anxiety that it would undermine the cherished ideals of British national character, defined chiefly in terms of autonomy from the state. In a volume of essays provocatively titled *The Man versus the State* (1884), Herbert Spencer, for one, was alarmed by what he called "the unhesitating belief . . . that evils of all kinds should be dealt with by the State" (47). Major initiatives to provide state education receive some of Spencer's sternest disapproval. For example, ventriloquizing a rising sentiment against the practice of parents paying for education in favor of the state taking on that responsibility, he writes,

> The payment of school-fees is beginning to be denounced as wrong: the State must take the whole burden. Moreover, it is proposed by many that the State, regarded as an undoubtedly competent judge of what constitutes good education for the poor, shall undertake also to prescribe good education for the middle-classes—shall stamp the children of these, too, after a State pattern, concerning the goodness of which they have no more doubt than the Chinese had when they fixed theirs. (22–3)

Girding his critique with steely irony, Spencer, too, engages in state fantasy inasmuch as he refers to an agential and coherent state that should stay out of private affairs of the economy or household. For him, "the State" assumes a burden, judges, undertakes to prescribe, stamps, and has no doubts. Moreover, it seeks to level social differences within England and, crucially, cultural differences between England and China, the horrifying authoritarian other that haunts so much of the anti-statist literature of late-nineteenth-century Britain. Representing a more traditional version of Liberalism, Spencer ultimately objects that the fantasy of the state as a heroic actor represented a return to the ancien régime: ". . . in so far as it has been extending the system of compulsion, what is now called Liberalism is a new form of Toryism" (29).

By the last decades of the nineteenth century, then, the state was felt by those invested in a certain model of liberal individualism to be exceeding its disciplinary and juridical capacities, emblematized by the diffuse courts of

Chancery that Dickens satirized in *Bleak House*. Correspondingly, late Victorian realist novels began to register this shift in state power and the fantasies that surrounded it. Consider an example that I shall explore more fully in Chapter 4: George Gissing's *The Odd Women* (1893) features two urbane, sophisticated characters, Rhoda Nunn and Everard Barfoot, batting the idea of a benevolent, interventionist state back and forth. The irony that coats their exchange belies the intensity of feeling that the idea of the state as a heroic actor occasioned. Gissing's narrow-minded feminist protagonist Rhoda draws the attention of the selfish and dilettantish Everard, who is attracted and repulsed by her radical politics. One afternoon, Everard calls upon Rhoda and his cousin, Miss Barfoot, who is Rhoda's employer. He playfully tells them a story about his old math tutor, Micklethwaite, who, after being engaged for seventeen years, is finally economically secure enough to marry. Barfoot remarks, "Pathetic, don't you think? I have a theory that when an engagement has lasted ten years, with constancy on both sides, and poverty still prevents marriage, the State ought to make provision for a man in some way, according to his social standing" (118). Rhoda joins the fun and mocks the classificatory and normativizing requirements of the state: "'If,' remarked Rhoda, 'it were first provided that no marriage should take place until *after* a ten years' engagement.'" She later adds, "'And no marriage, except where both, for the whole decennium, have earned their living by work that the State recognizes'" (118).

This scene exemplifies some key features of state fantasy in general. The speakers, like Skimpole, refer to the state with a big "S" and personify it. But, like Hobhouse, Rhoda and Everard engage in a historically new political grammar that assigns the state an ethical function: "The State ought to *x*." Like Spencer, they also ironize this grammar. Everard proposes that the state intervene economically to facilitate the entrance of a middle-class man and woman into marriage. The impossibility of Micklethwaite and his beloved marrying is overdetermined by a number of historical factors that interest Gissing: the low pay of educators or culture workers; the structural obstacles that prevent middle-class, respectable women from supporting themselves financially; the social expectation that married women will not work outside the home; and the hypocrisy of a state that sanctions all three injustices while still seeking to promote the rate of reproduction of its population, especially that of the middle classes. Everard's jab at the state thus indexes a specific historical moment. In the name of fostering the public good, the state takes as its concern the biological reproduction of the desirable members of its population and the alleviation of poverty, but does not recognize a version of middle-class poverty that prevents its members from marrying in a socially sanctioned style. Meanwhile, Rhoda's rejoinder reminds us of the disciplinary aspects of the state: the requirements, norms, and examinations that it institutes in order to manage the population. Her joke points out how these requirements actually disable the achievement of the ends that the state is seeking, which, in this case, are middle-class marriage and reproduction.

Considered in light of the whole novel, this scene becomes especially pertinent. Rhoda and Everard soon embark on a tortured romance in which the institution of marriage serves as the central crux. They imagine themselves to be new and modern kinds of people. Their modernity expresses itself as a critique of marriage as a state-sanctioned institution that kills love by containing it. Yet, as Gissing details, they nevertheless desire the form, for different reasons. For Everard, it provides social recognition and approbation. To love outside of the form is to be cast to the margins of their bourgeois social world. For Rhoda, it functions as the external expression of Everard's genuine desire for her. Their ambivalence reaches cruel heights as their story unfolds. The irony that saturates this early scene expresses their critical relation to marriage and the state, which serves as the grounds of their mutual attraction. But their irony also defends against their strong desire that an external, powerful authority might *actually* enable, rather than disable or appropriate, private pleasures.

As my examples suggest, while my archive includes political writings, letters, political speeches, and newspaper articles, I focus on novels because of their generic capacity to produce a sense of everyday life; to register the overlapping edges of what Raymond Williams, in *Marxism and Literature*, identified as residual, dominant, and emergent historical formations; and to construct new subjectivities during a time of historical flux. They are especially adept at exposing and meditating upon the contradictions and conflicts that attend people's fantasies about political authority. Posing liberal agency as a question, rather than a given, the late Victorian novels I examine in the following chapters analyze what it means for subjects to fantasize that the state is a heroic actor, meditating upon the tragic conditions of individuals engaging in state fantasy. The central tragedy concerns the painful condition of imagining oneself to be a liberal agent and thus independent from power-bearing institutions, yet knowing—consciously or unconsciously—that one is not. With varying degrees of ambivalence, these novels examine the intractable wish for a pure agency, that is, a free will that is unimpeded and uninfluenced by the desires of others or even by the contradictory desires of the self. This agency is at once so dear and so threatened that, in order to hold onto it, subjects project it away from themselves and onto "the State."

The historical uniqueness of the late Victorian state is at the center of long-standing debate. Some recent historians support A. V. Dicey's famous proposition in 1905 that the period from 1865 to 1900 witnessed a shift from individualism to collectivism. They maintain that the late nineteenth century saw an essentially new kind of state that predicted the coming of the twentieth-century welfare state. These historians emphasize a notable increase in legislation and intervention. Meanwhile, others argue that the state in the late nineteenth century was continuous with its previous manifestations and that to locate the welfare state in this period obscures its long historical making. They maintain that it is specious to posit a radical break between earlier Benthamite and mid-century centralization efforts and late-nineteenth-century interventionism. This disagreement raises the question of whether the charged distinction between "laissez faire" and "interventionist" is salient.

Not surprisingly, Gramsci's concepts feature prominently in the former camp of historians. For example, Stuart Hall and Bill Schwarz argue that this period witnessed the consolidation of monopoly capitalism, that is, the state control of capital, which led to a cultural revolution on par with the constitutional revolution of the mid–seventeenth century and the industrial revolution of the late eighteenth and early nineteenth centuries. Characterizing all three periods as "epochal" and as "time[s] of organic crisis," Hall and Schwarz deem the decades from the 1880s to the 1920s as "the most immediately formative for us" (8). David Lloyd and Paul Thomas also see a pronounced break in this period. Instead of pointing to changes in capitalism, however, they draw upon Gramsci to argue that the Reform Bill of 1867 and the Education Act of 1870 consolidated the hegemony of the ethical state. For them, the ethical state's defining feature is "the saturation of discourse on society with an 'idea of the state'" (115).

On the other side of the debate, Phillip Corrigan and Derek Sayer maintain that state intervention was a long-standing practice and not a phenomenon unique to the 1880s and 1890s. For them, the signs of state intervention in this period must be explained in terms of the Benthamite reorganization of state structures in the 1830s, which involved measures concerning poor relief, public health, and sanitation. In this view, the legislation of the 1870s and 1880s, while important, represents merely the "consolidation and administrative formalization of legitimate structured social relations long in being" (Corrigan and Sayer 169).

Despite their differences over the historical newness of this period, both camps agree that the idea of the state changed significantly during the closing decades of the nineteenth century. For example, Corrigan and Sayer concede that the "'social' recognition of labouring men" in this period is noteworthy (169). For them, the conceptualization of poverty as a social problem rather than as a sign of individual moral failure represents an important historical shift that was attended by a shift in the idea of the state: "Above all there was this sacred object recognized as there to be worshipped, worked, used and consolidated" (Corrigan and Sayer 173). They argue that the state underwent a process of fetishization similar to that undergone by commodities, emerging for the first time as a coherent entity: "To change the idea of 'the State'—to make it, in fact, visible as 'the State'—was an enormous accomplishment and one which much legitimation work has to labour to sustain" (179).

In material terms, the late nineteenth century did indeed witness an unprecedented proliferation of public services, municipal projects, and regulations designed to protect workers and consumers. Free education, unemployment insurance, municipalization, old-age pensions, guaranteed minimum wages, and a regulated labor market were passed into law. The increase in legislation demanded an increase in infrastructure. Jose Harris notes how employees of the government increased fourfold in the period from 1870 to 1914. The spending of central and local governments rose tenfold, while government agencies, such as Local Government Boards, the Labour Department of the Board of Trade, the Board of Agriculture, and the Board of Education, proliferated. The government also increased its public spending on a range of welfare provisions and in the process rearticulated the nation-as-family allegory, with the state occupying the role of paternal caretaker. Hobhouse's statement concerning the role of the state is emblematic of this tendency: the proto-welfare state of the early twentieth century reinforced patriarchal roles and, in the process, consolidated its own paternalistic relation to its citizens. Through a range of regulations and provisions, the state was now involved in life processes from birth to death and was articulating the rationality for such practices as the ethical defense of the overall health of the population.

As citizens projected a head onto this contradictory and incoherent assemblage of governmental operations, we can see a historically new kind of subjectivity emerging from novels. The doubleness inherent in the term "state personhood" is useful for describing the process by which the state became personified and people became "statified." By "statified," I am referring to how people became shaped not only by the material and governmental practices of the state, but also by their fantasies of the state. My readings of certain novels suggest that some late Victorians granted heroic personhood to the state as a way to defend themselves against the confusing implications of the dispersal of power outside of the state. In the process, they entered into modern state personhood, a mode of personhood characterized by ambivalent feelings—oscillating among love, hate, need, and fear—in relation to political authority. Rhoda and Everard are examples of this type. Battling the sense that the state was saturating and appropriating every aspect of human life, they desire to be independent from "the State" but they are unconsciously distressed by their sense of wanting it to intervene in their lives, as well.

To provide a sense of the political discussion in which novels were intervening, I would like to return to Spencer's *The Man versus the State* and consider it alongside a rebuttal launched by Webb in his essay, "Historic," published in *Fabian Essays in Socialism* (1889), a volume edited by George Bernard Shaw. As I mentioned earlier, Spencer bemoaned "the notion, always more or less prevalent and just now vociferously expressed, that all social suffering is removable, and that it is the duty of somebody or other to remove it" (32). Adhering to an organic view of society, he argued that suffering is natural and that there is no ethical obligation to relieve it. The problem with Liberals, he complained, was that they wrongly figured society as a made thing that could be engineered. Behind the conviction that the state ought to intervene lurked "the tacit assumption that Government should step in whenever anything is not going right" (Spencer 46).

Spencer's text exposes how the state was by no means the coherent, consistent, animated, discrete, or agential entity that it appears to be in syntax. Spencer started his critique of late-nineteenth-century British political culture with a diatribe on the downtrodden and even the respectable poor being quick to appeal to the state. But he also condemned solid middle-class citizens, who, goaded by the promises of politicians and idealistic reformers, imaginatively consolidated what were actually disparate, irrational, and contradictory functions, services, administrations, laws, spaces, rationalities, practices, discourses, and career bureaucrats into a single entity and then felt optimistic about its capacity to change their lives. The performance of appealing to the state—whether privately, as in moments of daydreaming or collective problem-solving, or publicly, in the courtroom or other civic spaces—granted to the state a coherence, an agency, and an ethical duty, which, for Spencer, it simply did not intrinsically have.

To make his point, Spencer detailed the growing number of ways in which the average citizen was daily more coerced since the 1860s. Arriving at the current Gladstone Ministry, he listed acts and regulations that protected the bodies of workers and the minds of children:

> We have, in 1880, a law which forbids conditional advance-notes in payment of sailors' wages; also a law which dictates certain arrangements for the safe carriage of grain-cargoes; also a law increasing local coercion over parents to send their children to school. In 1881 comes legislation to prevent trawling over clam-beds and bait-beds, and an interdict making it impossible to buy a glass of beer on Sunday in Wales. In 1882 the Board of Trade was authorized to grant licences to generate and sell electricity, and municipal bodies were enabled to levy rates for electric-lighting: further exactions from ratepayers were authorized for facilitating more accessible baths and wash-houses; and local authorities were empowered to make bye-laws for securing the decent lodging of persons engaged in picking fruit and vegetables. (20–1)

The arc of Spencer's list highlights the wide-ranging powers of the state, producing a sense of an arbitrary, overwhelming, and paralyzing web of regulations and laws in which citizens conducting their business in the private sphere are caught.

Spencer targeted the late-nineteenth-century New Liberals and Socialists in particular, but the Liberal Party from the 1860s more generally. He complained that they had perverted the traditions of liberal critique, which had originally set itself against state intervention in the name of personal freedom, into a version of state-loving Toryism. For Spencer, this state love both grew from and further strengthened a dangerous culture-wide sacralizing of state power into an idol, an animated agent who ought to "step in" to mitigate personal and collective suffering (46). Spencer was most irritated by the way that politicians and common men alike seemed to be gladly surrendering their own agency and granting it to "the State" in the act of viewing it in this light. For Spencer, by wrongly endowing the government with this ethical sanction, citizens were responsible for the state impinging on their own individual freedoms, while depriving concerned critics like Spencer of any recourse to challenge its ever-increasing scope of action.

Spencer's diatribe elicited a direct response from Webb. In "Historic," Webb celebrated the pervasiveness of the "tacit assumption" that the state should regulate industry, provide resources, and ultimately control the means of production as a sign of national morality. Collapsing the state and the nation, he wrote, "In the teeth of the current Political Economy, and in spite of all the efforts of the millowning Liberals, England was compelled to put forth her hand to succor and protect her weaker members" (1889, 46). He cast this cultural consent as evidence of "the statesman's unconscious abandonment of the old Individualism, and our irresistible glide into collectivist Socialism" (1889, 60). For Webb, the incremental chipping away at the hallowed precepts of private property indicated the manifestation of the latent principles of both official British political philosophy and its unofficial counterpart, the ordinary citizen's common-sense awareness of the economic defects of industrial individualism. Throughout the essay and elsewhere, Webb argued that local governments had already achieved the principles of socialism long ago: "The general failure to realize the extent to which our unconscious Socialism has already proceeded . . . is due to the fact that few know anything of local administration outside of their own town" (1889, 50).

Webb also deployed lists, but he went beyond the purely legislative to capture a sense of how the late Victorian state in fact produced the very sense of the everyday in ways that its subjects were no longer aware. Webb's list is remarkable for its density:

> It [the community as expressed through local or national government] provides for many thousands of us from birth to burial—midwifery, nursery, education, board and lodging, vaccination, medical attendance, medicine, public worship, amusements, and interment. It furnishes and maintains its own museums, parks, art galleries, libraries, concert-halls, roads, streets, bridges, markets, slaughter-houses, fire-engines, lighthouses, pilots, ferries, surfboats, steamtugs, lifeboats, cemeteries, public baths, washhouses, pounds, harbours, piers, wharves, hospitals, dispensaries, gasworks, waterworks, tramways, telegraph cables, allotments, cow meadows, artizans' dwellings, schools, churches, and reading-rooms. It carries on and publishes its own researches in geology, meteorology, statistics, zoology, geography, and even theology. (1889, 47–8)

The list moves from those issues concerning the biological functions of man as human, to the culturally hegemonic (the moral and civilizing mission), to the capitalist (aiding the profit-making of private corporations through the provision of infrastructure), and finally to the disciplinary (the funding of scientific knowledge). Webb also engaged in state fantasy, referring to a knowable agent behind all of these concerns: "Besides its direct supersession of private enterprise, the State now registers, inspects, and controls nearly all the industrial functions which it has not yet absorbed" (1889, 48).

Foucault's discussion of biopower helps make sense of the copious lists that Spencer and Webb use rhetorically. Any discussion of state power and subjectivity in the late nineteenth century must reckon with Foucault's work on discipline and biopolitics. Here I want to suggest that late Victorian state fantasy was a psychic response to the succession, convergence, and ultimately triangulation of the three modes of power that concern Foucault: sovereignty, discipline, and governmentality, which he elsewhere calls regulation and biopower (1991, 102). In his monumental study of modern European war, Foucault sought to dismantle the dominance of sovereignty, boiled down to the credo of "the right to take life or let live," in contemporary political theory by arguing that it was eventually overtaken by disciplinary power in the eighteenth century. In *Discipline and Punish*, Foucault describes discipline as a mode of internalized power that addressed the individual body and involved surveillance, the establishment of norms, and examinations. The modern prison, with its emphasis on rehabilitation, is a primary instance of disciplinary power and, according to Foucault, was replicated architecturally throughout society in institutions like schools, factories, and hospitals. This new form of power was then joined and to some extent subsumed in the nineteenth century by regulatory power, or biopower, summed up in the phrase, "the power to 'make' live and 'let' die" (2003, 240–1). While sovereignty concerns the protection of territory and discipline concerns the surveillance, training, and punishing of individual bodies, biopower addresses the individual as a member of a species. Modeled on war, this mode of power sought to protect society not against invaders, but against enemies that lurked within, such as disease, threatening the general health of the population. It addressed biological processes ranging from "birth to burial," to borrow from Webb above, producing statistics and information and establishing institutions, such as life and accident insurance and mandatory savings, to safeguard the health of the population against risk. In "Governmentality," Foucault argued for a new way of thinking about the state exercise of power, one modeled on biopower, that involves the management of the population within a territory and, more specifically, with the "right disposition of things" (93).

Biopower lumps individuals into a group that share the same biological processes. As such, it is a genre of power that seems to call for the convention of lists. For example, when Foucault expands on the kinds of things that government manages, he, too, like Spencer and Webb, resorts to a catalogue:

> The things with which in this sense government is to be concerned are in fact men, but men in their relations, their links, their imbrication with those other things which are wealth, resources, means of subsistence, the territory with its specific qualities, climate, irrigation, fertility, etc.; men in their relation to that other kind of things, customs, habits, ways of acting and thinking, etc.; lastly, men in their relation to that other kind of things, accidents and misfortunes such as famine, epidemics, death, etc. (1991, 93)

Foucault's sense of the general form of management that the government undertook in the nineteenth century captures the anxiety and elation, respectively, of Spencer's and Webb's essays.

But Foucault's schema is less satisfactory for framing the historical question of agency, a question that is indeed vexed—did subjects first have a fantasy of the state as a heroic actor that facilitated the interventionist measures of the state, as Spencer and Webb both contend? Or did the state start intervening and then its subjects developed the fantasy as a compromise-formation? The fantasy of the state as a heroic actor, of course, has ties to an earlier age of sovereign power and may very well have eased the transition to state interventionism. At the risk of radically reducing history, one might say that nineteenth-century British liberals, in particular, were wishing the interventionist state into existence out of nostalgia for an idea of the ancien régime—a mode of power that earlier historical classes of British liberals had worked to dismantle. If that is the case, then the psychological conflicts attending this wish cut both ways. In the seventeenth and eighteenth centuries, the bourgeoisie sought to free themselves of the monarchy and the clergy and to locate sovereignty in the individual. In the nineteenth century, the bourgeoisie longed for a sovereign figure and projected sovereignty back onto the representative government that replaced the ancien régime. Conflicted about such longing, they also resented a strong interventionist state, which they experienced as inhibiting freedoms. In the novels I examine, the interventionist state seems to signal the emergence of a citizen-subject who both criticizes and craves subjection to a powerful other. As I explore in Chapter 2, these conflicts have had material effects outside of Britain, as well. For example, they have influenced the modern production of Afghanistan, an extremely precarious imperialized site.

What is odd about this fantasy is that it occurred in a nation that so strongly celebrated its freedom from the state. The liberalism of nineteenth-century England proclaimed the autonomy of the individual from the tyranny of sovereign power and sought to locate sovereignty in the individual instead. As Goodlad has argued, Victorian liberalism harbored a contradictory impulse around centralized authority. It entertained a tension between negative and positive conceptions of liberty that by the end of the nineteenth century had materialized in a split between anti-statism and statism (2003, 36). The anti-statist position, exemplified by Spencer, derived from a liberal discourse that advocated limited government and citizen's self-reliance. Adherents of this position exalted the free market and voluntarism. Meanwhile, statists, like Hobhouse, argued that citizenship required looking out for all members of society and that the state, not the market, was necessary for securing the public good. The first ideology presupposes a subject who is agential and self-transparent, knows his or her desires, and can act without conflicts to achieve them as long as the state does not interfere. The second presupposes a subject who constitutionally, both in the legal as well as ontological senses, lacks plenitude and the power of self-determination, not because of his or her own moral failings, but rather because of historical circumstances.

The novels included here explore the tension between these two conceptions of the subject. They show how these conceptions fuel each other and can be found within a single individual's self-understanding. On the one hand, the subject, regardless of sex, profession, or social position, holds herself to be autonomous and free in the liberal tradition and, on the other, remains unconsciously attached to structures of power. Thus, the conscious fixation on autonomy from the state paradoxically belies a tenacious and anxious attachment to the state and other institutions of authority. We see this dramatically in Sarah Grand's *The Heavenly Twins* (1893). As I discuss in the last chapter, this bestselling New Woman novel is ridden with conflicts and contradictions, which expose how the more the subject struggles to be free, in the style offered by liberal thinking, the more entrenched in social structures she finds herself.

On the most essential level, these novels reveal how state and non-state institutions could not operate without the fantasies of those they interpellate. My focus on the state is not motivated by the belief that it lies at the core of power. Instead, I am interested in how British subjects—some with tenuous relations to citizenship, as my chapter explorations of colonial settlers and women will uncover—fantasized about the state during a time of historical transition. Despite evidence to the contrary and despite conscious knowledge that power resided not only in other institutions, but also within themselves, these subjects often recentered and at times even eroticized the state in their conscious and unconscious fantasies of how power works.[3]

My readings of novels bring to light another crucial aspect of the late Victorian liberal state and non-state institutions, an aspect often obscured by political theory, but quite palpable in the earlier quote from Hobhouse: even as liberalism might move us away from the vaunting of a sovereign masculine figure, the king, to the promotion of a democracy of abstract equivalent individuals, its institutions still rely upon a fantasy of sexual difference to function. In other words, the state in state fantasy is always masculine. The work of feminist psychoanalytic thinkers like Jacqueline Rose and Teresa Brennan usefully establishes this essential aspect of modern power. For them, the fantasies upon which institutions rely not only reveal the role of the unconscious in the formation and maintenance of institutions, but also must be understood as tied to "the most fundamental images of sexual difference (adoration to the male, chaos or exclusion to the female) on which the wider culture so centrally turns" (Rose 4). The novels chosen for this study highlight a feature that the state and social institutions share: the privileged position of a paternal figure, whether Prime Minister, M.P., magistrate's clerk, father, gentleman, or doctor, and the precarious position of a feminine figure. These are not biologically essential categories, of course. Women can pass through a historically masculine position and momentarily pulse with power to the awe of those who are then placed under them. Examples include Felice Charmond, the landlady in Thomas Hardy's *The Woodlanders* (1887), who rules the rural folk of Little Hintock, and Rhoda Nunn, a political activist and entrepreneur in George Gissing's *The Odd Women* (1893), whose vigor positively electrifies the other, exhausted odd women. Likewise, men can occupy a subordinate position, like Waldo, a working-class, colonial settler in Olive Schreiner's *The Story of an African Farm* (1883), who falls under the hypnotic sway of an imperial administrator, or Giles, a rural yeoman (small businessman) in *The Woodlanders*, who trembles at the thought of how a single law might give him his heart's desire. The sexual difference that propels the meanings of these fantasies reminds us of the deep contradictions inherent in liberal notions of freedom and individuality. These abstract concepts cannot be separated from the historical contexts in which they were conceived and need further interrogation, even when invoked positively in current critical theory.

By focusing on state fantasy, my study casts new light on the British realist novel of the 1880s and 1890s. An anomalous period in British literary history, these years have been classically described as "the interregnum" (Raymond Williams, 1983, 161) and as an exhausted state of mind (Max Beerbohm, quoted in Frierson, 35). More recently, literary critics have described the period in terms of the breakdowns of Victorian philosophical and literary realism (George Levine and Elizabeth Ermarth). This breakdown narrative has in turn been historicized in terms of a collapse in the liberal subject's confidence in his capacity to apprehend reality and his subsequent reliance on the institutions of the nation-state to ground him (Irene Tucker 25–6). Many literary critics of the fin-de-siècle have also read the period's novels in the context of the construction of the New Woman, that icon of modernity and gender transgression, as well as the marriage question (Ann Ardis); the rise of commodity culture (Rachel Bowlby); loss and the emergence of scientific theories of degeneration (Stephen Arata), eugenics and hysteria (Angelique Richardson); and the specter of imperialism (Laura Chrisman). However, these critics tend to cordon off changes in the material practices of the state, the novelty of characters' feelings about the state, and the fetishization of disciplinary and regulatory practices into "the State." While their works illuminate crucial aspects of fin-de-siècle culture and realism, it is striking that they do not address how the state appears in some of the most libidinally intense scenes in key late Victorian novels. These scenes, I have found, feature fantasies about the state and bring to light hopes and fears about the possibilities for liberal agency and freedom within a range of relationships, including, most crucially, those between citizens and the state.

In the novels I examine, public works, municipal spaces, and laws emerge as events, while state officials and functionaries beam the love of the state onto the local level. As arms of the state, these elements embody, abstract, locate, and dislocate characters, narrators, and readers in dramatic ways. For instance, in Hardy's *The Woodlanders*, the road's official state function as a unifier of the nation is defeated both by a remembered history of the marginalization of the rural local and by contemporary tensions between local and central governments. Meanwhile the woodlanders' belief that the law can transform individual destinies is rendered pathetic and tragic: the state does not facilitate an escape from history or fate. In Gissing's *The Odd Women*, municipal spaces emerge as sites of gendered state subjectification and are also shaped by the very social tensions that urban planners explicitly designed them to resolve. Meanwhile "the State" as a heroic actor, as I mentioned briefly, appears as an object both of irony and of suppressed desire. Through its metonyms, the state as a site of optimism appears in both novels tragically and ironically, testifying to these authors' self-conscious pessimism regarding its transformative powers, a stance that may ultimately have contributed to their novels' contemporary and future literary value.

Extending this line of interpretation, I argue that while earlier realist novels construct marriage and culture as primary sites of optimism for social mobility and as critical standpoints outside the state, the late-realist novels I examine in the following chapters cast them as fully saturated by the state and thus anachronistic and impotent. These novels register how the state in this historical moment superseded marriage and culture as the dominant fantasmatic site of optimism for change while having colonized them through legislation and the production of civic spaces. With subtlety and ambivalence, the novels index how this emergent state culture increasingly defined individuals in terms of a fundamental lack that only a benevolent yet monolithic state could address.

The project's primary texts are major realist novels, but I attend as well to a variety of minor subgenres in order to convey better the variety of attachments to the state. They include a colonial novel (Olive Schreiner), an adventure novel for boys (G. A. Henty), a detective story (Arthur Conan Doyle), a rural novel (Hardy), an urban novel (Gissing), and a New Woman novel (Grand). While I might have chosen more explicitly state-related works by the same novelists, such as Hardy's *Jude the Obscure* (1895), with its characters' conflicts about marriage; Gissing's *Demos* (1886), which features workers' demands for rights; or Schreiner's *Trooper Peter Halket of Mashonaland* (1897), a harsh critique of Cecil Rhodes's state-sanctioned seizure of lands in Africa, I deliberately selected novels that, at least on the surface, do not appear to be about the state. By making my roster of novels heterogeneous and by treating novels whose content is not directly related to the state, I hope to show the cultural pervasiveness of state fantasy and the concerns it generated.

Victorian critics considered novels by Schreiner, Hardy, and Gissing to be "serious" literary fiction, while those by Grand, Henty, and Doyle bore the damning label of popular fiction. Yet they maintain a basic characteristic of the nineteenth-century realist novel, one that fulfills Georg Lukács' description: on some level, they seek to liberate their readers from false consciousness by exposing the doctrines and norms that bind them. But they also betray anxieties about the novel form's capacity to do this work of critical demystification. These anxieties appear not because the characters are presented as duped. At times, as in the case of Schreiner's liberal feminist Lyndall; Gissing's enlightened city dwellers, Rhoda and Everard; or Grand's morally balanced New Woman, Mrs. Malcomson, they are extremely articulate about the doctrines and norms they see around them. Rather, these anxieties appear in the narratives because of an apprehension that the state and its subjects are powerfully interlocked and that fantasy serves as the binding force that glues them together. The novels each feature moments of fantasy that interrupt the flow of daily activity. As realist novels, they are generically obligated to describe the material features of everyday life, but their attention to characters' dreams about the state and its metonyms, such as the law, tell us how such dreams were becoming recognized as a meaningful aspect of everyday life toward the end of the century. These late Victorian novels betray the sense that, because of the power of fantasy, critical demystification fails to deliver the subject from either external or internal repression. It fails not because fantasy distracts the subject from the horrors of political reality. In fact, as Slavoj Žižek has argued, the horrors of political reality, even the most physical and brutal, are mediated through fantasy (1997, 7). It fails because fantasy binds subjects to this political reality, teaching them to desire their own oppression and even to find pleasure in sustaining it. The novels I discuss betray a helpless and impotent awareness of how people remain unconsciously attached to figures of power despite consciously knowing how such figures limit and control them.

Because they struggle within the legacy of liberalism, aestheticizing—or lyricizing—the feelings of unpoliticized characters toward a mysterious and magical state, one could classify the novels in my archive as liberal-realist novels, in contradistinction to an important subgenre of the late nineteenth century that I do not discuss: socialist novels. The 1880s and 1890s witnessed the publication of a number of socialist and socialist-feminist realist fictions, including Florence Dixie's *Gloriana: Or, The Revolution of 1900* (1890) and Gertrude Dix's *The Image-Breakers* (1900). Socialist utopic novels also appeared, such as William Morris's *News from Nowhere* (1890) and H. G. Wells's *A Modern Utopia* (1905). Late Victorian socialist novels often feature characters working toward a socialist state—in which case the liberal, possessive-individual manifestation of the state has been abolished—or, if the novel is utopic, waking up in a socialist world. They typically do not feature libidinally intense scenes in which characters fantasize about the state as a person who could take care of them. It is not that these novels lack an unconscious or psychic depth. But, because they are often invested in imagining worlds in which collective efforts result in a new kind of stateless society or in which the state and society are fully merged, they are not motivated in the same ways to represent characters' complicated attractions to the state as heroic actor, a process that "statifies" the subject and subjectifies the state in liberal cultures. In other words, while it would make sense that socialist novels might want to critique an emergent liberal welfare state, their sights tend to be set in alternative, visionary directions.

By not including socialist novels or a fuller discussion of the different kinds of socialist movements in the period, I am mindful that I run the risk of foreclosing on the different historical possibilities that they opened up. My account could ultimately then be seen as suggesting that the early-twentieth-century liberal welfare state was inevitable. This would be regrettable because I do not wish to put forward such a totalizing, teleological narrative. As Ruth Livesey and Diana Maltz have recently argued, these decades witnessed the flourishing of different kinds of socialisms and charity movements that vaunted the power of art to transform people's lives. For Livesey, who explores the diverse works of socialist writers, including William Morris, Edward Carpenter, and Clementina Black, art became a privileged means for imagining a world not dominated by commodification or capitalist modes of production. Meanwhile, Maltz has argued that the late nineteenth century witnessed the emergence of "missionary aestheticism," a term she uses to describe a range of philanthropic efforts to improve the lives of the poor by uplifting their souls through art.

I do wish to suggest, however, that a fantasy of the state as a heroic actor—i.e., a liberal as opposed to socialist fantasy of the state—dominated the popular imaginary in the last decades of the nineteenth century and it is that fantasy that I wish to trace in this book. The liberal-realist novels I have chosen feature members of the population who, at least according to the novels, are not—or not yet—politicized in self-conscious ways and are thus, I would argue, represented as powerfully shaped by liberal ideology. These include rural workers, déclassé middle-class women, and colonial settlers, for whom, the novels suggest, this particular state fantasy is compelling, distracting, and formative.

The book begins in the settler colony of South Africa with a reading of Schreiner's *The Story of an African Farm* (1883). Published just before the discovery of diamond mines and the Berlin Conference in 1884, which led to the multi-national Scramble for Africa, *The Story of an African Farm* is set at a time when South African settlers felt that the British state had lost interest in them. Schreiner's novel provides an origin story for late Victorian state fantasy. Detailing how colonials felt rejected by the imperial state, the novel invests one particular relationship with intense libidinal energy: that between Waldo, a colonial subject, and "the stranger," a low-level state official. To develop my argument, I turn to Hannah Arendt's discussion of what she terms the "aloof rule" of British imperial practice. A variant of liberal governance, aloof rule is more resistant to critical demystification than tyrannical rule, which Arendt associates with French imperialism. *The Story of an African Farm* self-consciously exalts the novel form as a key technology for teaching subjects to see through the empty charade of tyranny. But it implies its own limits in undoing aloof rule, which, it argues, shapes the critical subject's very sense of self.

From the colonies, I move geographically back to Britain and temporally forward into the 1880s to examine domestic representations of an anomalous imperial product, Afghanistan. I argue that Afghanistan functions as a repressed homology for British subjects' feelings of their own vulnerability toward, subjection by, and yet fascination with a new turn in official power, the kind exercised by the interventionist state. Afghanistan's status as imperialized but not colonized enabled the flourishing of fantasies that compensated for anxieties about material and symbolic changes in the British state. First, I turn to nineteenth-century writings to identify what I call "Victorian Afghanistan," a complex cluster of images, ideas, and affects that crystallized across the nineteenth century. I examine William Gladstone's *Midlothian Speeches* (1879), which occasions a look backward to Sir Walter Scott's "Culloden Papers" (1816) and Sir Mountstuart Elphinstone's *An Account of the Kingdom of Caubul* (1816). I then turn to Henty's adventure novel for boys, *For Name and Fame, or Through Afghan Passes* (1886), and Doyle's detective novel, *A Study in Scarlet* (1887). In all five texts, Afghans appear primitive, savage, and lacking in discipline, the antithesis of liberal selfhood. However, they also appear ruggedly individualistic, freedom loving, brave, and hospitable—qualities belonging to British ideals of liberal selfhood and civility. This uneasy mix of attributes indicates how racial stereotypes rationalize imperial practices. The British were not motivated to colonize Afghanistan, yet they wished to control its foreign policy. The imperative to cast Afghans as docile or civilizable is thus absent. In its place is a romanticization that marks Afghans, like the Scots Highlanders, as odd stand-ins for England's own pre-liberal individual selves, poised to emerge in opposition to absolutist power over the seventeenth and eighteenth centuries.

Chapter 3 moves from the peripheries of the empire to the peripheries of the home nation. Here I examine Hardy's novel of rural life, in which fantasies proliferate almost as wildly as the lichen and ivy that choke the stalk and sapling in its eco-system. *The Woodlanders* locates the effects of late

Victorian state fantasy in the hinterlands of the nation, denaturalizing a process that was becoming everyday in the metropolitan spaces of England. Here characters dream of a new law that will release them from the bonds of marriage and even erase the past. Hardy attends pointedly to the vagaries of love and pity among characters and on the part of readers for characters. In light of historical shifts in the political imaginary of the 1880s and 1890s, we can read such moments as meditations on the relations between a benevolent, sympathetic state and its subjects. Ultimately, while *The Woodlanders* seems to foster sympathy for how rural folk get caught up in state fantasy, it ultimately indicts this social feeling and, by extension, the emergent modern welfare state, which was appropriating it. Through the flows of feeling and projections that it describes and induces, *The Woodlanders* exposes how the practice of sympathy is founded on distance, deferral, and moral judgment, thus complicating attempts to receive or mobilize it on either an individual or governmental scale.

From the rural setting of southern England, I move to metropolitan London to a reading of Gissing's *The Odd Women*. Critics often interpret *The Odd Women* solely in terms of what it has to say about the surplus in eligible women, the gendered division of labor, and the author's notorious pessimism about the possibilities for gender equality. In this chapter, I maintain that the novel also critiques the state's encroaching powers, both actual and imagined. In particular, through the description of how municipal spaces shape characters' interiority, Gissing expresses the fear that the state, as mediated through local government, was in the process of appropriating marriage and culture. As the lynchpins of nineteenth-century bourgeois liberal individuality, these institutions furnished imagined sites from which one could both escape and critique the political. Gissing's novel registers the subtle process by which, through common law courts, the state began converting marriage's religious identity into a primarily civil one. The novel also records the state's active provision of education and public spaces, seen as the incubators of culture, to the masses. I propose that *The Odd Women* expresses Gissing's anxiety that the two institutions of marriage and culture were thus becoming disarmed as traditional liberal sites of opposition to the state. In their place, he describes a model of critical consciousness based on novel reading, which comes to offer British subjects a possible position outside of the state.

In the last chapter, I turn to Grand's landmark New Woman novel, *The Heavenly Twins*. Published the same year as *The Odd Women*, Grand's novel explicitly sets out to dramatize the injustices experienced by women. Unlike

Gissing, however, Grand is less interested in the economic deprivations afflicting middle-class women. Rather, she attacks the social and political structures that endanger their physical health. Of all the novels I have discussed in this book, *The Heavenly Twins* as a feminist protest novel strains most self-consciously toward a political argument. I show how the novel's explicit desire to be political accounts for the many contradictions that it has generated for contemporary and recent readers. These contradictions bring to the surface the complexity of this historical moment in liberalism: the very claim for freedom can constrain the liberal subject. In other words, the more the liberal subject fights to be free in a certain way, the more she upholds the structures that subordinate her. Grand figures the relationship between the injured citizen and the healing state as a sexual one between a failed feminist, Evadne, and a physician who is also a baronet, Dr. Galbraith. Galbraith represents the ideal state in Grand's text. A professional expert who is also landed, he combines two kinds of disinterest and virtue. But Grand also expresses reservations about the kind of power such a state might wield. Ultimately, political hopelessness and sexual pleasure, elsewhere excised by the bourgeois moral economy of the novel, converge at the end of *The Heavenly Twins* in the spectacle of the heroine's hysterical submission to and withholding from the hero.

As the introduction suggests, this book is primarily concerned with the affective complexity of turn-of-the-century British citizenship. It focuses on the psychic aspects of the subject called into being through the exercise of indirect power and shows how a crucial feature of this psyche is its production of a particular, historical version of state fantasy. I do not wish to imply that fantasy was not always already a crucial mediating factor in earlier political formations. In the first chapter, for instance, I argue that Schreiner's *The Story of an African Farm* compares the fantasies that attend sovereign power with those that attend disciplinary and regulatory power. I do propose, however, that the late nineteenth century in Britain witnessed the emergence of a new state fantasy and a new mode of being defined by opacity, lack of clarity, and a split between conscious and unconscious thoughts.

As I indicated previously, the mode of being that defines modern state personhood is connected to material changes in the late Victorian state, but is also relatively detached from them. Scholars such as Lauren Berlant have noted that while Foucault derided critics for falsely locating the state as the center of power, his own analyses unfailingly return to state practices (2007). As Mitchell has argued, this tendency tells us that the border between the state and society is less salient than our conceptions of either imply. While

Mitchell and other political scientists might look at the material practices of the state, I focus on novels to examine this duality: as the liberal political project disperses power from the state, its subjects simultaneously fetishize the state as capable of benevolent, transformative acts. My close readings also demonstrate that fantasies about the state incorporate other dominant Victorian institutions, such as the family, marriage, culture, education, philanthropy, religion, and medicine. As the subject was increasingly regulated by an array of such institutions, the need to locate a center, and a benevolent one at that, likewise intensified.

Most importantly, while my work contributes to political theory, it shows how novels do things that political theory cannot.[4] Political theory might abstract and analyze the material processes or even the psychic ones by which the state operates, but novels set them in specific historical conditions and embody them in diverse characters, showing how this phenomena affects the ways that stories can be told and how they might be read. Specifically, late Victorian novels show us that complex psychic and emotional processes attend modern liberal citizens' attachments to centralized authority. Ultimately, the late Victorian novels I discuss in this book expose how the wish for autonomy in liberal political fantasies becomes tangled with the wish for salvation, throwing into question the supposed opposition between these two conditions.

1. *An Imperial Origin Story*

Aloof Rule in Schreiner's *The Story of an African Farm*

Olive Schreiner's *The Story of an African Farm* (1883) stages the origins of late Victorian state fantasy in the precarious and tenuous zone of empire. Set in South Africa from the 1860s to the 1880s, the novel dramatizes the grand historical shifts and events that profoundly shaped the last decades of the century. These events include the slowing down of an earlier phase of colonialism and the acceleration of imperialist expansion; fierce multinational competition over diamond and gold mines; the intertwined formalizations of administrative rationality, bureaucracy, and modern racism; and the rise of nationalisms. These decades also witnessed the emergence of a new mode of state power that claimed to grant freedom, but actually occupied subjects' emotional and sexual lives in such a way that they felt free and bound at the same time.

Recent scholarship on *The Story of an African Farm* frequently focuses on how its experiments in style communicate the contradictions and stresses that the nation form underwent symbolically in the South African colonial context. For example, Jed Esty describes the novel as "a kind of Southern exotic or literary platypus whose ungainly combination of parts and functions seems to flummox both classification and periodization" (408). He has written eloquently about the novel's colonial temporality and its unwriting of the nineteenth-century bildungsroman, a subgenre of the novel that ties the individual to the nation. Drawing attention to its "proto-modernist" features, Deborah Shapple remarks upon the novel's purposeful juxtapositions of different genres, such as realism and romance, and modes, such as letters and dreams. She draws upon ethnographic studies to argue persuasively that Schreiner characterized the white protagonist Waldo as a colonial indigene who then problematically displaces the native Africans as the basis for a postcolonial South African national identity.

Thus, both critics have interpreted the novel's famous formal experimentation as a literary attempt to capture the tension white colonials in South

Africa felt between the organic notions of unity that underwrote nationalism and the realities of life in the peripheries. However, far less attention has been paid to the state and the kinds of meanings that attach to shifts in political power in the symbolic economy of *The Story of an African Farm*. To be sure, literal references to "the State," either local or imperial, do not appear in the world of the novel. In fact, even material signs of the state are difficult to find, obscured by the dreamy, allegorical cast of the novel. Herbert Spencer's concatenation of labor and consumer legislations and Sidney Webb's local schools, hospitals, and telegraph cables are nowhere to be found in the loose-limbed social body that haunts the novel. Even in Thomas Hardy's remote rural locations, which I address in Chapter 3, the presence of the centralized, interventionist state can be felt through the road system and the circulation of the idea of a divorce law or, in other words, in the captivating, contagious idea that the state can grant new life. Meanwhile, George Gissing's urban setting, the subject of Chapter 4, appears as a grid of municipal projects and cultural institutions trained upon the cultivation of the individual. In contrast, Schreiner's novel gives us open spaces, social paucity, isolation and, crucially, the feeling that no one is watching. The isolated farm at the novel's center does not appear to be on the radar of the British government or any party outside of the family.

Nevertheless, two of the most libidinally intense scenes in the novel feature arms of the state, first, in the form of a liberal functionary of the colonial state and, second, in the setting of a state-funded public space. An aloof stranger randomly traverses the farm one day and has a strong emotional exchange with the overseer's son Waldo. The stranger is foreshadowed in the novel's preface, in which the writer explains her method as anti-romance. Strangers who come and go without reappearing, thus denying formal closure, produce the Barthesian reality-effect of this novel, a reality streaked with violence. Despite the narrator's disavowal in the preface, the stranger's second appearance in Waldo's life does indeed produce a denouement—it leads to an end of Waldo's self-narration within the novel. Crucially, this encounter occurs in the state space of the Grahamstown Botanical Gardens.

In this chapter, I show how Schreiner's novel turns to the colonial state to make meaning out of the fragments or, as I shall call them, unattached surfaces of colonial life, which inhibit any kind of coherent social and cultural reproduction. The novel organizes complex historical changes into a contest between an older, tyrannical version of state sovereignty (power with a head and the right to cut off its subjects' heads) and a newer, detached version of liberal governance (a headless, dispersed power that gets into its subjects' heads). While the novel's critique of the first mode of power would seem to invite the installation of the latter, The Story of an African Farm actually exposes this new mode of liberal governance as more difficult to resist and in some ways more insidious because of the fantasies of wholeness and recognition that it inspires in colonial subjects. These fantasies bind colonial subjects into a new sort of thralldom. Liberal thinkers, old and new and sometimes even socialist, such as Matthew Arnold, John Stuart Mill, Spencer, L. T. Hobhouse, and Webb often described or assumed liberal personhood to be the expression of the innermost authentic self that needs only cultivation to be simultaneously developed and accessed. In contrast, Schreiner's colonial subjects experience such personhood as a condition that the liberal state can give or withhold at whim.

An Unsound Social Body and a Partial Body Politic

The Story of an African Farm follows the destinies of three children on a family farm in the semi-desert outreaches of the Cape Colony: the orphaned English cousins, Em and Lyndall, and the German boy, Waldo. The children suffer under the abusive care of Em's stepmother, the Boer Tant' Sannie, who runs the farm until Em comes of age. The other characters include Tant' Sannie's bilingual Hottentot maid, who facilitates much of the action of the plot; the German settler Otto, who is Waldo's father and the overseer of the farm; the villainous Irish interloper, Bonaparte Blenkins, who usurps Otto and indirectly causes his death, leaving Waldo an orphan; and the tepid English farmer, Gregory Rose, who replaces Blenkins once the latter has been deposed.

As this synopsis suggests, Schreiner's novel takes great pains to identify characters by their nationality and ethnicity so that they come to embody the different groups that were in conflict in modern South Africa: native Hottentots and Zulus; the Dutch settlers, or Boers, who invaded in the mid–seventeenth century; the Germans who followed them; and, finally, the English, who entered the multi-front fray at the end of the eighteenth century. Even though it would appear that the children are all born in the Cape Colony, the narrator consistently identifies them by their parents' nationality. In this fractious, heterogeneous settler colony, there are no "South Africans." The constant reference to the characters' national or ethnic identities is just one example of the novel's relentless refusal to allow the reader to imagine that a harmonious South African social body exists. The title also reflects the lack of an overarching identity that would transcend differences. The story told might be distinct ("the story"), but the farm itself is only one of many ("an African farm") and while the title's one descriptive term ("African") indicates that the farm is not on the British Isles, it does not specify a location within the enormous continent.

The novel begins as an earlier stage of British colonialism was beginning to wane. During this stage, the British actively sought to control South Africa because they feared that the Napoleonic Empire would try to seize the Cape in order to encroach upon India. At the end of the eighteenth century, the British entered a brutal playing field established by the Dutch who had been engaged in colonization efforts in the Cape since the mid–seventeenth century. The British were able to capture the Cape peninsula from these earlier European competitors in 1795. The Dutch momentarily regained control of the Cape from 1803 to 1806, but war in Europe caused Britain to redouble its efforts. In 1814, the European peace settlement secured British sovereignty over the Cape Colony (Saunders and Smith 597–623). At this point, Britain found itself ruling not only a large native population that outnumbered its settlers, but also non-British European settlers, a situation that differed from Canada, Australia, and New Zealand.

Schreiner's novel then takes us into the 1870s and 1880s when diamond fields and gold mines were discovered and the era of high imperialism began.[1] Once these extremely lucrative resources were found, Britain's interest in its settler colony increased dramatically, as did the interest of other European powers. Germany and Belgium began to fight for a portion of the wealth to be attained in South Africa. Such international competition led to the infamous Scramble for Africa, which was capped by the Berlin Conference of 1884. The heightened expansionism that characterizes this era had two major effects. First, it spurred the development of finance capitalism to fund excavation of the mines. Second, it led to the simultaneous contraction and expansion of the nation form as Western European states extended beyond their national borders for economic gain and their colonies began to demand independent national status.

Neither the narrator nor the characters refer to the numerous bloody conflicts that occurred between European settlers and African natives and among settlers and entrepreneurs upon the discovery of diamond fields and gold mines. The military presence of the state creeps into the story only through cultural fragments: a scrap of a military poem recited here, a written reference to a military song heard there. The novel's transmuting of the political situation into these details renders it a kind of museum of charged bits and pieces rather than a historical novel, emitting a vision of an unhealthy and meager South African social body and a nonexistent body politic.

The lack of cohesion—which prevents the appearance of a transcendent, abstract conception of the social with which the characters can identify—is communicated through the landscape scenes, as well. As mentioned previously, critics have noted how Schreiner's prose style captures the fragmentary nature of this violent colonial world. Her representation of landscape also emphasizes surfaces and horizontality. The opening paragraph establishes a South African terrain that is reflective, as opposed to vertical or historical, denying the reader's search for depth or meaning:

> The full African moon poured down its light from the blue sky into the wide, lonely plain. The dry sandy earth with its coating of stunted "karroo" bushes a few inches high, the low hills that skirted the plain, the milk-bushes with their long finger-like leaves, were all touched by a weird and an almost oppressive beauty as they lay in the white light. (47)

Unlike H. Rider Haggard's adventure novel, *King Solomon's Mines* (1885), Schreiner's landscape depictions of South Africa do not inspire feelings of ownership, nostalgia, or even sublime tragedy.[2] While Schreiner's opening scene has an aesthetic quality that can be found in Haggard's imperialist fiction, the feelings it conveys are far more ambivalent. The interplay of active and passive natural objects partly accounts for this. The moon may be said to be the most active agent in the scene, pouring its light down. The elements of the land, such as the sandy earth, the skirting hills, and the groping bushes, then passively reflect the light back, rendering the landscape an assemblage of surfaces "touched" by light, glinting and reflecting.

For a brief moment, we might imagine that Schreiner's moonlight has the potential to homogenize or unify the disparate elements of the landscape and the social world of the novel, as it does in *King Solomon's Mines*.[3] It shines down on the plain and then on the home, and finally forces its way inside, where we are introduced to the first human character: "In the farmhouse, on her great wooden bedstead, Tant' Sannie the Boer-woman, rolled heavily in her sleep" (47). The theme of surfaces continues with the novel's human subjects. The narrator tells us that Tant' Sannie's bad dreams are "only of the sheep's trotters she had eaten for supper that night," and thus not the sign of psychic depth (48). The weak promise of the unifying force of the moon definitively ends in the next paragraph, when the moonlight occasions a reference to African labor, but only in its negligent absence: "In the next room, where the maid had forgotten to close the shutter, the white moonlight fell in a flood, and made it light as day" (48). The moonlight not only fails to link isolated people to something national or global, but also draws attention to a society that cannot even be said to be crumbling or in fragments because those processes imply a prior state of wholeness.

Nor do the scraps of a print public sphere that appear in the narrative offer an "imagined community," to borrow from Benedict Anderson, that might bind the population of South Africa. The novel continues its theme of discontinuity and surfaces with Lyndall's and Gregory's obsession with magazine and newspaper photographs. Unlike the elements of the human population or landscape, which do not adhere or add up to an imagined whole, the pieces of magazine that float through the novel did at one time belong to an originary wholeness—physically, that of the bound issue from which they were taken, and symbolically, that of a far-away metropolitan public sphere that imports images of itself to the colonies.

Despite their temperamental and philosophical differences, Lyndall and Gregory are similarly attracted to aspirational images of English success, beauty, celebrity, and power, not to the small print of local colonial politics. Their absorption in these cutouts acts as a measure of their own sense of internal incoherence and desire to inhabit a perfected, idealized body that comes to them from the imperial center. As a small child, Lyndall is drawn to the magazine picture that hangs over Tant' Sannie's bed. Desperate to escape a present in which she has no power, Lyndall's fantasy of her future omnipotence incorporates the photograph. For Lyndall, knowledge and material wealth are fully conjoined. She tells Em and Waldo,

> "When I am grown up" . . . the flush on her delicate features deepening at every word, "there will be nothing that I do not know. I shall be rich, very rich; and I shall wear, not only for best, but every day, a pure white silk, and little rosebuds, like the lady in Tant' Sannie's bed-room, and my petticoats will be embroidered, not only at the bottom, but all through." (57)

The narrator then explains, "The lady in Tant' Sannie's bed-room was a gorgeous creature from a fashion-sheet, which the Boer-woman, somewhere obtaining had pasted up at the foot of her bed, to be profoundly admired by the children" (57). Likewise, Gregory is drawn to surfaces and print. When he first arrives to run the farm, he decorates his one-room lodging with pictures clipped from the *Illustrated London News*. These images, the narrator informs us, feature "a noticeable preponderance of female faces and figures" (171). Ironically, Gregory's attraction to these figures does not point to a typical masculinist objectification of the female image. Instead, it suggests his need to identify with images from the imperial center and foreshadow his future donning of women's clothes.

Lyndall and Gregory seek wholeness in mirrors, as well, finding a unification of an image that is both reassuring but, because reflective and doubling, also unsettling. As an adult, Lyndall has learned the limits of attaining knowledge and becoming a beautiful, fashionable woman and is at a loss for other images to help her organize her intellectual aspirations and sexuality. Pregnant and unmarried, she decides to disappear into the unchartered territory of the Transvaal. Alone in her bedroom, before departing the farm, she looks at herself in a mirror, whispering, "We are all alone, you and I . . . no one helps us, no one understands us; but we will help ourselves" and "We shall never be quite alone, you and I . . . we shall always be together, as we were when we were little" (233). Similarly, Gregory uses a mirror to stabilize uneasy feelings. Upon first arriving at the farm, he writes a self-pitying letter to his distant sister. Starting the letter with an address, he then looks into the mirror: "It was a youthful face reflected there, with curling brown beard and hair; but in the dark blue eyes there was a look of languid longing that touched him" (172). The image inspires him to include an account of his image in his letter. He writes, "When I look up into the little glass that hangs opposite me, I wonder if that changed and sad face—"; he stops when he considers that it "sounded almost as if he might be conceited or unmanly to be looking at his own face in the glass" (172). Gender norms in the colonial context inhibit Gregory from enjoying a singular moment of absorption in an external image of himself, a pleasure that other British colonizer characters in the novel appear to be denied, as well.

Through landscape, cutout photographs, and mirrors, the novel thematizes surfaces that break apart, glimmer, and reflect; lights that do not unify fragments, but rather double them; and the absence of depth or a core to the social world. With its emphasis on antagonisms among groups over commonality and surfaces over depths, *The Story of an African Farm* dismisses the organic concepts sacred to nineteenth-century political and social theory. Most especially, it dismisses the idea of reproduction, which is tied to the organicism that underwrites modern political theory.

Schreiner's dedication initiates the theme of reproduction—and its extreme circumscription—by encouraging us to equate a writing utensil to a birth canal: "To My Friend Mrs. John Brown Of Burnley, This Little Firstling Of My Pen Is Lovingly Inscribed Ralph Iron" (37). Analogizing cultural and biological reproduction is a familiar literary convention, but

Schreiner's dedication makes some unsettling associations. First, it inserts the act of inscription into both kinds of reproduction. To inscribe something is to devote it to someone else, but it can also mean to mark a surface, an act that may in fact be part of the process of devotion. In this instance, the surface is not only the paper on which the novel is written, but also, metaphorically, living flesh ("firstling").

What is inscribed is a name, which, in the syntax of the dedication, slips between two positions: Schreiner's pseudonym "Ralph Iron" dedicates the novel/offspring and transfers his name to it, collapsing subject and object. Whether in the patriarchal family, the imperialist mode of acquisition, or the classificatory, administrative rationality of bureaucratic government, the act of naming people and places is, of course, central to ownership and control. The name of the dedicatee, Mrs. John Brown, also evokes the nineteenth-century subsuming of women into their husbands' bodies, signified by the wife casting off her given name and taking her husband's.

That the author inscribes his first novel/offspring "lovingly" scarcely mitigates the proprietorial and violent aspect of the ceremony of naming. Furthermore, the author's act of naming the text after himself suggests both the loss and the doubling of the self in one's own products, which in turn weakens the idea of an authentic, singular self who masters the objects that surround him. The status of the name in question, "Ralph Iron," Schreiner's prosthetic identity, implies a further displacement of self. Finally, the choice of pseudonym, "Ralph Iron," calls to mind iron manacles, as well as branding irons, both of which reinforce the association of reproduction and violence.

To reproduce, an entity—whether commodity, person, culture, or society—must have a coherent identity, some kind of internal integrity. Reproducing thereby ensures continuity into the future, establishing a connection between the present and the future and, inasmuch as the present reproduces the past, between the past and the future, as well. The idea of reproduction is crucial for national ideology, which requires that the national subject feel himself to be a member of a homogeneous population, all of whom share a past and thus can imagine a progressive destiny for themselves, as well. But the novel shows that only violence and custom have enough coherence in the partialized, disjointed world of the novel to reproduce. After all, none of the main characters reproduce biologically within the novel. Lyndall's baby dies, along with Lyndall. Even if Em and Gregory, unenthusiastically engaged at the end of the novel, do have children together, they will be the offspring of defeated parents. Only Tant' Sannie and the illiberal views she spouts unthinkingly will reproduce with any vitality, leaving the reader at the end of the novel with a frightful vision of the future of South Africa. This condition sets the scene for the state's entry into Waldo's erotic and intellectual life.

While inter-European and European-African violence would have been occurring all around the farm, violence only explicitly enters the narrative with the appearance of the Irish interloper Bonaparte Blenkins. Narrated through the conventions of melodrama, he is referred to as Bonaparte throughout the novel, standing in for a French-style imperialism that, on the surface, appears brotherly and benign, but is actually tyrannical and brutal. Through the negative example of Otto's worship of Bonaparte, the novel theorizes how an earlier imperialism managed to install itself by operating on subjects' irrational and masochistic subjection of themselves. However, what follows in the linear time of the novel's plot brings its own pains, as well. An aloof magistrate, representing liberal colonial governance, appears in the more standard conventions of realist description. Revealingly, even this latter scenario is undercut with allegory, as I explain later in this chapter.

Humanitarian Tyranny and Aloof Rule

For Hannah Arendt, South Africa represented a particularly vexed example of British imperialism, which she compared with French imperialism. The Napoleonic Empire sought to assimilate natives into a political structure in which they had double identities as fellow citizens and consenting subjects of French civilization and progress. The so-called humanitarianism of this mission often devolved into tyranny because its oppressive example tended to inspire counter-nationalisms that the French military then attempted to quell with brutal force, violating the principles of its own national institutions. Thus, for Arendt, French, or Napoleonic, imperialism most dramatically exposes the contradiction between the nation form and conquest.

Arendt contrasted this form of rule with a British style that remained aloof. The British sought to control the native populations through the latter's own governmental structures. Arendt ascribed the relative, if limited, success of British imperialists to their ability to obscure the stark contradiction between national ideals of liberty and equality and the bloody injustices of conquest through this strategy. British officials sought to keep their legal and cultural institutions as separate as possible from those of the colonized. This distancing mechanism signaled, Arendt writes,

... a curious mixture of arrogance and respect: the new arrogance of the administrators abroad who faced "backward populations" or "lower breeds" found its correlative in the respect of old-fashioned statesmen at home who felt that no nation had the right to impose its law upon a foreign people. (176)

Arrogance became an effective instrument of rule while its correlative, respect, only managed to set certain restraints on its exercise, such as the abolition of the slave trade and later slavery in the British Empire. Although immensely significant, these abolitions did not fundamentally alter social hierarchies or economic conditions. Arendt draws attention to how the British imperative to respect difference rested upon exclusion and the adoption of superiority. Aloofness, Arendt argued, was in fact more insidious than outright tyranny because it kept the natives at a distance, disallowing any kind of exchange, even bribery, between ruler and ruled.

In what follows, I transpose Arendt's distinction between French and British imperialism onto Michel Foucault's distinction between sovereignty and biopower. As I mention in the Introduction, in his writings on war, Foucault exploded the dominance of the idea of sovereignty in political theory, arguing that sovereignty, boiled down to the credo of "the right to take life or let live," was eventually overtaken in the nineteenth century by a new mode of power, biopower, summed up in the phrase, "the power to 'make' live and 'let' die" (2003, 240–1). While sovereignty concerns the protection of territory, biopower refers to the management of the population within a territory. I read these two theories together, so that Arendt's key terms of respect, arrogance, and aloofness in the British imperial context appear as the affective code words or rhetorical face for the British government's operations of biopower at home and abroad. I call this mode of detached, biopolitical power "aloof rule." While Arendt's distinction is synchronic and Foucault's distinction is diachronic, Schreiner's novel sets these national and historical distinctions on the same temporal plane, presenting one as succeeding the other and comparing their modes of forming subjects.

Bonaparte first insinuates himself into the family by inspiring Otto with religious awe and trying to seduce Tant' Sannie, thus harkening to an older form of patriarchal power found in Christianity and kinship. Otto encounters Bonaparte first, inviting him to stay and eventually viewing him as a figure for Jesus. When Bonaparte slyly expresses his wish to lead the Sunday Service, Otto, despite his pleasure in that role, happily and masochistically hands it over. When Bonaparte then protests that his clothes are too shabby to perform the service, Otto gives him his own best suit: " 'It's not the latest fashion, perhaps not a West End cut, not exactly; but it might do; it might serve at a push. Try it on, try it on!' [Otto] said, his old grey eyes twinkling with pride" (76). His pleasure and excitement build as he continues to add to the splendor of Bonaparte's image with his own material goods.

In the novel's restaging of French imperialism, the pleasure that comes from self-renunciation misleads subjects into giving power to those who destroy them: "Bonaparte drew [the boots] on and stood upright, his head almost touching the beams. The German looked at him with profound admiration. It was wonderful what a difference feathers made in the bird" (76). Bonaparte then uses these clothes and a series of performances to insinuate himself into Tant' Sannie's good graces. Flirting in English, translated into Dutch by the Hottentot maid, Bonaparte courts the matron. Seeing his opportunity when some sheep are missing, Bonaparte lies to Tant' Sannie, telling her that Otto had confessed that Tant' Sannie wanted to marry him and that he would kill her. Flying into a rage at what she perceives to be Otto's impudence and threat to her life, Tant' Sannie orders the old German to leave.

As Otto lies in his cabin on the last night before his departure, he rereads an old storybook, a conventional melodrama featuring aristocrats and an innocent maiden. Despite its fanciful trappings, Otto takes it for reality: "To the old German a story was no story. Its events were as real and as important to himself as the matters of his own life" (101). The narrator encourages us to view Otto as a naïve reader, one who does not distinguish between fiction and reality. The way he reads a melodrama is how he reads his life, in a perpetual state of surprise and then with retroactive claims to having known better all along: "Occasionally, as his feelings became too strongly moved, he ejaculated, 'Ah, I thought so!—That was a rogue!—I saw before!—I knew it from the beginning!' " (102). Sometimes, the novel seems to be saying, the melodramatic exists in reality, but melodramas have failed to train Otto to detect the villain in his own life. Perhaps they have even disabled him from detecting real-life villains. Defining its own realism against this suspect subgenre, *The Story of an African Farm* indicts melodramas, romances, and other kinds of novels for consoling the reader and distracting him or her from "seeing" through the pretense of power.

While the adults on the farm appear to be in power and thus must be wooed by Bonaparte, the white children and the black South Africans are merely terrorized. The latter are dumbfounded by his appearance, "star[ing] stupidly at the object of attraction" (62). Their stupefaction forms the neutral background of the drama, marking a possible imperviousness, but also a passivity suggesting that they will succumb to whomever force dominates. In the political imaginary of the novel, the children and the black servants do not form an alliance against this external imperial force, whether in French or British form.

Bonaparte continues his seizure of power by seeking to dominate the now fully orphaned Waldo. He speaks to the child in the rhetoric of duty and obligation: "I am to be master of this farm now; and we shall be good friends, I trust, very good friends, if you try to do your duty, my dear boy," later "looking benignly at the candle" while committing acts of injustice, such as tripping Waldo (109). As he did with Waldo's father, Bonaparte trumps up charges against the boy to ingratiate himself with Tant' Sannie. One day, he sees Waldo leave the attic and notes that his face is flushed. Turning over various possibilities—drinking wine, fooling around with a girl—and summarily dismissing them, Bonaparte concludes, "sagaciously," "Did not Tant' Sannie keep in the loft 'bultongs,' and nice smoked sausages? There must be something nice to *eat* up there! Aha! That was it!" (115). Unable to speak Tant' Sannie's language, he uses pantomime to accuse the boy of eating her stored supplies in the attic. She replies that the only food she had stored in the attic were salt and dried peaches, the latter being inedible, but Bonaparte, not understanding her and not particularly interested in rational explanations, proceeds with his plan, pulling out a horsewhip. Tant' Sannie readily consents and laughs, for reasons not clear to herself: "There was something so exceedingly humorous in the idea that he was going to beat the boy, though for her own part she did not see that the peaches were worth it" (125).

The absurdity of Bonaparte's formal language signals the absurdity of administrative rationality:

> Waldo, it grieves me beyond expression to have to summon you for so painful a purpose; but it is at the imperative call of duty, which I dare not evade. I do not state that frank and unreserved confession will obviate the necessity of chastisement, which if requisite shall be fully administered; but the nature of that chastisement may be mitigated by free and humble confession. Waldo, answer me as you would your own father, in whose place I now stand to you: have you, or have you not, did you, or did you not, eat of the peaches in the loft? (125)

Waldo refuses to respond, thereby refusing to speak in terms that cast him as victim or perpetrator. His silence makes Bonaparte self-conscious about his own performance. Pushing Waldo to confess, he forgets himself, but then, "feeling that he had fallen from that high gravity which was as spice to the pudding, and the flavour of the whole little tragedy, he drew himself up" (126). To punish Waldo for refusing to answer, if not for taking the peaches, Bonaparte sends him into "solitary confinement," a term that fully renders the extent to which the small farm has become a military state.

In this scene, Schreiner draws attention to the ways violence and political authority are wildly in contradiction and, consequently, terrifyingly effective in controlling subjects. She also emphasizes the connections among violence, political authority, and sexuality: "[Bonaparte] drew his mouth expressively on one side, and made the lash of the little horsewhip stick out of his pocket and shake up and down" (126). After locking him in the fuel-house, Bonaparte then ties Waldo to a wooden post, slits his shirt open at the back, and savagely whips him. At the end of this brutal scene, Bonaparte asks him if he has something to say now: "The boy looked up at him—not sullenly, not angrily. There was a wild, fitful terror in the eyes. Bonaparte made haste to go out and shut the door, and leave him alone in the darkness. He himself was afraid of that look" (128). Bonaparte identifies with the terror in Waldo's eyes, for it is his own terror reflected back to him—another example of surface over depth.

Despite its violence, however, Bonaparte's exercise of tyranny can be interrupted. Even as a child, Lyndall understands how Bonaparte's position is sustained by the acts of pleading, the masochistic self-renunciation, and the sheer belief of those he seeks to dominate. Her solution represents a kind of fantastical will to out-Napoleon the Napoleon figure. After the brutal whipping, Waldo remains locked in the fuel-house. Em cries and tells Lyndall that she has been begging Bonaparte to let Waldo out, to which Lyndall replies, "The more you beg the more he will not" (129). When Em sees that Lyndall will neither share her grief nor comfort her, she turns against her, seeking to injure Lyndall and thus pass on this flow of violence: "'Oh, but it's late, and I think they want to kill him,' said Em, weeping bitterly; and finding that no more consolation was to be gained from her cousin, she went off blubbering—'I wonder you can cut aprons when Waldo is shut up like that'" (129). Em's parting shot does motivate Lyndall to act: "A flush rose to her face: she opened the door quickly, and walked in, went to the nail on which the key of the fuel-room hung" (129). Bonaparte and Tant' Sannie watch her, asking her in unison what she wants. Lyndall replies, "[t]his key" and holds it up while looking at them. The two adults then bicker:

"Do you mean her to have it?" said Tant' Sannie in Dutch.
"Why don't you stop her?" asked Bonaparte in English.
"Why don't you take it from her?" said Tant' Sannie. (130)

As the Hottentot maid translates their bewildered, accusatory questions to each other, Lyndall walks to the fuel-house with the key and releases Waldo.

The Story of an African Farm displays faith in critique and, in particular, the novel's capacity to teach its readers how to see clearly through tyranny and injustice and to experience themselves as having already known how to do so. It achieves this by asserting the superiority of the literary mode of realism over melodrama. However, the novel also narrates a different form of power against which it appears less able. As it dissects how this power takes hold, the novel argues for its own limits in teaching readers to use rationality and will to extricate themselves from it. Hegemonic and aloof, this other form of power manages to get beyond surfaces. One simply cannot have knowledge, refuse its gaze, or do what one wants, because this form of power locks even the critical thinker in a scene of his own fantasy. As we shall see, the novel is ultimately pessimistic about breaking out of the subjectifying bind that shapes the subject in the realm of this kind of fantasy.

The Long Arms of the State: Shame, Citizenship, and Aloof Rule

In a scene that marks an abrupt rhetorical transition from realist narrative to fable and metaphysical meditation to realism again, the dark-skinned, dispossessed German laborer Waldo meets a stranger who displays the class markings of a gentleman. The stranger's official function is not mentioned in the novel. In keeping with the text's aesthetics of contingency laid out in the preface, he just passes through (41). However, if we turn to a letter Schreiner wrote to Havelock Ellis in 1884, she reveals that this episode between Waldo and the stranger refers to a real-life encounter of her own with a stranger who dropped in on her in Basutoland one rainy night.[4] He turned out to be a recently appointed clerk to the magistrate at Dordrecht in the Eastern Cape Colony.[5] This biographical detail opens up the scenes between Waldo and the stranger into explorations of what happens when a marginalized settler, previously with no conscious relation to the state, encounters a figure of the state and becomes entwined in a performance of aloof rule. The encounters represent two sides of an exchange: first, a colonial desire for understanding, benevolence, and sympathy from a State Other, which adds up to the desire for a coherent, livable identity in an environment that consistently and pervasively shreds attempts to build one; and, second, a state functionary's interiority, which is defined through the shame that springs from his recognition of himself as the screen upon which others project their fantasies. Attending Waldo's wish for recognition is the novel's fearful pessimism about the British state's capacity to do so without violence to its subjects, for the novel also exposes the social and political limits of this desire in the public space of the colonial state.

The first scene occurs a few years after Tant' Sannie has run Bonaparte off the farm for wooing a younger, wealthier relative of hers—a fatal foreign policy mistake on his part. Waldo lies on the ground near his father's grave, carving a wooden totem. A stranger approaches, alights from his horse, and looks down upon the prostrate Waldo, asking him what the marks on the wooden carving mean. The novel takes great care to describe the stranger as afflicted by a complex of feelings: "The questioner looked down at him—the huge, unwieldy figure, in size a man's, in right of its childlike features and curling hair a child's; and it hurt him—it attracted him and it hurt him. It was something between pity and sympathy" (157). This feeling of pity and sympathy implies a mix of disidentification and identification and prompts the stranger to offer to buy the carving. But because Waldo is making it for his father's grave, he refuses. Still viewing Waldo as a primitive fixture of the land, and thus provincial, backward, and superstitious, or, in other words, a Boer, the object of strong British prejudice, the stranger mockingly questions Waldo. Why, he asks, carve a totem for his father's grave if he believes his father will rise again? To the stranger's surprise, the boy lobs his arch question back at him. The stranger then laughs and replies, "I am a man who believes nothing, hopes nothing, fears nothing, feels nothing" (158).

The stranger's declaration of a belief in nothing fills the lonely, seeking Waldo with love, which prompts him to explain the story carved into the post. After Waldo finishes, the stranger retells his account in expansive detail. Waldo replies, "All my life I have longed to see you" (167). The stranger closes with advice to Waldo that he should remain on the farm: "Live on here quietly. The time may yet come when you will be that which other men have hoped to be and never will be now" (170). After this moment of identification, the stranger then becomes immediately ashamed by his own earnestness. Resuming his decadent affectation and defensive posture of carelessness, he gives Waldo an old brown volume. Schreiner tells Ellis in the same letter mentioned previously that it was meant to be Spencer's *First Principles*. The scene encapsulates the kind of rule Arendt ascribes to British imperialists. Although a functionary and not seemingly having direct power over Waldo, the stranger's relay between arrogance and shame, distance and intimacy, becomes an allegory for British rule in South Africa, at least over its European settlers.

We already know that liberal thought enlivens Waldo—as I discuss in the previous section, Bonaparte had accused Waldo of stealing food from the attic. In fact, Waldo had been reading Mill's *Principles of Political Economy*, a book that had belonged to Em's now deceased British father. Instead of considering political or intellectual excitement, the crude tyrant thinks Waldo's elation has to do with the sating of a physical appetite of some kind, whether food, sex, or alcohol. Waldo's reading experience is described as a kind of consumption and possession, another form of conquest, but one with fewer human consequences: "All he read he did not fully understand; the thoughts were new to him; but this was the fellow's startled joy in the book—the thoughts were his, they belonged to him. He had never thought them before, but they were his" (114). Men's ideas, not images of women's bodies, sexualize his adolescent body:

> The boy's heavy body quivered with excitement. So he was not alone, not alone. He could not quite have told any one why he was so glad, and this warmth had come to him. His cheeks were burning. (115)

Waldo imagines that the stranger, too, harbors these ideas inside himself, which will similarly excite him.

For Waldo, this encounter marks an intense falling in love in which he feels his best self, as Arnold might describe it in *Culture and Anarchy*, being recognized and cultivated. The intensity of this feeling is only matched by an intense rejection, by the individual, the state, and the imperial body politic. Toward the end of the novel, Waldo returns to the farm after a long journey and composes a letter to Lyndall. He emerges as a kind of realist novelist, detailing the loneliness and disappointments that attend alienating one's labor under a capitalist regime. However, his imagined reader, Lyndall, is not only physically absent, she is actually dead, suggesting that the South African realist reader may also be extinct. A different kind of reader and a different kind of literary style are needed to overcome the kind of oppression that Waldo feels, but the future seems quite bleak.

The emotional climax of the letter concerns a key scene in the Botanic Gardens in Grahamstown where Waldo spends his half-holiday. Here he experiences shame and the deep, self-loathing pangs of bourgeois aspiration.

Botanic gardens, like parks, were state-funded initiatives that became popular throughout the nineteenth century. Their proponents argued that in addition to educating the public on plant variety and science, they would end up fostering the social order by exposing those from the working class to the middle classes and inspiring them with aspirations toward respectability, while heading off social malcontent. In the mid-1850s, the Governor of the Cape Colony granted the land and starting funds for the Grahamstown Botanic Garden. Its history was interrupted by violent frontier wars, mentions of which, as I noted before, are conspicuously absent from the novel. Instead, as Waldo enters the garden, we get his careful description of a long raised avenue, artfully arranged flowers, and well-dressed ladies and children strolling about the park: panoplies of leisure and the family form, broadcasting advertisements of the white family, the romance plot, domesticity, and bourgeois respectability. Then the military band starts up, a lone signal to the reader of the constant presence of war.

At first, Waldo writes, the music is like everyday life. It then transports him out of himself and, yet, curiously, brings him closer to his objects of desire, which are not material, but transcendent. When the music stops, he spots the stranger once again sitting between two well-dressed ladies. He writes to Lyndall, "I could not see anything while [the music] was playing; I stood with my head against the tree; but, when it was done, I saw that there were ladies sitting close to me on a wooden bench, and the stranger who had talked to me that day in the karroo was sitting between them" (247). They are talking, not listening to the music, and he stops listening as well, growing painfully hyperembodied:

> When I was listening to the music I did not know I was badly dressed; now I felt so ashamed of myself. I never knew before what a low, horrible thing I was, dressed in tan-cord. That day on the farm, when we sat on the ground under the thorn-trees, I thought he quite belonged to me; now, I saw he was not mine. But he was still as beautiful. (248)

Flooded with shame and suddenly aware of his body, he sees how the stranger does not, as he puts it, belong to him. As they mount a phaeton and drive away, one of the ladies drops her whip. At her peremptory demand, Waldo retrieves it. The lady then throws a sixpence on the ground in front of him. This humiliating gesture implants the desire for material goods in Waldo and teaches him the ineffectiveness of groping for a political or intellectual community: "I might have gone back to the garden then, but

I did not want music; I wanted clothes, and to be fashionable and fine. I felt that my hands were coarse, and that I was vulgar. I never tried to see him again" (249).

The public gardens—ostensibly open, accessible, and inclusive—become instead the stage of exclusivity, difference, abjection, and shame. Instead of fostering intellectual and cultural development, they instill the desire for material wealth and emphasize the impossibility of democracy in a capitalist, imperialist society. In this way, the novel aligns Waldo with the black servants on the farm; unable to participate in the drama of power or on the stage of history, they are nevertheless necessary as spectators for power to function properly. This experience permanently marks Waldo and, as he returns home, he starts to crave the material things that go along with bourgeois respectability. Love involves the desire to acquire, to have, to incorporate an object, to blur boundaries. He is no longer happy with the possession of men's thoughts:

> I did not love books; I wanted people. When I walked home under the shady trees in the street I could not be happy, for when I passed the houses I heard music, and saw faces between the curtains. I did not want any of them, but I wanted some one for mine, for me. I could not help it. I wanted a finer life. (248)

The stranger had expanded Waldo's intellectual, private interiority, but seeing the stranger's intimate life in a public space that is also a staging of state power reminds Waldo of the exclusions and contradictions of the public sphere. These exclusions are at once economic and sexual, articulated through the heterosexist cult of domesticity in which respectable men and women arrange themselves within marriage and set about to reproduce, socially and biologically. Waldo's desires not to reproduce but to project himself outward intellectually and emotionally into the world cannot be satisfied. His explicit encounters with the state elevate and depress him in proportionate degrees, sending him out into the world and back to the farm again, where the novel closes in a famously inconclusive way with the death of Waldo's consciousness. *The Story of an African Farm* reveals how the power of the British state relies upon the fantasies of the marginalized, a point that Michael Taussig has argued: It is not only fear of violence that keeps people willing subjects of the state, ready to believe its official version of them, but also love and desire that keep subjects spellbound.

Conclusion

Ultimately, *The Story of an African Farm* compares sovereignty and biopower in their South African manifestations to argue that sovereignty is in fact easier to resist. One can reverse the violence and terror that motivates it or one can simply refuse to acknowledge it, while aloof rule, the novel suggests, is far more intractable and resistant because it is not motivated by terror. Nor is it susceptible to critical demystification. In the barren terrain of this colonial outpost, the reader apprehends how this new mode of power shapes the subject's very sense of self, operating on the level of sexuality, affect, and fantasy: liberal governance or biopower makes the claim of enabling its subjects to be their best selves and therefore, as one's best self, to be loved by the State Other. This is not to say that sovereignty as a mode of power acting on subjects does not also involve these human faculties, but in the case of biopower, the subjects feel themselves to be finding their authentic individuality—along with their freedom, choice, and will—in the same act that, first, results from power acting upon them and, second, locks them in a relation of desire with another entity.

2 *"Rather a Geographical Expression Than a Country"*

State Fantasy and the Production of Victorian Afghanistan

> If the frontiers of India are insufficiently delineated, those of Afghanistan are a thousand times more vague.
>
> —W. P. Andrew, *Our Scientific Frontier* (1880)[1]

In the previous chapter, I argued that Schreiner's *The Story of an African Farm* charted the psychic vicissitudes undergone by colonial subjects as the logic of biopower began to overtake that of sovereignty. In this chapter, I reverse the direction of my analysis. Instead of examining representations produced in the outlying areas of the empire that reflect back upon its center, I examine the center's representations of Afghanistan. In what follows, I propose that these representations were profoundly shaped by British anxiety about the emergence of the fantasy of the state as a heroic actor. I also contend that they contributed to the material and symbolic making of modern Afghanistan.

To say that Afghanistan presents a hermeneutical problem for the West is perhaps to say the obvious. It certainly appears self-evident to the narrator of G. A. Henty's *For Name and Fame, or Through Afghan Passes* (1886), a popular adventure novel for boys set during the Second Anglo-Afghan War (1878–81). To account for the lack of patriotism on the part of Yossouf, the young Afghan attendant of William, the novel's British protagonist, the narrator patiently explains to his readers, "It must be remembered that Afghanistan has for centuries been rather a geographical expression than a country" (231).[2] Henty's metaphor efficiently accomplishes several functions at once: It casts the country in a perpetual condition of prenationhood that keeps its meaning as well as its frontiers open and malleable. It also serves to explain why Afghans, like Yossouf, lack national or any other collective feeling, as well as individual sovereignty. These deficiencies render Afghans labile, untrustworthy, and inferior. In other words, the obvious is precisely the site of the ideological and we can view the narrator's use of abstract metaphors and a self-assured tone as a strategy for containing the potentially destabilizing perplexity inherent in British perceptions of Afghanistan. In this chapter, I frame Afghanistan's symbolic and territorial vagueness in late-nineteenth-century British discourse less as an empirical question of geography, foreign policy, or central intelligence than as an ideological opportunity. Afghanistan arguably appeared protean and unclear, a "geographical expression" rather than a country, throughout the nineteenth century. By the late nineteenth century, those qualities served specifically to defend against the conflicting feelings aroused by shifts in state power and its disturbing implications for the fate of liberal individuality.

Afghanistan rarely appears, if at all, in literary criticism, cultural studies, or historical accounts of the Victorian period or of the British Empire. For example, it is altogether absent from Eric Hobsbawm's *The Age of Empire, 1875–1914* (1987) and David Cannadine's *Ornamentalism: How the British Saw Their Empire* (2001), two key works on nineteenth-century Western imperialism. When Afghanistan does appear, for example, in Edward Said's classic *Culture and Imperialism* (1993), Patrick Brantlinger's important *Rule of Darkness* (1988), and the ambitious, multi-volume *Oxford History of the British Empire* (1999), edited by Andrew Porter, it does so merely as a footnote, marginal to the kinds of stories unfolding in relation to India, South Africa, or the Caribbean. Why this scarcity of reference?

In part, we can assume that it has something to do with the fact that Afghanistan was not officially colonized. Ania Loomba, for one, makes a significant material distinction between colonialism and imperialism. Modern Western European colonialism refers not only to the conquest and control of other countries' lands and peoples, but also to the restructuring of the subjugated territories' economies, "drawing them into a complex relationship with [the conqueror's] own, so that there was a flow of human and natural resources between colonized and colonial countries" (Loomba 3). More generally, Loomba writes, imperialism is "the process which leads to domination and control" and which subsumes colonialism: Imperialism can exist without colonialism, but colonialism cannot exist without imperialism (6–7).

Recent studies of the British Empire tend to focus primarily on colonies, their imbricated economies within the empire, and the dialectical formation of the self and other that marks colonial discourse. They thus overlook what we might call imperialized sites such as Afghanistan, Mongolia, Tibet, China, Siam, Japan, and Ethiopia.[3] Of course, one does not have to look very far from imperialized sites to find contested colonized ones. In the case of Afghanistan, the British military sought strategic control of the area and the right to decide who could enter its territory in order to shore up their possession of India against Russian incursions. To that end, they sought to instantiate their influence over the country's foreign policy and its borders. Thus, rather than the kind of complex exchange of goods, people, and ideas characteristic of colonialism, the British pursued a one-directional mode of control. While postcolonial theory tends to cast relations between the British and its colonized subjects as one of master to slave, giving rise to Said's well-known conceptual model of the mutually constitutive, interlocked dyad of self and other or the hybridized status made famous by Homi Bhabha, the imperialized site of Afghanistan suggests that other modes of identification and fantasy existed under empire. In particular, because the British did not seek to colonize Afghans, they could use their image to assuage contemporary anxieties. That is, the British could project onto Afghans certain positive qualities that they feared they had themselves lost in the aftermath of modernity. At the same time, because Afghanistan was so difficult to conquer—given its geographical terrain and its radically decentralized population—those same qualities could rationalize British failure to control the region.

In short, British objectives across the nineteenth century entailed consolidating the region into a recognizable unit, a nation-state, limited and sovereign, with secure boundaries and an overarching ruler sympathetic to British interests. British nation-building in Afghanistan alternated between two operations, epitomized by the First Anglo-Afghan War (1838–42) and the Second Anglo-Afghan War. The British military either fomented preexisting tribal disputes into local rebellions in order to usurp recalcitrant rulers (i.e., leaders that resisted British influence and/or seemed too friendly with the Russians) and replace them with those willing to ally with the British, or quelled local rebellions against those handpicked leaders, when they were denounced by factions within Afghanistan for being puppets of the British.

Thus, when viewed through Western discourse, Afghanistan as a modern nation emerges from the outside, materially and symbolically, encroached upon from the pressures of other nations' desires, investments, and conflicts. When Afghanistan does appear in histories of empire or in postcolonial studies, it is always tangentially, in connection with India, as the primary terrain on which Britain and Russia waged their Great Game. We could conclude that the British decision not to view Afghanistan as a colonial prize has in fact made it marginal to most theories and histories of the modern world, which in turn passively reflect this status. However, I would like to suggest instead that recent scholarship in effect discursively repeats the British government's own divergent, strategic treatment of Afghanistan and tends to overlook it even when it is present.

In this chapter, I turn to three particularly evocative late-nineteenth-century British texts: Henty's *For Name and Fame*; William Gladstone's Midlothian campaign speeches (1879), in which the famous British statesman excoriated the Tory government for invading Afghanistan and thereby established his own political viability; and Arthur Conan Doyle's first Sherlock Holmes detective novel, *A Study in Scarlet* (1887), which launched the famous series' starting point in Afghanistan. By virtue of their literariness, these texts helped to establish and maintain what I call "Victorian Afghanistan," a complex cluster of images, ideas, and affects, which crystallized in the late nineteenth century. In what follows, I consider how the historical rise of the fantasy of the state as a heroic actor informs the meaning and the cultural work that these texts called upon Victorian Afghanistan to do.

These works illustrate not only how Afghanistan appeared marginal and obscure in Victorian culture, as it does in current criticism and in our own culture at large, but also how Victorians suffused the idea of Afghanistan with powerfully ambivalent meanings. What drives this ambivalence may in part explain the tendency of Afghanistan to appear "vague" and diffused or obliquely as a highly charged detail. This formal quality of references to Afghanistan is part of their content, as well. When specifics are provided, these works cast Afghans as, on the one hand, primitive, savage, ruled by passion, lacking in discipline, and impossible to categorize. For example, in W. P. Andrew's *Our Scientific Frontier*, Afghans' religious status ranges from being so varied as to defy categorization to being utterly fanatical, while their racial status remains incoherent, obscured by a profusion of ethnicities and tribes. In other words, they appear as the antithesis of the ideal liberal individual. They even appear fundamentally excluded from achieving this form through education, a promise held out to Indians and certain other colonized subjects. On the other hand, these writings assign to Afghans the values of rugged individualism, such as love of freedom, military fierceness, bravery, and hospitality—qualities belonging to ancestral British ideals of personhood.

Informing this particular mix of romantic qualities in the late nineteenth century is an older imaginary historical linkage to that antique origin, and casualty, of British modernity—the vanquished, obsolete Scottish Highlanders. This chapter rewinds to the early nineteenth century, a critical and violent time of early nation formation, to touch briefly upon two works. Appearing in the years following the war with France and the success of the Clearances in Scotland, these works each compare eighteenth-century Scottish Highlanders and contemporary Afghans: Sir Mountstuart Elphinstone's 1815 travel narrative to Afghanistan and Sir Walter Scott's 1816 review of the Culloden Papers. These texts form the unconscious of late-nineteenth-century representations of Afghanistan in which the country once again appears as the scene of attempted ideological resolutions for conflicts about individual autonomy, state power, and national identity. By reading late-nineteenth-century representations of Victorian Afghanistan alongside these earlier accounts, we can see how Afghans serve as odd stand-ins yet again for England's own pre-liberal individual self, poised to emerge gradually, if ardently, in opposition to absolutist power over the seventeenth and eighteenth centuries.

By attending to historical shifts in British governance from a more coercive to a more hegemonic, interventionist mode and to corresponding shifts in the popular political imaginary, we can read the ambivalent status of Afghans and the generic vagueness and marginality of Afghanistan in the late nineteenth century as a symptom of Britain's own fascination with a culture it deemed an uncanny and impossible allegory for itself. This identification shows how Afghanistan served as a repressed, homologous case for British subjects' feelings of their own vulnerability toward, subjection by, and yet fascination with a new turn in official power, the kind exercised by an interventionist state. To put it somewhat differently, Afghanistan by the end of the nineteenth century was conceived in the Victorian imaginary as a raw, inhospitable space that could be made into a protective zone against Russian attempts to invade India. At the same time, it provided the setting for the destabilization and reformulation of British national identity during the years when the circulation of state fantasy generated conflicting feelings of hope and anxiety. If we remain locked in the self/other dyadic structure of much recent postcolonial studies, we risk reducing the texture and complexity of different modes of identification and projection that function to maintain uneven relations of power under empire.

"Remember the rights of the savages": Gladstone's Comeback Campaign and the Circulating Afghan Signifier

One of the longest serving politicians in British history, Gladstone played a significant part in the increase in state intervention that characterized the latter part of the century. Gladstone had started his career as a Tory, serving as chancellor of the Exchequer. In this role, he sought to balance the national budget, curtail central government spending, abolish protective tariffs, and equalize the number of direct and indirect taxes. Although he was interested in lowering central government spending, Gladstone was not averse to expanding its administrative powers. He tightened Treasury control over a professionalizing civil service and established the Public Accounts Committee to ensure financial accountability.

In the mid–nineteenth century, Gladstone's political views began to change and he switched to the Liberal Party. From this point onward, he rose to prominence. In 1868, he became Prime Minister for the first of four times. His government distinguished itself by being one of the most reformist of the nineteenth century, including among its many acts the establishment of a national education system. After a series of government scandals and the failure to win a general election, Gladstone retired, briefly, in 1874. He reentered politics in 1879, making a bid to represent Midlothian in Parliament. To that end, he traveled to Scotland to deliver what would become a famous set of foreign policy speeches. Radiant with Gladstone's charismatic oratory skills and sometimes as long as five hours, these public speeches and the large crowds they drew are often credited with contributing to the consolidation of the mass electorate. As we shall see, Afghanistan features prominently in their symbolic economy, figuring as the emotional lynchpin around which Gladstone built his critique of the current government and the legitimacy of his return to politics.

By drawing on imagery from Sir Walter Scott's historical romance, *Waverley* (1814), Gladstone linked the Afghans ravaged by the Second Anglo-Afghan War with vanquished mid-eighteenth-century Scottish Highlanders. These phantom Highlanders functioned in turn, as scholars have pointed out, as the imagined ancestors of contemporary British citizens. They particularly appealed to the Scottish constituency whom Gladstone wished to persuade, but also to the British nation as a whole. In the popular imaginary, the figure of the Highlander had come to stand for a violent past disavowed, but mourned. Over the nineteenth century, the Highlanders' mythic love of independence became core to a British culture in need of national origins and was folded into a conception of British national identity as liberal individuality. Gladstone's linkage between Scottish Highlanders and contemporary Afghans showcased their warlike, impassioned spirits, crushed by an authoritarian English government. It also transitively placed current British citizens in the same position in regard to a despotic Tory government, the bugbear of Gladstone's speeches. Despite his drive to produce an empathetic identification between the British and Afghans, however, Gladstone required their fundamental difference to complete the image of the current government's illegitimacy. Afghanness thus floats through the speeches. In some instances, it signifies Scottish Highlanders' rugged individualism, an identification that invites Gladstone's audience to identify with them against the encroaching state. In others, it signifies a savage, illiberal, unregulated past mode of warfare and incivility that the current Tory government dangerously echoed.

While addressing domestic issues, the Midlothian Speeches are particularly famous for setting out Gladstone's oppositional foreign policy principles. They critique the aggressive and expansionist tendencies of the Tory government led by Gladstone's longtime rival, Benjamin Disraeli (his second ministry, 1874–80). In the speeches, Gladstone accuses the ruling party of depleting the surplus left by his first ministry (1868–74) on unnecessary and immoral imperial endeavors, spending precious resources in the vain pursuit of acquiring more land, and jeopardizing foreign policy relations with other European powers. In his Third Midlothian Speech, Gladstone meticulously lists his foreign policy principles in the following order: "to foster the strength of the Empire by just legislation and economy at home"; "to preserve to the nations of the world—and especially . . . to the Christian nations of the world—the blessings of peace"; "to keep the Powers of Europe in union together" (115); to "avoid needless and entangling engagements"; "to acknowledge the equal rights of all nations" (116); and to "be inspired by the love of freedom" (117).

Gladstone structured his critique around several recent sites of imperial activity, including the Transvaal in South Africa and Turkey. But his attack focused on the government's starting of the Second Anglo-Afghan War: "I have got now as far as the Anglo-Turkish Convention. What is the next? The next is Afghanistan. A war was made in Afghanistan to the surprise and astonishment—I might almost say to the horror—of this country. . . ." (35). When Gladstone delivered this speech, the British public had already ceased to protest the magnitude of the British military reaction to the Afghan insurgency and had moved on to worries about domestic economic issues (Quinault 31). Here Gladstone appeals to both economic and humanitarian concerns by combining the two: The government, in his language, had exhausted the nation's economic and moral resources. In this way, he restages the Tory government's actions overseas as a domestic issue. The Anglo-Afghan War becomes an emblem of the Tory government's deliberate scare tactics, jingoism, and moral bankruptcy:

> I am only now illustrating to you the manner in which a series of surprises, a series of theatrical expedients, calculated to excite, calculated to alarm, calculated to stir pride and passion, and calculated to divide the world, have been the daily employment and subsistence, the established dietary of the present Government. (36)

In this excoriation, Gladstone casts the Tory government as having become an authoritarian, fearful dictatorship, sowing anxiety in the population at home with their military aggression and imperial heavy-handedness abroad, and using the fear that they have fabricated in turn to justify their actions. His vision of the state-society relationship figures the state as a machine that perpetually runs on a population's fear and its own offensive attacks on the world at large. Gladstone reads from a letter sent to his electors in which he catalogues the Tory government's divisive and scaremongering transgressions:

> I hold before you . . . that by the disturbance of confidence, and lately even of peace, which they have brought about, they have prolonged and aggravated the public distress; that they have augmented the power and influence of the Russian Empire, even while estranging the feelings of its population; that they have embarked the Crown and people in an unjust war (the Afghan war), full of mischief if not of positive danger to India; and that by their use of the treaty-making and war-making powers of the Crown they have abridged the just rights of Parliament and have presented prerogative to the nation under an unconstitutional aspect which tends to make it insecure. (37–8)

By embarking on an unjust war and by violating the constitution, the Tory government has compromised the very character of Britain, undercutting its citizens' autonomy and individuality and breeding dependence on its power.

Once the Second Anglo-Afghan War is established as an emblem of the Tory government's profoundly illiberal and nondemocratic show of power, it serves as the occasion for Gladstone to articulate his own version of government in which emotion is regulated and feelings of superiority are contained:

> ... the great duty of a Government especially in foreign affairs, is to soothe
> and tranquillize the minds of the people, not to set up false phantoms of
> glory which are to delude them into calamity, not to flatter their infirmities
> by leading them to believe they are better than the rest of the world and so
> to encourage the baleful spirit of domination; but to proceed upon a prin-
> ciple that recognises the sisterhood and equality of nations, the absolute
> equality of public right among them; above all, to endeavour to produce and
> to maintain a temper so calm and so deliberate in the public opinion of the
> country, that none shall be able to disturb it. (36)

Gladstone constructs an image of political power hypostasized in a body whose harmonious working of faculties will, in effect, "tranquillize" the population, while serving as an impenetrable and imperturbable shield against foreign aggression. Paradoxically, this political power both doses the population into tranquility and serves as a model of individual agency for the population to emulate. Rather than the dependent, fearful population of the Tories, Gladstone's measured Liberal government will foster the development of similarly measured British citizens.

In the service of preaching the equality of other nations and cultures, though, Gladstone reinscribes the inferiority of Afghans, exposing the limits of his culturally relativist liberal critique. Unlike the inhabitants of South Africa and Turkey, Afghans are singled out and given specific details that romanticize them:

> ... we have, by the most wanton invasion of Afghanistan, broken that
> country into pieces, made it a miserable ruin, destroyed whatever there was
> in it of peace and order, caused it to be added to the anarchies of the Eastern
> world, and we have become responsible for the management of the millions
> of warlike but very partially civilised people whom it contains, under
> circumstances where the application of military power, and we have nothing
> but military power to go by, is attended at every foot with enormous diffi-
> culties. (49–50)

Gladstone's description of Afghans as "warlike but very partially civilised" reminds his listeners of the alterity and backwardness of the natives that the British are seeking to control and regulate and dooms such efforts appropriately. In the Second Midlothian Speech, Gladstone again singles out Afghanistan from other countries Britain had recently invaded by describing its inhabitants as violent and uncivil: "There is no strength to be added to your country by governing the Transvaal, by overrunning Zululand, by undertaking to be responsible for Egypt, or for the vast mass of mountains in Central Asia, and for keeping in order their wild and warlike tribes" (64–5).

While such references may seem minor, the work that they do becomes more apparent as Gladstone warms up to making an unconscious, tacit analogy between the British and the Afghans under Tory rule. If the speech uses strong critical language to forge a connection between the war-mongering Tories and the warlike Afghans, it also uses romantic analogies to connect noble British civilians, yoked to a war they do not want, with noble Afghans, provoked into retaliation and insurgency. This romanticization, activated by an implicit linkage to Scottish Highlanders, shows how Gladstone uses an image of a violated Afghanistan to mirror a violated England back to the constituency he wants to win over: "I really have but one great anxiety. This is a self-governing country. Let us bring home to the minds of the people the state of the facts they have to deal with, and in Heaven's name let them determine whether or not this is the way in which they like to be governed" (50). In Gladstone's rhetoric, the Tories trample not just upon Afghans' rights, but also upon those of the British. Through this association with Scottish Highlanders, Gladstone could suggest that contemporary Afghans be imagined as distant versions of an original British race and reliving, in a different time and place, an imagined travesty.

This theme is picked up again toward the end of the Second Midlothian Speech. Here Gladstone specifically addresses the women in the audience. They do not have the vote, but he presumes that they have influence over men's votes. Gladstone appeals to, and prescribes, their sentimental attachments to the idea of domesticity and family: "I speak to you, ladies, as women; and I do think and feel that the present political crisis has to do not only with human interests at large, but especially with those interests which are most appropriate, and ought to be most dear, to you" (90). This moment dramatically marks a turn toward the emotional life: "The harder, and sterner, and drier lessons of politics are little to your taste. You do not concern yourselves with abstract propositions. It is that side of politics, which is associated with the heart of man, that I must call your side of politics" (90). Comparing the war in Afghanistan with the one in South Africa, Gladstone intones, "Go into the lofty hills of Afghanistan, as they were last winter, and what do we there see? I fear a yet sadder sight than was to be seen in the land of the Zulus" (91). The sadder sight, which Gladstone will vividly depict, describes a previous winter's strike against an Afghan village that had attacked British forces. In retaliation, the British military had burned it down. Gladstone unfolds a scene that he admits is only partial, filtered through inadequate reports. In his telling, he emphasizes the independence of the villagers from any centralized power: "We know that that was done for the most part not strictly in the territory of Afghanistan proper, but in its border lands, inhabited by hill tribes who enjoy more or less of political independence, and do not own a regular allegiance to the Afghan ruler" (91–2). He then rhetorically punctuates a matter-of-fact description with an emotional question, one designed to evoke in the imagination the horror of war: "You have seen during last winter from time to time that from such and such a village attacks had been made upon the British forces, and that in consequence the village had been burned. Have you ever reflected on the meaning of these words?" (92). He casts the hill tribes as uninvolved in the conflict between the British and Afghan governments and punctuates their innocence with a provocative question: "Those hill tribes had committed no real offence against us. We, in the pursuit of our political objects, chose to establish military positions in their country. If they resisted, would not you have done the same?" (92).

According to Ruth Clayton Windscheffel, Gladstone's question would have evoked in his Scottish audience memories of the final Jacobite rebellion, in which Charles Edward Stuart, the Young Pretender, attempted to regain control of the throne of England and Scotland after the deposition of his grandfather James II and IV during the Glorious Revolution of 1688. Gladstone's question refers to the Battle of Culloden in 1746, the mid-eighteenth-century disaster in which the English army decisively crushed the forces of Charles's Highland supporters. Gladstone wraps up this segment with the graphic evocation of Afghan hill-tribe women and children forced from their homes and dying in the harsh winter elements:

> And when, going forth from their villages they had resisted, what you find is this, that those who went forth were slain, and that the village was burned. Again I say, have you considered the meaning of these words? The meaning of the burning of the village is, that the women and the children were driven forth to perish in the snows of winter. Is not that a terrible supposition? Is not that a fact—for such, I fear, it must be reckoned to be—which does appeal to your hearts as women, which does lay a special hold and make a special claim upon your interest, which does rouse in you a sentiment of horror and grief, to think that the name of England, under no political necessity, but for a war as frivolous as ever was waged in the history of man, should be associated with consequences such as these? (92)

Windscheffel argues that Gladstone's imagery evokes the moment in Scott's *Waverley* when the protagonist arrives upon a sentimentalized scene of excessive destruction. The English army has just defeated the Jacobite rebellion and burned their homes:

> The place had been sacked by the King's troops, who, in wanton mischief, had even attempted to burn it; and though the thickness of the walls had resisted the fire, unless to a partial extent, the stables and outhouses were totally consumed. The towers and pinnacles of the main building were scorched and blackened; the pavement of the court broken and shattered; the doors torn down entirely, or hanging by a single hinge; the windows dashed in and demolished; and the court strewed with articles of furniture broken into fragments. (1985, 433)

Windscheffel goes on to claim that Gladstone's strong attachment to Scott's novels and other writings informed not only his identification with his Scottish lineage, but also his sense of British identity and nationality and, later, his approach to the political future of Scotland.

Gladstone's forging of a connection between contemporary insurgent Afghan hill tribes and eighteenth-century Highlanders, both decisively defeated by the English army, tacitly builds upon and reverses a connection made in Scott's writing. In "Culloden Papers" published in 1816 in *The Quarterly Review*, Scott reviews the 1815 publication of letters, state papers, and the memoirs of Duncan Forbes, written from 1625 to 1748. The review provides a history of the ancient Highlands, including the brutal suppression of the Jacobite Rebellion at the Battle of Culloden in 1746, through the ongoing process of modernization that finally defeated them, the Clearances. From the eighteenth to the nineteenth century, Scottish landlords attempted to evict tenant farmers in order to use the land for sheep farming. Scott viewed the loss of the Highland way of life in the face of modernization and economic speculation with sorrow and melancholy.

Ironically, Scott's writing contributed to the very modernization process that his literary works criticized. As Ian Duncan and James Chandler have argued, Scott followed Scottish Enlightenment thinkers in conceiving of English nation formation in terms of temporality. His grand narratives of the birth of the modern English nation required that spatial difference be rendered temporal. Scotland, a place, became England's past and thus an essential element of its pre-modern identity. To narrate England's having already entered modernity, as Scott's novels do, required the postulation of a violent, insurgent Scotland as its own prehistory. Safely consigned to the past and sanitized of its threatening elements, this imaginary Scotland could be subjected to an aestheticized melancholy and serve as the collective origins of the imagined community of the British nation.

Duncan frames Scott's discursive work as an instance of Scottish Enlightenment epistemological chronotoping. Drawing on Reinhart Koselleck's work, he argues that this transformation of a place into a time is characteristic of the world-historical epistemic project. As Europeans traveled across the world from the sixteenth century on, they encountered different cultures, coexisting synchronously in time. European intellectuals ordered these cultures according to a scale of progress, placing some further back on an evolutionary timeline. What was once synchronic and simultaneous became diachronic and progressive: "Cultural differences fall into a receding, insatiable past" (Duncan 98). Scott's literary works cast a synchronous place and culture (the Scottish Highlands and the Highlanders) into a diachronic earlier time (a storied British past). Gladstone's speech resurrects the Scots Highlanders, becoming, in effect, synchronic once more, but with a difference.

One of Scott's most famous Highland romances, *Waverley*, forges an identification between the protagonist and the reader. Both come to view Highland clan society as disappearing into the past, a sad but necessary sacrifice for the inrush of modernity. In the novel, the Scottish Highlands and its warlike inhabitants represent a premodernity that is poised on the brink of obsolescence. Scott achieves this effect by using the sentimental romance. This subgenre transforms potentially destabilizing feelings about the inherent violence of nation formation into much safer, pleasurable feelings of nostalgia: "The contemplation of this lost world converts our disaffection from the imperial violence of modern state formation into a luxurious, aestheticized melancholy" (Duncan 98). Discussing the similar operations performed by Jane Austen's novels, Nicholas Dames has argued that such aesthetic nostalgia served to unite the disparate regional and social populations of the nation by proffering a shareable past.

Interestingly—and in keeping with my earlier claims about the marginalization of Afghanistan—neither Duncan nor Chandler refers to Scott's prominent use of Afghanistan to consolidate the pastness and exoticness of the Highlanders and thereby fortify British national identity. For instance, in "Culloden Papers," Scott draws on Sir Mountstuart Elphinstone's *An Account of the Kingdom of Caubul* to make the connection: "Indeed, when we took up the account of Caubul, lately published by the Honourable Mr. Elphinstone, we were forcibly struck with the curious points of parallelism between the manners of the Afghaun tribes and those of the ancient Highland clans" (288). In his account, Elphinstone had written,

> To sum up the character of the Afghauns in a few words; their vices are revenge, envy, avarice, rapacity, and obstinacy; on the other hand, they are fond of liberty, faithful to their friends, kind to their dependents, hospitable, brave, hardy, frugal, laborious, and prudent; and they are less disposed than the nations in their neighbourhood to falsehood, intrigue, and deceit. (vol. I, 253)

Scott writes that the ancient Highland clans "resembled these oriental mountaineers in their feuds, in their adoption of auxiliary tribes, in their laws, in their modes of conducting war, in their arms, and, in some respects, even in their dress" (288). He goes further in establishing their cultural correspondence: "The genealogies of the Afghaun tribes may be paralleled with those of the clans; the nature of their favourite sports, their love of their native land, their hospitality, their address, their simplicity of manners exactly correspond. Their superstitions are the same, or nearly so" (289). Noting the independence from laws that the Highlanders and Afghans share, he writes,

> The Afghaun, who, in his weary travels, had seen no vale equal to his own native valley of Speiger, may find a parallel in many an exile from the braes of Lochaber; and whoever had remonstrated with an ancient Highland chief, on the superior advantages of a civilized life regulated by the authority of equal laws, would have received an answer something similar to the indignant reply of the old Afghaun; "We are content with discord, we are content with alarms, we are content with blood, but we will never be content with a master." (1816, 290)

For Scott, as Duncan has argued, similarities between cultures point to a diachronic and progressive view of history in which circumstances can be universal and lead inevitably to a similar stage of progress: "But our limits do not permit us further to pursue a parallel which serves strikingly to shew how the same state of society and civilization produces similar manners, laws, and customs, even at the most remote period of time, and in the most distant quarters of the world" (Scott, 1816, 290).

Gladstone's and Elphinstone's respective representations of Indians provide a counter-example. In his Glasgow Speech in December 1879, Gladstone critiques repressive laws in India as unjust because India's subjects are amenable to order and have "been distinguished by an extraordinary docility, and a disposition, wonderful in an Asiatic population, to submit to the restraints of order and of law" (203). Similarly, if we review Elphinstone's summary of Afghans, we see how he distinguishes them as being "less disposed than the nations in their neighbourhood to falsehood, intrigue, and deceit" (vol. I, 253). Elphinstone goes on to imagine how two travelers, one coming from England, the other from India—both unmarked in Elphinstone's text, but implicitly British, white, male, and genteel—would each experience Afghanistan. The man traveling from England to Afghanistan would follow a devolutionary temporal schema, finding a nation in disorder, lacking an organized government or police, and thus acting as a breeding ground for lawlessness. Perpetuating the continuously doubled representation of Afghans throughout the nineteenth century, Elphinstone writes:

> Yet, he would scarce fail to admire their martial and lofty spirit, their hospitality, and their bold and simple manners, equally removed from the suppleness of a citizen and the awkward rusticity of a clown; and he would probably, before long, discover among so many qualities that excited his disgust, the rudiments of many virtues. (149)

The English traveler from India, though, Elphinstone writes, would travel forward in a temporal progression, receiving a fully favorable impression. He would enjoy the coldness of the region and the "wild and novel scenery" (think Scottish Highlands). While noticing the scarcity of population as compared to India, he would also observe, with moral approval, that the people are "not fluttering in white muslins, while half their bodies are naked, but soberly and decently attired in dark-coloured woolen clothes, and wrapped up in brown mantles, or in large sheep-skin cloaks" (150). Furthermore, the traveler comparing Afghans to Indians "would admire their strong and active forms, their fair complexions and European features, their industry and enterprise, the hospitality, sobriety, and contempt of pleasure which appear in all their habits; and, above all, the independence and energy of their character" (150).

Significantly, Elphinstone locates one of the major reasons for the difference between Afghans and Indians in the form of government that shapes them. In India, a colonial government represses its population and is found everywhere: "In India, [the traveler] would have left a country where every movement originates in the government or its agents, and where the people absolutely go for nothing" (15). Passing into Afghanistan, the same traveler "would find himself among a nation where the control of the government is scarcely felt, and where every man appears to pursue his own inclinations, undirected and unrestrained" (150). The example of the "stormy independence of [the Afghan] mode of life" would make the traveler from India "regret the ease and security in which the state of India, and even the indolence and timidity of its inhabitants, enable most parts of that country to repose" (150). Elphinstone concludes,

> On the whole, his impression of his new acquaintances would be favourable; and although he would feel that, without having lost the ruggedness of a barbarous nation, they were tainted with the vices common to all Asiatics, yet he would reckon them virtuous, compared with the people to whom he had been accustomed, would be inclined to regard them with interest and kindness, and could scarcely deny them a portion of his esteem. (150)

In sum, the traveler from England would be "struck with the despotic pretensions of the general government" while the traveler from India would be most surprised by "the democratic licence which prevails in the government of the tribe" (151).

At stake in these contrasting descriptions are contrasting ideological imperatives. The British did not seek to colonize Afghanistan, but they did want to possess India, thereby requiring different perceptions of their inhabitants. Not wanting to colonize Afghanistan but to control their foreign policy, the British could project fantasies of independence and military fierceness onto them. At the same time, they could make an identification that allowed them to mourn their own present perceived as constricted by a too willful government. The correspondence between eighteenth-century Scottish Highlanders and early-nineteenth-century Afghans informs Gladstone's appeals to his audience. He reinforces Afghans' difference from the British but at the same time plays on an underlying cultural identification of the British with Afghans, all in the service of critiquing the current administration and shoring up support for his bid on office: "Remember the rights of the savage, as we call him. Remember that the happiness of his humble home, remember that the sanctity of life in the hill villages of Afghanistan among the winter snows, is as inviolable in the eye of Almighty God as can be your own" (94).

The political speeches of Gladstone, the romantic historicism of Scott, and the proto-ethnographic travel writing of Elphinstone process Afghans and other natives, including the Scottish Highlanders and colonized Indians, through British frameworks of political philosophy and the ideology of British superiority. They cast the unfamiliar into the familiar, seeking to contain its threatening elements, while reflecting upon their own present political context. By suggesting parallels between contemporary Afghans and eighteenth-century Highlanders, these three authors at different historical moments could tacitly critique a growing interventionist state and mourn an imagined loss of independence and autonomy. When we turn to fiction, we see how this image of Afghanistan performs similar cultural work, but to assuage a different, if related, set of anxieties. In the next section, I turn to Henty's 1886 adventure novel, *For Name and Fame*. One of the few late Victorian fictions set in Afghanistan, if only partially, the novel positions Afghanistan explicitly as the scene of self- and nation formation, while Britain emerges as weakened, overly domesticated, and symbolically unmoored.

Birthmarks: Identifying British Masculinity in Henty's For Name and Fame

Henty's *For Name and Fame* intersperses generic episodes of swashbuckling with didactic passages that explain the history and culture of Afghanistan and the events of the Second Anglo-Afghan War. Unlike Scott's *Waverley*, written some seventy years after the historical events it describes, Henty's novel appears just five years after the war that is its setting. In brief, its protagonist, the workhouse foundling William Gale, performs singular acts of military stratagem, physical strength, and gentlemanly conduct in Afghanistan, enabling him to rise through the ranks, despite a lowly birth. As he ascends the social ladder, he rubs shoulders with gentleman officers, one of whom turns out to be his real father from whom he was kidnapped at the age of two. Like other late Victorian adventure novels written for boys, *For Name and Fame* teaches the lesson that manhood is achieved by defending the empire.[4] In boys' adventure novels, as well as in other colonialist discourses, ideal masculinity was of course nationally, racially, and class-coded: The white British gentleman was necessary for guarding and reinforcing the values of British culture and for whipping both white British working-class troops and nonwhite native troops into shape. Characterized by military quickness, stoicism, physical strength, respect for hierarchy, and loyalty, Henty's version of masculinity was meant to counter perceived domestic threats to British manliness. These threats included the sexual decadence of the upper classes, the suffocating dominance of the feminine in the middle classes, and the moral and biological degeneration of the lower classes in late Victorian England.[5] To this well-rehearsed list, I would add a perceived weakening of autonomy in the face of an interventionist state that claimed to embody liberal ideals while being experienced by its subjects as undercutting them.

Two overlapping and contradictory discourses overdetermine manhood in Henty's novel: first, late Victorian liberalism, which emphasized self-cultivation, and, second, biological determinism, which gave rise to a genetic fatalism. Manhood in the novel then accordingly comes to rely upon two contradictory narratives. First, the poor, no-name, orphaned protagonist William must choose to model himself as a white British gentleman through sheer willpower, hard work, and fastidious moral discipline. Second, his virtuous and heroic acts perform in the present the proof of his genteel past, fulfilling a prophecy that is implied in the beginning pages by virtue of the social status of his parents. Different presumptions underlie the two intertwined narratives of masculine identity in *For Name and Fame*, but I am interested in what they share: a vaguely understood imperial scene as setting, changeable native others as supporting cast, and a historical moment marked by a shift from a coercive to a hegemonic mode of governance at home.

Henty's text might seem to be the most generic and least complicated of the fictional texts I examine in this chapter. After all, its explicit desires are normative and its characters lack psychological depth. As a child and later as a soldier, Will (a nickname that has meaning) is steadfast and devoted, eager to please others, full of initiative, hungry for promotion, and eminently teachable. He is in this sense very different from Kipling's much more interesting Kim who loves lying for its own sake, has no interest in economic or professional advancement, and is conflicted to the point of breakdown. Henty's novel is fairly average in its racism, as well. The native others in *For Name and Fame* include Malays, "the most bloodthirsty pirates in the world" (77), and Afghans, who receive the conventionally ambivalent treatment we have already discussed. They have virtues: "In these pages you will see the strength and the weakness of these wild people of the mountains; their strength lying in their personal bravery, their determination to preserve their freedom at all costs, and the nature of their country" (iii–iv). And they have shortcomings: "Their weakness consists in their want of organization, their tribal jealousies, and their impatience of regular habits and of the restraint necessity to render them good soldiers" (iv).

However, upon examination, the novel exceeds this reading and is, I suggest, far more interesting than its surface suggests. First of all, while explicitly invested in class hierarchy, the novel betrays enormous anxiety about the stability of the upper-class Britishness that it promotes as the safeguard of the nation and the empire. As I have indicated, the story clumsily proceeds on the contradiction that ideal masculinity is achieved through one's acts *and* is the result of one's lineage. This is a conundrum that Charles Dickens's *Oliver Twist* (1838) also carries along in its narrative, except in its case, it is more specifically moral character, not genteel masculinity, that is both performative and ontological. Second, the novel begins with the by now familiar ambivalent mixture of qualities ascribed to Afghans, but the emphasis on their positive virtues, like bravery, love of freedom, and willingness to fight, quickly recede. Instead, Afghans' changeability emerges as their most distinctive characteristic. This changeability, I suggest, acts to shore up the unstable outlines of the British hero's identity. The less understood Afghan culture is and the more labile its inhabitants, the more solid the actually nebulous, underdeveloped character of William Gale, né Tom Ripon, appears. In other words, Afghans' changeability diffuses the fundamental contradiction between the liberal narrative of self-cultivation and the more traditional, conservative narrative of high birth and good breeding, given a scientific sheen by eugenic discourse. Without such screening, the contradiction threatens to impede the reader's apprehension of William Gale's virtue.

While *For Name and Fame* argues directly for the aggressive defense of India against Russia and for the subjugation of Afghan insurgents, it is equally invested in the domestic scene of England. In fact, England itself emerges as another front to defend, this time against feminine influence and lower-class degeneration. If India needs a secure buffer in the shape of Afghanistan, England needs the paternal governance and regulation of gentleman magistrates to replace the suffocating influence of mothers, as well as the incompetence of lower-class policemen.

The opening establishes the novel's masculine contempt for feminine emotional attachments to smaller, defenseless creatures, such as birds and, later, children. The first chapter, "The Lost Child," starts with the cries of an unnamed lady in distress: "My poor pets! . . . They all knew me so well, and ran to meet me when they saw me coming, and seemed really pleased to see me even when I had no food to give them" (9). This opening cry joins feminine emotional attachment, with its loop of food/need and love, to an instable social in which a crime has been committed. Given the title of the chapter, the reader might be led to think that "poor pets" refers to children. We soon learn, however, from the lady's husband, Captain Ripon, that it refers to her prize fowls. Captain Ripon vows to find the thieves, but in the meantime he makes light of his wife's anguish and criticizes her indulgence. To her sad remembrance that they seemed happy to see her even when she bore no food, he sarcastically rejoins, "Which was not often, my dear" (9). Changing his tone, he declares he will find the thief: "However, it is, as you say, too bad, and I will bring the fellow to justice if I can" (9). The justice is necessary less because of her emotional loss, than because of his own economic one: "There are twelve prize fowls worth a couple of guineas apiece, not to mention the fact of their being pets of yours" (9). What particularly seems to gall him, however, is the thought of lowly criminals misreading signs of social distinction as mere sustenance: "[they have been] stolen, probably by tramps, who will eat them, and for whom the commonest barn-door chickens would have done as well" (9).

Inspecting a broken panel, Captain Ripon suspects gypsies as the criminals and, accordingly, sets about producing them as such. The disparity between the domestic situations of the genteel Ripons and the impoverished gypsies is striking and serves as an example of how a text that appears unconflicted about class difference and its necessity in the defense of empire exposes contrasts of social class. As scholars have long argued, such exposures make class disparity available for critique and suggest, in fact, a logical causality between poverty, or bare existence, and theft, or social crime: While Mrs. Ripon keeps hens as pets, the gypsies are in want of food; while the Ripons live in a house, in which a panel could be broken and which sits on a park that abuts a village, the gypsies occupy a temporary encampment, consisting of four low tents, a wagon, and an emaciated horse.

When Ripon and the police officers find the gypsy camp, they encounter a communal scene, "the women weaving baskets from osiers, the men cutting up gorse into skewers" (10). They also find feathers, which convinces them to haul several of the gypsy men to the jailhouse. The chief magistrate informs Captain Ripon that the feathers do not constitute enough evidence for the crime of fowl abduction, but he nevertheless extends the courtesy of detaining the unconvicted men for twenty-four hours until the captain can find more evidence. Captain Ripon, however, declines the favor, producing a prime piece of evidence out of memory: a footprint he found near the henhouse, "made by a boot which has got hobnails and a horse-shoe heel, and a piece of that heel has been broken off" (13). One of the men admits that it is his boot and is subsequently convicted of the crime. In what will become a significant plot turn, the charged man's wife turns up at the Ripons' door and begs that he not testify against her husband. When the Captain refuses out of principle, the gypsy woman then delivers threats, which he brushes off. When Mrs. Ripon suggests fearfully that he should comply, he yet again dismisses her concerns in the name of masculine, patriarchal duty.

The birth of the Ripons' son occasions the novel's tacit endorsement of the captain's critique of his wife's femininity as indulgent. She interprets the baby's gurgles as fully articulated words, while Captain Ripon denies such a claim: ". . . while willing to allow that they might be perfectly intelligible to her, [he] insisted that to the male ear they in no way resembled words" (18). He continues, "Tom is a fine little chap, and I am very fond of him in his way, principally, perhaps, because he is your Tom; but I cannot see that he is a prodigy" (19). After allowing that perhaps it is a good thing for mothers to care so much, because fathers would surely neglect their children, he makes an interesting, rather odd concession: "[B]ut I suppose we should take to it, just as the old goose in the yard has taken to that brood of chickens whose mother was carried off by the fox" (19–20).

Captain Ripon's humorous but grudging claim that men could become mothers if forced inaugurates the novel's proliferating showcase of identities that blur and change. This blending betrays anxiety about the very malleability of identity per se, as well as the novel's fantasy of a world in which either mothers did not exist or, as we shall see, doled high-quality but low-quantity attention. Instabilities in class, gender, and ethnicity extend the criminal plot from the theft of fowls to the abduction of little Tom. These instabilities in turn give rise to the text's continual return to the themes of identification, interpretation, and the potential threat of signifying practices in general. At the age of two, little Tom disappears while playing in the garden. Left in his place is the very boot that served as the incriminating evidence against the gypsy. Captain Ripon rightly reads the boot as signifying that the gypsy's wife has made good on her threat and has taken his son from him in revenge for his taking her husband from her. Fears about authentic identity—how do you identify bodies in the global battlefield of the empire in which death is the final social leveler?—are now brought to the surface. After searches fail to find the toddler, Mrs. Ripon recovers enough from her suffering to be thankful for what she had once lamented, a birthmark on her son's neck: "No other child can be palmed off upon us as our own; when we find Tom we shall know him, however changed he may be!" (24). Just as a footprint leads to a boot that leads to the thief and then a boot substitutes for a child, signifying revenge, a birthmark ceases to be a blemish when it can serve as a signature, a distinctive mark belonging only to a single person and inherited from his family. The birthmark will prove to be the authentic sign that guards against imposters and reestablishes the true family and the social hierarchy it represents by the end of the novel. The fluidity of identity remains the lurking evil here. It is, after all, because the gypsy woman who kidnapped him could pass as a "decent-looking Irishwoman," working in a laundry in Notting Hill, that they never find her or the child (24).

While the gypsy woman is bad enough, the suffocating emotional attachment of middle-class women is even more to blame for this chaos of shifting shapes. In the novel's world, the traditional domestic family structure dominated by the mother has the malignant power of inhibiting the expression of good breeding. In its place, the novel proffers an alternative. *For Name and Fame* counters an earlier anti-workhouse fiction, Dickens's *Oliver Twist*, from which it borrows the idea of the orphan of high birth. In *For Name and Fame*, the gypsy-woman leaves Tom at the gates of a workhouse shortly after kidnapping him. Here, unlike Oliver, he flourishes. The narrative attributes young Tom's successful childhood in part to the fact that the only maternal attention he receives is from the workhouse porter's wife, Mrs. Dickson, a perhaps ironic reference to Dickens. Attached to the foundling right away, whom she and the porter name William Gale, Mrs. Dickson is also busy with the care of the institution and can only give him a very partial attention. However, the precious time she expensively lavishes on him in small doses is the right amount to enable him to thrive: "The affection of the good woman had brightened his life, and he had none of the dull, down-cast look so common among children in workhouses" (31). He thus receives the novel's ideal education. Rather than being idolized by a mother who treats him as a prodigy, Will grows up having to prove himself. An essentially pro-Tory novel, even its workhouse, the legacy of early Victorian Utilitarians whom Tories did not fully support, appears as an ideal environment for the male youth of Britain since it diffuses toxic maternal affection to a healthful amount.

Signs and the act of interpretation continue to motivate the plot. Will moves in a world in which people across social classes are well versed in the physical markers of good breeding. They read his noble body against his humble context in wonder. For instance, when one of the workhouse guardians says he looks like a gentleman's child, Mrs. Dickson seconds his appraisal, adding, "Look at his white skin; see how upright he is, with his head far back as if he was somebody; he is different altogether from the run of them. I always said he came of good blood, and I shall say so to my dying day" (32). Mrs. Dickson regularly repeats to Will that his parents were gentlefolk and that he must therefore groom himself accordingly:

Now, mind, it does not make one bit of difference to you, for it ain't likely you will ever hear of them. Still, please God, you may do so; and it is for you to bear it in mind, and to act so as, if you were to meet them, they need not be ashamed of you. You have got to earn your living just like all the other boys here, but you can act right and straight and honorable. Never tell a lie, Billy, not if it's to save yourself from being thrashed ever so much; always speak out manful and straight, no matter what comes of it. Don't never use no bad words, work hard at your books and try to improve yourself. Keep it always before you that you mean to be a good man and a gentleman some day; and, mark my words, you will do it. (33)

The working-class wife of a workhouse porter articulates here, in bad grammar and lowly accent, the precepts of liberal individuality as theorized by such dignitaries as John Stuart Mill and Matthew Arnold: economic independence, moral behavior, honesty, disinterested reflection, commitment to self-cultivation, and disciplined labor.

Beyond the workhouse, Will's appearance and his deeds continue to inspire wonder and speculation. After being released into the world, Will serves as an apprentice on a fishing vessel, then becomes a shipwrecked survivor fighting Malays, before being rescued by a ship sailing to India. This ship is, in turn, attacked by pirates, but saved ultimately by Will's ingenuity. Upon arriving in Calcutta, the ship's captain relays the story of Will's heroism to an audience consisting of the agent of the firm that owns the ship and two military officers, who demand more information about this unlikely figure. Fascinated by the paradox between his working-class status and his heroic, gentlemanly acts, they wonder what he is like in person. Captain Mayhew replies, with what will become a generic characterization of the divergence between Will's appearance and comportment and his scandalously humble origins,

> He is surprisingly well-mannered. Had I met him elsewhere, and in gentleman's clothes, I do not think that I should have suspected that he was not what he appeared. His features, too, somehow or other, strike one as being those of a gentleman; which is all the more singular when, as a fact, he told me had been brought up in a workhouse. (124–5)

The two captains ask to meet the boy and later introduce him to their colonel. The colonel echoes the ship's captain's response, but with a difference that neatly encapsulates the ideological contradiction that structures the novel. Addressing Will, he says,

> . . . certainly your appearance and manner go far to sustain the belief that the tramp who left you was not your mother, and that your parents were of gentle birth. I do not say that a man's birth makes much difference to him; still, it does go for something, and in nine cases out of ten the difference both in face and figure is unmistakable. Unless I am very wrong your father was a gentleman. However that is not to the point: it is your quickness and activity, your coolness in danger, and the adventures which you have gone through which interest us in you. (130)

The colonel's speech doubles back on itself, bellowing clouds of smoke as he equivocates. He at first denies that he is saying that birth matters, an indirect statement that leaves untouched what his beliefs might be, and finishes off with the equally obscure statement that birth "does go for something." The colonel then proposes that William enlist in the service, in which a "steady respectable man is sure to rise" and mentions the stirrings of the Second Anglo-Afghan War: "There is trouble in Afghanistan, and an ultimatum has just been sent to the ameer that if he does not comply with our terms it will be war, and we hope to be there in time for the beginning of it" (130).

Once again, William proves himself through noble acts of courage, physical strength, and military ingenuity. Readily rising through the ranks, the battlefields of Afghanistan become the setting for what we could paradoxically describe as the performance of his essential identity and thus the settling of the questions surrounding it. Meanwhile, Afghans appear all the more malleable and protean. This malleability is signaled early in the novel. In the preface, after listing the good and the bad along the lines we have already seen in Gladstone's, Scott's, and Elphinstone's texts, the narrator then describes Afghans as a perpetual problem. Afghans escape a fully romanticized status, maintaining their potential to be a threat that endlessly erupts into the future. Dispersed throughout the land, this infinitely regenerating fighting spirit can be redeemed, however, the narrator argues, if articulated through the logic, force, and economic incentive offered by the British:

> Crushed one day, they will rise again the next; scattered, it would seem hopelessly, they are ready to reassemble and renew the conflict at the first summons of their chiefs. Guided by British advice, led by British officers, and, it may be, paid by British gold, Afghanistan is likely to prove an invaluable ally to us when the day comes that Russia believes herself strong enough to move forward towards the goal of all her hopes and efforts for the last fifty years, the conquest of India. (iv)

This passage tries to contain and harness the irrepressibility of the Afghans for British purposes in their Great Game against Russia. The novel groups Afghans with other colonized subjects, like the so-called martial races, such as the Rajputs, Sikhs, and Pashtuns, enlisted into the British Indian Army. Afghans are raw materials that can be transformed into good soldiers. But while Afghans are inferior and must be led, they are still "invaluable allies," which implies a level of equality in sovereignty and status.

Henty's characterization of Afghans as closely resembling Indians and yet different may have something to do with Afghanistan's status as a nation. As mentioned previously, Afghans were compelled into nationhood, belying the myth of the generic nation as an expression of organic essence or will. In other words, the British imposed the nation form upon a disparate assemblage of tribes because it suited their imperatives to ghost up an ally in the region in their fight against another national competitor, Russia. But such wishing troubles the sacred notion of the nation. Henty displaces this contradiction into meditations upon Afghans' changeability, incompetence, and incapacity to have abstract feeling or a historical destiny equivalent to the British.

The few Afghans who are named and described in the story bear out the theme of changeability. They include the chief ruler, the Amir Sheer-Ali, and Will's native assistant, the young Yossouf. The Amir's decision to allow a Russian envoy to be sent to Kabul while refusing a British one is technically what begins the war. But the narrator provides a history, explaining the Amir's actions as due, in fact, to the isolationist approach of Gladstone's first Liberal government (1868–74), which had preceded Disraeli's second Tory ministry (1874–80):

> Sheer-Ali was not wholly to be blamed. He had for many years received an annual present of money and arms from the British government; but upon the other hand he saw Russia marching with giant steps toward his northern frontier, and contrasting the energy and enterprise of the great northern power with the inactivity which he may have supposed to prevail among the men who governed England, he became more and more anxious, and asked the English definitely to state whether he could rely upon them for assistance should he be attacked by the Russians. (189)

The narrator here seeks to forge sympathy with the Amir, while critiquing Gladstone's first ministry for not having done enough, thus placing the Amir, "between the hammer and the anvil" (189). Establishing this chain of causality, the narrator presents the Amir's actions as understandable, if feminine: ". . . as he could obtain no guarantee of assistance from England he determined to throw himself into the arms of Russia" (189). Under the current Tory government, such an action now meant war: "Unfortunately for the Ameer, the government of England had now changed hands, and the ministry at once sent to Sheer-Ali to demand that he should receive a British resident" (190). The British government sends an envoy, accompanied with strong military forces, which overtakes the Amir's forces. More uprisings follow and the Amir subsequently flees: "He was no longer a powerful ally, but a broken instrument; and heart-broken with disappointment and failure the unfortunate Sheer-Ali was seized by fever and died in an obscure village almost alone and wholly uncared for" (190). His son Yakoob Khan takes over, but because of his time in prison, he has become weak, "no better than a reed to lean upon," explains Yossouf (203). While Yakoob signs a treaty with the British, other Afghan tribes overwhelm them. A battle around Kabul ensues and the British eventually defeat, for the moment, the insurgent Afghans.

At this point, the narrator details for us the psychic life of young Yossouf, who is in some ways the most psychologically complex character in the novel. The narrator tells us,

> Yossouf had throughout the morning been swayed by conflicting emotions and wishes. At one moment he hoped that his countrymen might conquer, then the fear that after victory the Hindoo quarter might be sacked and his English friend discovered and killed, overpowered his feeling of patriotism. (231)

Yossouf's inner conflict incites the narrator to expostulate at length about Afghan character: "Its population is composed of a great number of tribes without any common feelings or interest, and often engaged in desperate wars and conflicts with each other" (231). This lack of collective feeling accounts for the young Afghan's changeability: "Thus Yossouf had grown up without understanding the meaning of the feeling which we call patriotism. He had, it is true, been taught to hate the unbelievers, but this feeling had disappeared on his acquaintance with Will Gale, and he now ranked the safety and happiness of his friend far before any national consideration" (232).

The uncertainties of Will's identity are therefore displaced onto the shaky lines of Afghan character, as well as territory, the lines of Afghanistan shifting through the battles. But the final moment of reunion between father and son attempts to seal over any doubt about Will's identity. The reader has known Will's true identity all along, but it cannot be asserted until the father recognizes his birthmark. The moment of reunion comes in Kandahar when three Afghans attack Colonel Ripon, now an Indian official on a special mission. Will saves him, but gets wounded in the fray, exposing the birthmark on his shoulder that leads to the emotional reunion. But this moment of recognition resulted from Will's own actions in the military, which caused him to rise up the ranks and be in contact with his father.

On one level, *For Name and Fame* is a conservative story that attributes Will's superiority to his birth. Yet, at the same time, it is a classically liberal tale of self-development: It teaches its readers how to cultivate themselves into bourgeois selfhood. I would like to suggest that this unease about the indeterminacy of British national identity is displaced onto the created indeterminacy of Afghan identity. In more than one sense, Afghans are this novel's raw materials. It is their identity, not that of the British, that is made to be protean. Whether it is Afghan warriors who can be turned into good soldiers of the Empire, an Afghan Amir who is batted back and forth between the Russians and the British, downgrading from "a powerful ally" to "a broken instrument" (204), or young Yossouf, Will's attendant, who switches loyalty from the Afghans to the British without trouble, Afghans appear to be in a constant state of identity crisis in Henty's novel.

In the next section, I examine Doyle's first Sherlock Holmes story, *A Study in Scarlet*. Published a year after *For Name and Fame*, the novel takes up the theme of empire in intimate ways. Critics such as Stephen Arata and Joseph McLaughlin have noted that the Sherlock Holmes tales evoked cultural fears of the return of a malignant empire upon an anemic metropolis and the waning of British imperial power as other European nations entered the scramble for territorial acquisition. Like Henty, Doyle was a staunch imperialist, but his fiction betrays a less than enthusiastic view of empire's effects, costs, and risks. In *A Study in Scarlet*, crimes committed beyond the nation and empire, in the ex–British colony of the United States and in the imperialized site of Afghanistan, return upon the imperial center where their surprising similarity threatens to invalidate the moral legitimacy of empire.

What Happened to Watson at the Battle of Maiwand?

Toward the beginning of *A Study in Scarlet*, Dr. John Watson reads a newspaper article on the emergent science of deduction, which he later learns was written by his new roommate, Sherlock Holmes. The article claims that an observant man can learn much by systematically appraising the detail: "The writer claimed by a momentary expression, a twitch of a muscle or a glance of an eye, to fathom a man's inmost thoughts. Deceit, according to him, was an impossibility in the case of one trained to observation and analysis" (16). The Holmes series, as D. A. Miller and Laurie Langbauer have noted, is driven by the fantasy of the synecdoche, in which a part can lead to a whole. Watson reads on, "'From a drop of water,' said the writer, 'a logician could infer the possibility of an Atlantic or a Niagara without having seen or heard of one or the other. So all life is a great chain, the nature of which is known whenever we are shown a single link of it'" (23).

If we attend to the pedagogical compulsions of the text, what then are we to do with the detail of Watson's return to London from the Second Anglo-Afghan War? This return inaugurates the beginning not only of the novel, but also of the Sherlock Holmes series. Despite its structural importance, interpretations of *A Study in Scarlet*, like those by Arata and McLaughlin, tend to leave this particular detail behind. Arata argues that the novel contributes to the male romance genre through its carving out of a male homosocial space of erotic pleasure in the act of paying attention, while McLaughlin argues that it compensates for the closing of the American frontier by exoticizing the modern city. But each of these very rich accounts also interprets the beginning of the novel as Watson's return from fighting in the "colonies."[6] Unless one counts his sick stay in Peshawar as fighting, Watson actually returns from military action in the imperialized site of Maiwand, which lies solidly within Afghanistan and outside the reach of British colonialism. Britain was, in fact, engaged in several colonial contests at the time, including the Anglo-Zulu War (1879) and the Transvaal War (1880–81). Taking a cue from the novel's vaunting of the detail, this section attends to Doyle's choice of the Second Anglo-Afghan War and rereads *A Study in Scarlet* in light of what I have been calling "Victorian Afghanistan."

First of all, the choice of Maiwand allows us to reframe the novel's bizarre detour in Part II. In "The Country of the Saints," Watson's first-person narration of 1880s London abruptly shifts to an omniscient narration of 1840s Utah. Doyle's description of the Mormons is uncannily similar to contemporary texts' descriptions of Afghans. Each culture shares a mountainous and severe terrain, a suspect fusion of church and state, a fanatical religion headed by elders, and the distasteful practice of polygamy. Lydia Fillingham has observed that British authors also felt ambivalent about Mormons. Some, including Doyle, described them as primitive, uncivilized, and, because polygamous, unable to restrain themselves. But the same authors also professed admiration for the industriousness that enabled the Mormons to wrest economic success from a formidable Utah desert. The brevity of Watson's allusions to Afghanistan and the large narrative space devoted to Utah suggest that the conflicts represented by the former location have been displaced to the latter where they can be more safely explored.

Second, by focusing on the detail of Afghanistan, we can reread the detective novel's meditation on the difference between revenge and justice to expose how it suggests, only to repress, the decisive role of national boundaries. The central mystery concerns two American Mormons, Enoch Drebber and Joseph Stangerson, found murdered in London. The culprit, Jefferson Hope, is an American frontiersman. Hope had been chasing Drebber and Stangerson, the privileged sons of Mormon Elders, for twenty years, seeking revenge for two crimes that they had committed in Utah. Their first crime was to force Hope's fiancée, Lucy Ferrier, to marry Drebber, a polygamist with several wives already, an event that causes her to sicken and die. Their second crime was the murder of Lucy's adoptive father, the wealthy farmer, John Ferrier.

The novel poses the following question: Is Hope's act of double homicide merely an act of revenge and therefore primitive and immoral, a crime that upsets the social order, or is it an act of justice and therefore reasonable and moral, a public service that reestablishes the social order? As the novel unfolds, these murky questions become inextricable from a consideration of national borders. When a national commits an atrocity within his or her nation and the state responds with violence within its borders, the state's action is likely to look like justice. But what happens if the actors involved cross national borders, as in the case of *A Study in Scarlet*? What does it mean for a national (Hope) to leave the boundaries of his nation (the United States) where the initial atrocities (the forced marriage and murder) have been committed and enter another nation (Britain) to respond with more violence (the double homicide)? The double homicide starts to look more like revenge, which counts as another atrocity in need of a just response from the state in whose territory the violence has occurred.

This situation gives rise to some troubling speculations. Watson's terse, if powerful, references to his experience in Afghanistan each serve as "single link[s]" that join the novel's murder plot and its consideration of the difference between revenge and justice to larger questions about the integrity of the imperialist state. Is it revenge or justice when the British invade Afghanistan, supposedly a sovereign nation, because the Amir is courting favor with the Russians? Is it revenge or justice when the "murderous Ghazis," seeking to oust the invaders, wound Watson and soundly defeat British soldiers at the Battle of Maiwand? What about Watson's own bitter feelings toward the British state, which he turns against himself? Justice or revenge?

The novel struggles with the precept that violence committed in response to violence within a national territory is just, but committed outside the nation looks more like the retrogressive, primitive, and illiberal act of revenge. Because Afghanistan lies neither within the proper boundaries of the British nation nor its empire, the novel hesitates to declare whether British military strikes committed there are simply revenge, and thus socially disruptive, or in fact just, and socially restorative. The implications of a liberal state engaging in warfare in an imperialized site, one whose economies are not imbricated with those of Britain and which thus has a kind of nominal sovereignty, are finally so disturbing that they are repressed by the conclusion of the novel, which, ultimately, like Holmes himself, seems curiously to suspend judgment on Hope's actions.

Watson's post-war traumatized psyche becomes the subjective terrain for the posing of these difficult questions. As Lawrence Rothfield has argued, Watson is in many ways a stand-in for the generic liberal individual projected by Victorian realist fiction. At the beginning of the novel, Watson is having an extraordinarily difficult time reconstituting himself along such lines as theorized by John Stuart Mill some twenty years previously. For Mill, the ideal individual exercises all his mental faculties, including perception, judgment, discriminative feeling, and moral preference, but in balance, so that they are also harmoniously aligned.[7] But Watson's experience in Afghanistan has dismembered his sense of self and dissociated him from his past. It leaves him unable to navigate a present in which he is alienated from those who are blithely unaware and unappreciative of his service to the country and therefore do not recognize how it has robbed him of his old, certain sense of self. Before meeting Holmes, Watson's present is drained of pleasure, meaning, and stimulation, suggesting that Afghanistan was, however perversely, the ultimate scene of all three.

The frame of the novel simultaneously establishes and undercuts the prominence of Watson's individuality. Part I of *A Study in Scarlet* is ostensibly an excerpt from his memoirs, loudly proclaimed on the first page: "(BEING A REPRINT FROM THE REMINISCENCES OF JOHN. H. WATSON, M.D., LATE OF THE ARMY MEDICAL DEPARTMENT)." The proclamation raises questions at once: Who is speaking and excerpting? From the use of parentheses, we might deduce that the overarching narrator desires to be unobtrusive and thus whisks his own voice away as soon as he uses it. But it is still another voice and it is capitalized. When we get to the radically different "The Country of the Saints," we are reminded that Watson's perspective is inadequate. Recourse to an abstract, omniscient perspective will be necessary for the novel to tell the story it wants to tell. Even the return of Watson's voice is subsumed within Part II.

With an almost exaggerated realist impulse, Watson begins the story with the spatial and temporal coordinates of his professional identity. He delivers the facts levelly and without emotion:

> In the year 1878 I took my degree of Doctor of Medicine of the University of London, and proceeded to Netley to go through the course prescribed for surgeons in the army. Having completed my studies there, I was duly attached to the Fifth Northumberland Fusiliers as Assistant Surgeon. (3)

The Second Anglo-Afghan War has just started and his regiment is soon sent directly into the conflict.

In the next paragraph, Watson betrays more emotion, letting escape the profound bitterness of a person violently dissociated from his accustomed sense of futurity: "The campaign brought honours and promotions to many, but for me it had nothing but misfortune and disaster" (3). Watson's authoritative "I" and the stable professional identity it represents now begin to degrade. He tells us that he is injured at the infamous Battle of Maiwand (1880), in which the British sustained tremendous losses while failing to put down an insurgency. A Jezail bullet tears through and shatters Watson's shoulder bone, also ripping through his sense of impermeability and infallibility. If the bullet had not ended him, he notes, then surely falling into the hands of the "murderous Ghazis" would have (3). Watson is saved from such a fate by his loyal orderly, who puts his wounded, broken body on a packhorse and brings him safely back to camp. The bullet effects a total transformation in Watson's sense of self. From credentialed doctor serving his country, he becomes an inanimate object, like a good, something to be packed up and transported by a laborer. Also, instead of providing for his subordinate, his subordinate provides for him, upsetting a status hierarchy.

Watson's tone now becomes overtly emotional, a far cry from the novel's cool beginning. He classes himself with a "great" group of "wounded sufferers" all being shipped back, their stories and the particular details of their wounds effaced by a group status: "Worn with pain, and weak from the prolonged hardships which I had undergone, I was removed, with a great train of wounded sufferers, to the base hospital at Peshawar" (3–4). Watson's health improves to the point that he can bask on the verandah, but he soon contracts a fever, "that curse of our Indian possessions" (4). By referring to the fever as a curse, Watson subtly indicates his sense that India's inhabitants are not as uniformly submissive or amenable to British rule as official and popular British thought would have it.

As Watson recovers, his story starts to focus on the obstructive role of the state. The medical board determines from his weak and emaciated condition that he should be returned to England, whether to recover his health or because he can no longer serve the British Empire, it is not entirely clear. Watson sums up his imperial enterprise with the following acerbic statement, one that neatly links his sense of passivity in the face of the state with the state's own supposed fostering of the conditions of individuality: "I was despatched, accordingly, in the troopship Orontes, and landed a month later on Portsmouth jetty, with my health irretrievably ruined, but with permission from a paternal government to spend the next nine months in attempting to improve it" (4). His rage mounting, Watson displays an urbane, ironic, and cutting cynicism regarding a benevolent state that gives people permission to heal and thereby pretends to have authority even over the natural processes of the body.

If medical school made him a doctor and the war made him a cursed, broken object, the state makes him an "idler of the Empire." In this stage, government, money, and freedom become linked in troubling ways for Watson. The "paternal government" achieves its benevolent stance by giving him just enough money to live, but not enough to resume his former genteel identity: "I had neither kith nor kin in England, and was therefore as free as air—or as free as an income of eleven shillings and sixpence a day will permit a man to be" (4). The government thus practices a liberal paradox, setting him "free," but also delimiting the conditions of his freedom by giving him only a certain amount of money. Wounded and no longer agential, just resentful and cynical, Watson tacitly agrees to stay within its parameters, concluding that he ought to head to London: "Under such circumstances I naturally gravitated to London, that great cesspool into which all the loungers and idlers of the Empire are irresistibly drained" (4). Making recourse to metaphors of natural law and physics, Watson renders himself just another element subject to dictates out of the increasingly diminishing sphere of his control. It is only when his government pension runs out that he moves to action:

There I stayed for some time at a private hotel in the Strand, leading a comfortless, meaningless existence, and spending such money as I had, considerably more freely than I ought. So alarmingly did the state of my finances become, that I soon realized that I must either leave the metropolis and rusticate somewhere in the country, or that I must make a complete alteration in my style of living. (4)

Watson decides to make a change, but not of occupation. Rather, he decides to change his lifestyle to fit the money he receives from the state, complying with its injunction to lead a small life.

Watson finds little in society to help him, either. On the same day he decides he must move, someone from his past life taps him on the shoulder: "... turning round I recognized young Stamford, who had been a dresser under me at Barts. The sight of a friendly face in the great wilderness of London is a pleasant thing indeed to a lonely man" (4). He confesses to us that he was not close to Stamford in the old days. Nevertheless, he greets his former subordinate exuberantly, fearful about whether Stamford genuinely reciprocates the feeling: "In old days Stamford had never been a particular crony of mine, but now I hailed him with enthusiasm, and he, in his turn, appeared to be delighted to see me" (4). Overjoyed to see someone he recognizes who can perhaps restore an old sense of self to him, a sense of mastery and power in a professional hierarchy, he invites Stamford to lunch.

Stamford's reception of Watson contrasts with Holmes's later appraisal. As they roll off in a cab to have lunch at a posh restaurant, Watson detects something unsavory in Stamford's questioning of him: "'Whatever have you been doing with yourself, Watson?' he asked in undisguised wonder, as we rattled through the crowded London streets. 'You are as thin as a lath and as brown as a nut'" (4). Watson's use of "undisguised" to describe Stamford's wonder relays his belief that Stamford ought to have been aware of the Battle of Maiwand or the larger war, and, if not, then he should have politely faked it. In contrast, in the famous scene in which Watson and Holmes meet, the latter knows right away what Watson has been doing with himself: "'How are you?' he said cordially, gripping my hand with a strength for which I should scarcely have given him credit. 'You have been in Afghanistan, I perceive'" (7).

From this moment on, Watson finds an external diversion from his internal brackishness by contemplating the mystery of Holmes. Stamford warns Watson that Holmes pushes the logic of science to "cold-bloodedness" and to "excess." To Stamford, Holmes is too enthusiastic, too scientific. Holmes combines excessive passion with excessive objectivity, a paradoxical formulation if placed within Enlightenment discourse, which distinguished between rationality and emotion. Holmes's passionate objectivity performs two narrative functions. It overrides questions of justice and it throws the ideal liberal subject into relief.

Holmes's relation to justice is difficult to assess. After identifying that Watson has been in Afghanistan, Holmes proceeds to describe the result of his recent experiments. He has just found a re-agent precipitated only by hemoglobin, which will provide a way to test for bloodstains, old and new: "Had this test been invented, there are hundreds of men now walking the earth who would long ago have paid the penalty of their crimes" (8). Holmes is eager to collapse the time of the crime with the time of detection:

> Criminal cases are continually hinging upon that one point. A man is suspected of a crime months perhaps after it has been committed. His linen or clothes are examined and brownish stains discovered upon them. Are they blood stains, or mud stains, or rust stains, or fruit stains, or what are they? That is a question which has puzzled many an expert, and why? Because there was no reliable test. Now we have the Sherlock Holmes test, and there will no longer be any difficulty. (8)

Holmes appears to be seeking justice for past wrongs. But the novel undercuts this by a small detail indicating what Watson will later describe as akin to female vanity: "His eyes fairly glittered as he spoke, and he put his hand over his heart and bowed as if to some applauding crowd conjured up by his imagination" (8).

The conclusion of the novel confirms that Holmes is motivated less by justice and more by the thrill of abstract thinking combined with, and perhaps superseded by, a craving for celebrity. Soon after Watson and Holmes move in together, Lestrade and Gregson, Scotland Yard detectives, consult Holmes about a murder case. Bored and seeking to escape himself, Watson accompanies Holmes to the scene, an abandoned house in a London suburb. Lestrade and Gregson are not incompetent, but they misread the clues, including a word etched in blood, "RACHE," which Lestrade takes to refer to a woman's name "Rachel." Holmes rightly interprets it as German for "revenge," a nod toward insurgent German socialists intent on revolution. The contents of the dead man's clothes reveal his name, Enoch Drebber, and nationality, American. Contacting police authorities in the United States, Holmes is able to learn about a longstanding dispute between Drebber and Hope. Shortly after Holmes and Watson see the first body, Stangerson is found murdered, as well, and the rest of the plot concerns finding a way to lure Hope into their clutches. Holmes concocts a scenario that works and Hope is accordingly pounced upon and arrested.

The murders add fear and terror to a social world, previously just alienating and empty, which makes their solving crucial for the restoration of order. They particularly affect Watson, the surrogate for the reader, who explicitly links them to his battlefield experience. When he first looks upon Drebber, he tells us, "I have seen death in many forms, but never has it appeared to me in a more fearsome aspect than in that dark, grimy apartment, which looked out upon one of the main arteries of suburban London" (25). Later that day, Holmes even breaks out of his narcissism to note, "What's the matter? You're not looking quite yourself. This Brixton Road affair has upset you" (39). Watson agrees: "'To tell the truth, it has,' I said. 'I ought to be more case-hardened after my Afghan experiences. I saw my own comrades hacked to pieces at Maiwand without losing my nerve'" (39). News of the second murder, and the etching of "RACHE" again on the wall above the body, compounds Watson's feeling of dread: "There was something so methodical and so incomprehensible about the deeds of this unknown assassin, that it imparted a fresh ghastliness to his crimes. My nerves, which were steady enough on the field of battle, tingled as I thought of it" (56).

Watson seems even more upset at the figure of Drebber himself. Shortly after viewing the first body, he tells us, "If ever human features bespoke vice of the most malignant type, they were certainly those of Enoch J. Drebber, of Cleveland. Still I recognized that justice must be done, and that the depravity of the victim was no condonement in the eyes of the law" (39). While Watson describes both Drebber and Hope as savage, he sympathizes with Hope.

The narrative directs us to share Watson's emotional response. It does this first by abruptly shifting to Part II after Hope's arrest. Now Watson's narration is suspended and an omniscient narrator goes into detail, providing a reasonable explanation for Hope's actions, followed by Hope's own narration. Watson does not return as narrator until the final two chapters.

Watson briefly frames Hope's telling of his own story at the police station. Because too much time had lapsed since Drebber's and Stangerson's crimes, they could not be convicted within the United States: "I knew of their guilt though, and I determined that I should be judge, jury, and executioner all rolled into one. You'd have done the same, if you have any manhood in you, if you had been in my place" (107). Hope then picks up where the omniscient narration leaves off, describing his hunt of the murderers.

Watson describes the room as absorbed by the story: "So thrilling had the man's narrative been and his manner was so impressive that we had sat silent and absorbed. Even the professional detectives, *blasé* as they were in every detail of crime, appeared to be keenly interested in the man's story" (114). Their interest in the narrative, like the reader's, manages to soften what looks like revenge and makes it seem more like justice. Holmes alone seems impervious because he simply does not care. He breaks the silence to inquire how Hope had managed to elude him at an earlier moment. Finally, the narrative itself suspends judgment, by removing Hope. Before the magistrates can judge him, he dies of an aortic aneurism. Watson philosophically sums it up: "A higher Judge had taken the matter in hand, and Jefferson Hope had been summoned before a tribunal where strict justice would be meted out to him" (116).

Like "the curse" of fever that strikes Watson in Peshawar, revenge was considered in the nineteenth century to belong to a chivalric, romantic long-gone age.[8] Daniel Hack explains how Victorian ethnographers posited revenge as a feature describing nonwestern primitive societies, implying that it did not belong in the modern West, where the law and the court system properly mediated wrongs. In the face of the increased importance placed on the social emotion of sympathy, inflicting suffering on others became less appealing, but not less interesting to read about. As Hack points out, numerous Victorian novels feature plots of revenge, including *A Study in Scarlet*. Like ethnographic works, these novels tended to equate revenge with a backward-looking perspective. In their moral systems, wanting revenge signifies being stuck in the past, rather than being liberal and progressive. These novels comfortingly stage revenge's defeat by modernity: "The classic revenge story of modern life, then, is the story of the end of revenge, at least the end of revenge as an end in life, its supercession or sublimation or domestication or diminution under the conditions of civilization in general and modernity in particular" (279). But, Hack notes, figures of progress paradoxically appear as figures of revenge: ". . . the very characters specifically identified with such signal features of modernity as geographical and social mobility, self-making, breaking with the past, and technological innovation became instead—or as well—agents of revenge" (280).[9] The real fear structuring the plot of these revenge novels is then revealed to be modernity. By assigning revenge to the figure of modernity, Victorian novels could safely assign to the past certain disruptive qualities associated with the modern.

A Study in Scarlet assigns the desire for revenge, along with the crime of double homicide, to a national other, Hope, while Watson appears exonerated of any such motive or crime. However, Watson's time in Afghanistan raises two possible revenge scenarios. First of all, the British started the Second Anglo-Afghan War, ostensibly to protect India, but also to punish the Amir for appealing to the Russians. Like Hope, British forces leave the boundaries of their own nation and cross into another, where their actions are more likely to look like revenge. For the Afghans, seeking to kick out the more powerful British Army, whom they are momentarily able to defeat, the Battle of Maiwand might be seen as a kind of justice. Second, fighting a war that may be motivated by his state's desire for revenge, Watson in fact internalizes his own rage and his own desire for revenge. He is split between resentment for "the murderous Ghazis" and for his own paternal government that placed him in such peril and then discarded him. Watson does not claim revenge because he cannot let himself identify who has wronged him. The result is that his anger ravages his own body. Watson becomes bitter and broken, a man whose numbness serves as a protective coating for his exposed nerves and simmering rage.

The novel thus evokes, and then displaces, anxieties about British aggression in imperialized sites. It also tries to find ways to restore Watson's sense of self. On a first look, the novel seems to hold out the possibility that observing Holmes will help Watson achieve a liberal harmoniousness of faculties again. Holmes excites Watson's curiosity in direct proportion to the vacuity of the veteran's own life: "As the weeks went by, my interest in him and my curiosity as to his aims in life gradually deepened and increased" (12). Holmes's wild thinking and his emotional swings become the occasion for Watson's liberal subjectivity: "Leaning back in the cab, this amateur blood-hound carolled away like a lark while I meditated upon the manysidedness of the human mind" (37). Watson observes Holmes fastidiously, noting his dramatic height and leanness, as well as the sharpness of his facial features, which he reads as a sign of a determined character. He also notices how Holmes's hands, scarred by chemicals, are graceful and touch his instruments with great care.

To defend himself against the reader who may find such interest in Holmes's person inappropriate, Watson provides an explanation. First, he willfully misnames the reader's suspicion of homosexuality as the reader's imputation of his being a meddler:

> The reader may set me down as a hopeless busybody, when I confess how much this man stimulated my curiosity, and how often I endeavoured to break through the reticence which he showed me on all that concerned himself. Before pronouncing judgment, however, be it remembered how objectless was my life, and how little there was to engage my attention. (12)

Watson forces his national audience to recognize what he has sacrificed for them in the name of the nation and therefore seeks to deflect or mitigate social disapproval of what could be seen as a vice, homosexuality. Instead, he claims to have been ruined in the service of his country and to be seeking distraction outside of himself.

Watson also seeks to reconstitute himself dialectically by the example of Holmes's illiberality. Fashioned on liberal principles, Watson is shocked to learn that Holmes knows nothing of "contemporary literature, philosophy and politics" (13). Holmes's response is that those areas of knowledge are useless to his pursuits. The detective's knowledge of music, however, seems to redeem him slightly in Watson's eyes. But even his playing has an illiberal cast:

> That he could play pieces, and difficult pieces, I knew well, because at my request he has played me some of Mendelssohn's Lieder, and other favourites. When left to himself, however, he would seldom produce any music or attempt any recognized air. Leaning back in his arm-chair of an evening, he would close his eyes and scrape carelessly at the fiddle which was thrown across his knew. Sometimes the chords were sonorous and melancholy. Occasionally they were fantastic and cheerful. Clearly they reflected the thoughts which possessed him, but whether the music aided those thoughts, or whether the playing was simply the result of a whim or fancy, was more than I could determine. I might have rebelled against these exasperating solos had it not been that he usually terminated them by playing in quick succession a whole series of my favourite airs as a slight compensation for the trial upon my patience. (15)

Holmes's absent-minded strumming of the violin draws to mind the hapless Mr. Harding in Anthony Trollope's *The Warden*. Mr. Harding is prone to playing an imaginary violoncello, one hand holding an imaginary bow while the other presses imaginary frets. Elaine Hadley has argued that Trollope's Harding performs a version of liberal agency that takes the form of thoughtful emotion, what she calls "liberalism's social aesthetic, a certain fantasy of an elegant, cognitive agency in the public square" (2005, 95).[10] For Hadley, Trollope signals Mr. Harding's achievement of liberal individuality when he can engage in detached thought in the face of social difference. Mr. Harding's playing of an imaginary violoncello reflects this harmonious interiority (n. 4, 101). In the case of *A Study in Scarlet*, however, Holmes's playing is always audience-oriented. Alone, he does not play actual songs. Watson cannot tell if the playing helps his thoughts or are completely random. In short, unlike Harding's imaginary playing, Holmes's careless playing might signal detachment, but it does not signal the harmoniousness of the mental faculties.

Holmes's craving for fame also bars him from liberal individuality. Watson continually faults Holmes's love of praise and desire for fame—his love of being seen. However, as we have seen, Watson's most profound sense of restoration came initially from being detected and therefore recognized by Holmes, a version of the same recognition that Holmes seeks. While the paternal government fails to renew his life, Holmes's recognition does. Holmes is able to tell that Watson fought in Afghanistan, recognizing the scene and source of Watson's new self and giving him the pleasure of being found out. The mystery of how Holmes knows where Watson has been rouses him back to life, more so than his social contact with Stamford. Rothfield has argued that Holmes's detection is not limited to lowly criminals, but extends to all aspects of the social spectrum. Rothfield redefines Holmes's process of detection as not solely negative—guarding the purity of a social category of respectable middle class—but rather positive. It produces feelings in the detector and the detected. For Holmes, the act of detection is a distinctly erotic, bodily felt sensation. The text disavows the sexual nature of detection and Holmes appears repeatedly as professional and cold. Rothfield deems this the scandal of Holmes's detective reasoning: Its sadistic act of detection stimulates the detector and humiliates both the person detected and those who could not penetrate the mystery—i.e., Watson and the reader.[11]

Watson's pleasure at being found out by Holmes is, of course, ironically similar to Holmes's own desire for fame, that promised pleasure of the mass public sphere and that weakness of liberal individuality for which Watson faults Holmes. After all, it will be through Watson's written memoirs that Holmes will achieve the fame he seeks and Watson will achieve the kind of mass recognition he craves. After the arrest of Hope, the newspapers, quoted by Watson, give the two Scotland Yard officers all the credit. Holmes sulkily admits that he may only ever find private satisfaction in solving the crimes. Watson's reassuring words conclude the novel: "I have all the facts in my journal, and the public shall know them. In the meantime you must make yourself contented by the consciousness of success, like the Roman miser—'*Populus me sibilat, at mihi plaudo / Ipse domi simul ac nummos contemplar in arca*'" (121). Adapted from Horace's *Satires*, the quote converts Holmes's public trivialization into public disdain and the fact that he solved the crime into money in a vault: "The public hiss at me, but I applaud myself at my house when I think about the money in my strongbox" (n. 4, 129).

These moments of libidinal intensity point out how the modern subject has come to eroticize the ways that the imperial nation-state has identified and classified him or her. Pulverized by questions of the difference between justice and revenge in a world where sympathetic exchanges have been co-opted by the state, leaving personal ones insipid and anodyne, the modern subject swells up again by the process of being detected and recognized. However, the source of recognition is less the state, which is compromised, than mass culture, to which both Holmes and Watson turn.

Conclusion

This chapter has proposed that we view the openness and instability of Afghanistan in late Victorian works—and indeed in present political discourse—not as a reflection of empirical reality, but rather as the expression of unconscious wishes. Because the British did not want to colonize Afghanistan, the imperative to represent its inhabitants as docile or civilizable, as in the case of natives of India, was absent, enabling other feelings and fantasies to be staged. To control them, the British embodied Afghans with the contradictory attributes of savagery and civility. The British could thus imagine them as in need of Western discipline, justifying imperial, if not colonial, control in the region. And they could imagine them as pre-liberal versions of themselves, projecting internal conflicts onto them. In the latter case, identifying with Afghans enabled the British to critique their own present and mourn an imagined loss of independence in the face of an interventionist state that appeared to galvanize its subjects' hope for self-transformation. This process in turn dramatizes how the formation of modern Western liberal citizenship integrates and relies upon fantasies about othered cultures in order to assuage anxieties produced by its own internal contradictions.

3   *The Rise of the State as a Sympathetic Liberal Subject in Hardy's* The Woodlanders

> To hear these two poor Arcadian innocents talk of imperial law would have made a humane person weep who should have known what a dangerous structure they were building up on their supposed knowledge. They remained in thought, like children in the presence of the incomprehensible.
>
> —Thomas Hardy, *The Woodlanders* (1887)[1]

The British did not fantasize only about Scots and Afghans, of course. The middle classes, to be more specific, entertained a robust set of fantasies about the rural working classes within Britain. As scholars of regional literature and of modern European nationalism have observed, the British middle classes had been fantasizing about rural folk for about as long as the British nation and the middle classes can be said to exist. While the Highlanders and insurgent Afghans came to embody the contradictory qualities of savagery and civility in the late Victorian period, England's rural folk stood paradoxically for both physical baseness and metaphysical purity. Unable to vote because they did not meet property qualifications, agricultural laborers nevertheless represented iconic Englishness.

In this chapter, my examination of modern state personhood moves from novels set in colonial and imperial zones to one set in the English countryside. Specifically, I focus on *The Woodlanders* (1887), Thomas Hardy's rustic novel of thwarted love and living decay. Populated by dialect-speaking rustics, his rural novels fed a healthy appetite for picturesque scenes of the countryside. Hardy famously rebelled against this appropriative way of reading his tragic tales. In his 1883 essay, "The Dorsetshire Labourer," a lament about the alienating and deterritorializing effects of agricultural capitalism, he took a jab at the bourgeois view of farm workers as timeless and outside of history and politics: "[Agricultural laborers] are losing their individuality, but they are widening the range of their ideas, and gaining in freedom. It is too much to expect them to remain stagnant and old-fashioned for the pleasure of romantic spectators" (1883, 181). In this chapter, I suggest that Hardy questioned a political and social climate in which the state was intervening more in citizens' lives, but in unequal ways. In particular, he probed the implications of the fantasies and feelings that the idea of the state as a sympathetic person incited in rural subjects. Rural folk were not impervious to biopolitical management, but their experience of it, according to Hardy, differed from urban and semi-urban folks and was shaped by their marginal political status and geographic distance from the metropolitan centers of England.

In the epigraph, "Arcadian innocents" refers to the rural protagonists Grace Melbury and Giles Winterborne. The "imperial law" they appear to be discussing is a distorted version of the Matrimonial Causes Act of 1857, which they tragically believe makes divorce easily available to all. Throughout the majority of the novel, Grace, the educated daughter of a timber merchant, has been locked in a disastrous marriage. When the village's unofficial counsel, Beaucock, a disgraced former law clerk, informs her distressed father, Melbury, about the allegedly democratic divorce law, he races off from Little Hintock to the courts of London to try to obtain his daughter's freedom. Before galloping away, Melbury enjoins Grace to renew her interrupted courtship with Giles, a virtuous if reticent yeoman farmer and also her childhood sweetheart. Now, as the two would-be lovers wait for news from London, they anxiously turn over the bewildering details of the divorce procedure: the "legal part" and whether it is done ("not yet quite done and finished, as is natural") or almost done ("But father said it was *almost*—did he not?"); whether one signs a paper or swears an oath ("Yes, I believe so"); and how long the law has been around ("About six months or a year, the lawyer said, I think") (282).

In this scene, Hardy seems to be parodying the kind of political discussion that liberal thinkers such as John Stuart Mill argued were edifying for England's disenfranchised classes. In *Considerations on Representative Government* (1861), Mill describes a form of debate and deliberation that lifts a manual laborer, "whose way of life brings him in contact with no variety of impressions, circumstances, or ideas," out of his "small circle" and into the political nation, learning "to feel for and with his fellow citizens" and becoming "consciously a member of a great community" (328). In contrast, Grace and Giles's discussion of the divorce law, based on hearsay from an unreliable source, neither abstracts them from their regional, class, or gendered particularities nor fosters in them feelings of collective solidarity.

Rather, Hardy has their tremulous discussion of the law reduce them to childishly self-absorbed semi-citizens, caught between legal-political knowledge and ignorance. The painful spectacle of their verbal exchange, shot through with vivid depictions of their internal states, would even, the narrator tells us, inflict collateral damage on an observer, the theoretical "humane person."[2] A surrogate for the reader, the sympathetic observer presumably has enough of a liberal education to grasp that Grace and Giles are indeed wrong about the inclusiveness of the Matrimonial Causes Act and that their political illiteracy will soon lead to devastating disappointment.

We could read this scene as a typically depressing moment in Hardy, yet another bleak and unforgiving exposure of the brutalizing ignorance and structural cruelty bearing down on England's marginalized rural folk. However, Hardy's interest throughout *The Woodlanders* lies less in narrating what an innocent rustic or cultured urbanite knows or does not know about the law, than in theorizing about what differently located subjects think they know, the fantasmatic modes in which they experience themselves as knowing, and the subjects they become in the process. *The Woodlanders* investigates the fragmentary narratives characters across the social spectrum stitch together from the scraps of everyday life to project a sense of self and futurity in a rapidly changing world. Hardy does not cast the woodlanders' and readers' identities as a priori and fixed. Nor does he depict either of their respective relationships to language and politics as powerful and instrumental. Instead, he encourages us to see both parties as coming into being as wounded, incomplete, and marginalized by virtue of the fantasies that mediate their encounters with the historical present. As the epigraph implies, this present is marked by the material and imaginary force of an increasingly sympathetic, interventionist, and imperialist state.

Throughout the novel, fantasies of self-transformation intertwine with fantasies of the magical powers of the state, proliferating almost as wildly as the lichen and ivy that choke the stalk and sapling in its ecosystem. For instance, a few scenes earlier, the lovelorn Giles hesitates to believe that marriage can be undone by an appeal to the courts, but he wavers enough to imagine, albeit with heartbreaking diffidence, infinite possibilities for the official-political: "Yet a new law might do anything" (277). Meanwhile, the narrator couches Grace's private contemplation of the act in more explicitly sacred—and ironic—terms: "The 'new law' was to her a mysterious, beneficent, god-like entity, lately descended upon earth, that would make her as she once had been without trouble or annoyance" (278). While one could designate this recurrence of fantasies throughout the narrative as a sign of fin-de-siècle malaise or literary interest in the unconscious, I argue instead that these fantasies' specific references to the "new law" tie them to the emergence of a fantasy of the state as a heroic actor endowed with the capacities to step in and ameliorate one's pain. This fantasy is in turn integral to the formation of a decidedly modern, and familiar, political subjectivity. To rephrase my opening sentence, then, we could say not only that Grace and Giles are discussing the law, but also that the law is "discussing" them, articulating them as subjects of the modern state. This state subjectivity has come to count as a form of political belonging and selfhood characterized by confusion, hope, and isolating inwardness.

While *The Woodlanders* seems to foster sympathy for rural folk who get caught up and reconfigured in state fantasy, it ultimately indicts sympathy and, by extension, the emergent liberal state's appropriation of the rhetoric of sympathy. In light of historical shifts in the political imaginary of the 1880s and 1890s, Hardy's pointed attention to the vagaries of love and pity both among characters and on the part of readers for characters can be read as allegories of the relations between a benevolent, sympathetic state and its subjects. Through the flows of feeling and projections that it describes and induces, *The Woodlanders* exposes the practice of sympathy for seeking to maintain the fantasy of a fixed and coherent self. With its radical doubt about the stability of the subject and its incisive critique of the politics of compassion for rural folk, the novel undermines the project of receiving or mobilizing sympathy on either an individual or governmental scale. Such literary scholars as David J. de Laura, Patricia Ingham, and John Goode have advanced classic arguments about Hardy's modern angst, obsession with injustice, and active pessimism, respectively. Pointing to rigid class and sex/gender systems, moral codes, and economic depressions wrought by British industrialism, they have illuminated the historical conditions against which Hardy's works throb and rage. Nevertheless, Hardy critics have yet to consider how his gloomy philosophy might constitute a creative engagement with this dramatic and enduring shift in the development of the state and the cultural formation of state subjectivity.

In contrast to Herbert Spencer and Sidney Webb, whose responses to late Victorian state fantasy I discuss in the Introduction, Hardy's *The Woodlanders* neither explicitly criticizes nor advocates state intervention or optimism in the state. The term "State" does not enter either the speech of the narrator or any of the characters. Rather, Hardy tracks the sensations, thoughts, and feelings that precede state fantasy and the installation of "the State" in common speech. Optimism in the state may have started as an urban phenomenon, but the novel imagines that attenuated versions were trickling into the countryside possibly as early as the 1860s. Staging its gradual encroachment on the hinterlands of the nation, Hardy narrates how characters merge with and become entangled in the long arms of the state, represented by the road, marriage, and the divorce law. By setting it in the countryside, Hardy denaturalizes the process of state subjectification, more likely to be associated with the metropolitan spaces of England (to be examined in the next chapter).

As Hardy tracks the spread of state fantasy across the nation, he blurs and overrides the bold, clear lines of the rational citizen-subject presupposed by contemporary political thinkers. For Hardy, meaning emerges from the body and its sensations. As Elaine Scarry has eloquently argued, for him, these sensations never evaporate, but become absorbed by matter, so that the world itself becomes a material record of a universal history of sensations (116). In *The Woodlanders*, Hardy situates the new historical force of a sympathetic, interventionist, imperialist state within what is for him a universal tension between these embodied feelings of agency and helplessness. With a kind of bated wonder, he asks how it feels when specifically rural subjects, already circumscribed by state practices of which they may or may not be aware, consciously turn back toward the state and achieve new forms of subjectivity in the process.

The Woodlanders thus bears witness to and sounds out late-nineteenth-century formal transformations in laissez-faire government, the rational and unified liberal subject, and the Victorian realist novel. If we consider these so-called breakdowns in positive terms, that is, as the building of something new, and as interlinked rather than isolated processes, we can view the particular contribution of *The Woodlanders* to our understanding of modernity as theorizing new subjectivities during a time of historical flux. By turning to this novel's meditations on state fantasy, we can begin to track how the structural emergence of an interventionist state physically and affectively shaped the everyday environment of subjects endowed with unconscious and internal tensions and opacities. We can also see how these historical forces redesigned what Fredric Jameson terms "the realist floor plan." Finally, we can arrive at a new critical understanding of Hardy's forlorn yet strangely appealing prose.

Fear and Loitering in Little Hintock

The Woodlanders opens with a rambler, a road, and what amounts to an eviscerating warning about the state. A classic chronotope, the road has multiple functions: It registers and collapses the physical distance between two places, it is an archetypal metaphor for life as a journey, and it serves as a literal and figurative artery of the national social body. In *The Woodlanders*, the road is also a literary device that leads the reader first into the artificial world of the novel, then into the fictional woodlands it depicts (and thus into the symbolic core of England), and finally into the dream lives of British subjects caught in the approaching force of an interventionist state. Finally, and perhaps most prosaically, the road is an arm of the state.

Like the humane person in the epigraph to this chapter, the rambler stands in for Hardy's imagined reader, who also hovers on the threshold of new territory: "The rambler who, for old association's sake, should trace the forsaken coach-road running almost in a meridional line from Bristol to the south shore of England, would find himself during the latter half of his journey in the vicinity of some extensive woodlands, interspersed with apple-orchards" (5). Calling to mind the narrator of Samuel Johnson's eighteenth-century series, the rambler, we learn from this first line, is sentimental and cartographically inclined. He also starts his journey in Bristol. Birthplace of Thomas Chatterton and Robert Southey, Bristol had been a thriving international port and manufacturing center in the late eighteenth and early nineteenth centuries. During the nineteenth century, its sociospatial structure changed from a medieval configuration, with the elites in the center of the city, to a modern, socially divided one, with the emergent middle class moving to the suburbs that sprouted up around the city. Bristol's economy had suffered a decline in the mid–nineteenth century, but revived in the next third of the century during the period of *The Woodlanders*.[3] The rambler thus finds himself, as it were, beamed or teleported, with no intermediary passage, into a space that contrasts sharply with the socially segregated, commercial, and financial center from which he began.

The first line spins us among a dizzying number of spatial and temporal locations. The reference to the "forsaken coach-road" recalls a specific moment in British national history: the eighteenth-century heyday of coaches, particularly mail coaches, and the then-revolutionary techniques for building roads, before the advent of the railway made both mail coaches and coach roads increasingly obsolete.[4] Meanwhile, the term "meridional," referring to the imaginary lines that pass through the North and South Poles, positions us on the globe and in an abstract, fixed location. Drawing on Michel De Certeau and Benedict Anderson, we can say that this first line places us firmly within the everyday of the nation. For De Certeau, place is "the order (of whatever kind) in accord with which elements are distributed in relationships of coexistence" (117). It is produced through the mode of the map, which implies the dominant act of seeing and "the knowledge of an order of places" (De Certeau 119). In addition, because Hardy articulates the meridional line as one running between Bristol and the south shore of England, he conjures a notion of place that is not only stable and abstract but also "local" in relation to an abstract idea of the nation. In delineating the fictional region of Wessex, the narrator deploys the conditional and present verb tenses ("should" and "would"), which, following Anderson's notion of the imagined national community, we can see as producing the sense that the rambler and the reader are inhabiting the same temporality.

But we cannot ignore Hardy's use of the adverb "almost" to modify "meridional." This "almost" introduces a hairline fracture into the abstract stability of place that "meridional" implies and diverts our path from the lines of the map. The fracture deepens by the time we get to the end of the sentence as the rambler "would find himself during the latter half of his journey in the vicinity of some extensive woodlands, interspersed with apple-orchards." The road, first a stable and planned place, now turns into a space, defined by De Certeau as *"a practiced place"* (117).⁵ While place is produced by the representational mode of the map, space is enacted through that of the tour, which "spatializ[es] actions" (De Certeau 119). From this point on, the representational mode of the passage switches between those of the map and the tour, while the tone shifts from neutral and quasi-scientific to lyrical and melancholic and back again. The second sentence begins with the deictic "Here," which reasserts the principle of the map by reconstructing a stable and abstract place: "Here the trees, timber or fruit-bearing as the case may be, make the wayside hedges ragged by their drip and shade, their lower limbs stretching in level repose over the road, as though reclining on the insubstantial air" (5). Counter-intuitively, it is the hanging of the trees that dirty the implicitly clean line of the hedges. The following sentence then undoes this sense of place by returning us to a space composed out of directions and relations: "At one place, where Rubdon Hill is crossed, a bank slopes up to the trees on the left hand, while on the right spreads a deep and silent vale." The points of view of the narrator and rambler coincide as they represent this spot in the language of the map, then diverge as the narrator leads the rambler into a region that seems to come from the rambler himself and yet somehow transcends or exceeds the epistemological claims of a map. Finally, in the last sentence of the paragraph, we must undergo another shift: "The spot is lonely, and when the days are darkening the many gay ones now perished who have rolled over the hill, the blistered soles that have trodden it, and the tears that have wetted it, return upon the mind of the loiterer" (5). Now the bourgeois, pleasure-seeking rambler, tracing the old coach road out of nostalgia, becomes a passive, melancholy, indolent mind, haunted by the memories that rise up from the road and overwhelm him.[6]

For John Barrell, the shifting perspectives in Hardy's fiction stage a complex contest between regional epistemologies, while for Gillian Beer, they set different temporal scales in relation. The opening scene of *The Woodlanders* beautifully exemplifies these characteristics of Hardy's writing. But if we attend to the rather obvious fact that the road that opens *The Woodlanders* is an arm of the state, one steeped in local meanings that do not evaporate, we can view the opening passage's shifts in mode and tone as tenderizing the rambler-reader for some upcoming politico-historical revelations. As we read on, the narrator cannot remind us enough about the varied past. The next paragraphs refer to the "forsaken coach-road" as a "deserted highway" and indeed finally an "old turnpike-road" (5–6).[7] These references consolidate the spectral presence of many past historical moments in the road, rendering it a social text bearing the thick and crisscrossing traces of a complex political unconscious. But just what kind of text is it?

In hagiographic histories, the road emerges as a key element in the symbolic arsenal of the nation. Metaphorically cast as the arteries of the nation, roads, in this view, link the far-flung and sparsely populated outlands of the nation with its dense cosmopolitan nodes, thereby transfusing the anemic periphery with vital goods, capital, information, ideas, and people. In the nineteenth and early twentieth centuries, this nationalist view crossed liberal and conservative lines. In *English Local Government: The Story of the King's Highway* (1913), Fabian socialists Sidney and Beatrice Webb laboriously chronicle the history of the road from the eighteenth century to the 1830s, the era of centralization and Reformed Parliament. They spotlight the road as the sole means for exchanging information and commodities before the onset of new transportation and communication technologies:

> To-day, the railway and the tramway, the telegraph and the telephone, have largely superseded roads as the arteries of national circulation. But, barring a few lengths of canal in the making, and a few miles of navigable river estuaries, it was, throughout the eighteenth century, on the King's Highway alone that depended the manufacturer and the wholesale dealer, the hawker and the shopkeeper, the farmer, the postal contractor, the lawyer, the government official, the traveller, the miner, the craftsman and the farm servant, for the transport of themselves, and the distribution of their products and their purchases, their services and their ideas. (143–4)

The highway in the Webbs' history operates as the common denominator of the people, rendering a diverse set of professionals, craftsmen, and laborers as a collective of abstract, equivalent citizens. It also binds disparate, remote places into a single coherent nation.[8] In short, for the Webbs, the road enables liberal democracy to flourish.

For Hardy, however, the road does not neatly fulfill a narrative of triumph and unification. After all, the rambler is left a passive, loitering mind, not a productive, circulating citizen. If we refer to the state history of road maintenance in the nineteenth century, we can account for Hardy's ambivalent version of the road. This history reveals anecdotal evidence of forced division and repartition of territories, as well as competition over government resources. The General Highway Act of 1862 sought to empower local governments, but in a fashion that fulfilled central government's own administrative logics and goals, in effect dictating what local governments' concerns should be, how they should maintain themselves, and how they should govern. In some cases, the central government even repartitioned local districts in ways that conflicted with traditional boundaries and cultural ties. In other words, the state sought at once to establish and formalize the sovereign powers of local governments and to standardize their procedures and functions—effectively instituting an extended form of disciplinary individualism whereby the central power sought to achieve control over local governments by endowing them with individual will. In the specific case of turnpike roads, travelers' complaints about paying tolls and the well-publicized corruption scandals concerning the trusts that funded them made them increasingly unpopular. It was only a matter of time before a Committee of the Commons was formed to dismantle them. By 1887, the year the novel was published, only fifteen turnpike roads across England were in operation and in another eight years, the last one was taken down.

In keeping with his interest in representing a feudal past quickly disappearing in the face of modernity, Hardy begins the novel with a road that his readers would have likely recognized as on the brink of extinction. He does so precisely at a time when the sovereignty and boundaries of local parishes, particularly rural ones, were quickly changing in the face of state centralization. Our rambler then starts out on an obsolete turnpike road for "old association's sake." But these associations go only so far. The turnpike road is also appealing because it belongs to an imagined past in which local communities were discrete, autonomous, and somehow pre-political. The rambler may indulge in pleasant reflections of that time, but he neither attends to the structural forces that relegate such communities to the past nor considers the reality in which those communities consequently find themselves.[9]

In addition to state centralization, the rural landscape and its inhabitants were undergoing major cultural changes due to shifts in the regime of production—changes Hardy chronicled in novels such as *Tess of the D'Urbervilles* (1891) and *Jude the Obscure* (1895). As peasants found themselves increasingly unable to own farmland, they became migrant laborers *en masse*. This led to national concerns that the landowning peasant class, the origin and moral backbone of the nation, was disappearing.[10] Public anxiety over the shrinking of the landowning peasant class not only exposes the moral symbolic valence assigned to them, but it also reveals the ideological linkage between home and virtue: Without property, it was said, these peasants were at risk of losing their sentimental investment in the nation. This logic also structured the Reform Act of 1884. The act brought votes to a wider segment of the working population but still discriminated in rural cases on the basis of property ownership, in effect disqualifying agricultural laborers who did not own property. Even as late as 1908, Sidney Webb was decrying agricultural capitalism for turning peasants into mere "agricultural labourers, working always under orders, unconcerned either with the improvement of the soil or the profitableness of the farmer's venture; and possessing no more claim or attachment to the land they till than the factory operative has to the mill in which he works" (viii).

Consequently, reviving the peasant class became an important political issue during the 1880s. The most popular solution to counter what was perceived as their slow degradation from peasants to mere workers was to give them land.[11] The image of a countryside farmed by peasants was thus charged with the function of harboring the very character of the nation itself.[12] Mere "agricultural labourers," hired to work other people's lands, threatened this character by signaling the transformation of the farm country into factories that simply exchanged wages for abstract labor, producing no affective bonds or national sentiments (viii). Additionally, as rural workers began to demand the vote, they seemed corrupted by abstract ideas of democracy—an urban, industrial concern. Since these kinds of laboring relations were already established in the major industrial centers, it would seem that even more pressure was coming to bear on a class that actually no longer really existed.

At first glance, *The Woodlanders* seems to comply with the national fantasy of the local as the backbone of the nation. After all, Hardy goes on to describe Little Hintock as the "still water of privacy," while the worldly middle-class outsiders who pop up in it are by contrast theatrical and publicity-oriented (11). The rural locale itself materializes as a sparsely inhabited space that safeguards individuality, understood as affective intensity: "Where the eyes of a multitude continuously beat like waves upon a countenance they seem to wear away its individuality, but in the still water of privacy every tentacle of feeling and sentiment shoots out in visible luxuriance" (11). The novel thus appears to charge the remote woodlands with the symbolic responsibility of sustaining the individuality and authenticity of the British nation, qualities theoretically held in suspension while the political nation was involved in deliberating matters of national import. But the narrator also complicates this fantasy, casting the sympathetic reader who might be affiliated with the political nation as a trespasser. As the sentence just described ends, this individuality is suddenly cast as always potentially vulnerable to outside appropriation: "to be interpreted as readily as a printed book by an intruder" (11). No longer just aimless, out of place, or lingering with shady intent, the reader is now an unwelcome, uninvited presence. By criminalizing any sympathetic consumption of an idea of the rural and its actual inhabitants, the narrator reinscribes a division between center and margin, one not based on the center's picturesque fantasies of the margins, but on the margins' rejection of the center.

This tension also underlies the transformative work of the novel's opening paragraph in which ghosts rise up to overwhelm and disable the leisurely rambler. Hardy's is a post-Romantic culture, influenced by evolutionary notions of natural and social struggle, anxious about colonized hordes converging on the imperial isle, and fearful of working-class mobs rioting within it. His rambler may have redoubled his desire to cultivate an inner solitude or heightened individuality by walking alone in the rural outreaches of England, but the road is also a zone of intense libidinal memories. Hardy thus sets up a literary booby trap, leading his readers on by their own sentimentality until they trip over a traumatic past that cannot finally be displaced into a pleasurable, nation-uniting nostalgia.[13] The affective force of this past not only exposes the fallacy of liberal theories of personhood but also suggests that the alterity of the rural locale is the violent effect of uneven government policies and economic practices and, indeed, sympathy practiced from on high. The affective force of the past reproduces in the reader an emotional experience that closely resembles that of the woodlander dragged partially and haphazardly into the national context. Glued to a particular sense of place that at once symbolizes Englishness yet is politically, economically, and culturally situated outside of the privileges of abstract citizenship, Hardy's woodlanders figure as both icons of and exiles from the nation.

Unlike Spencer's or Webb's political writings, Hardy's implicit reference to the state by means of the metonym of the road cannot be reduced to a pro or con position on state intervention or belief in the salutary power of the state. But it does provide a lesson in regional and class politics. Through the road, Hardy connects the increasingly interventionist state and its promises of resources and recognition to local traumas that continue to cause pain. The road may be the artery of the nation, but it gushes and clots by turns as it establishes the very distances it claims to collapse and reinforces the same differences its ideologues praise it for bridging. The novel's opening passage, through its intense, irrational affects and oscillations, makes us feel conflicted and uneasy—in preparation for the forthcoming doubled image of the state as benevolent and judging, giving and withholding, hopeful-making and fear-inducing, unifying and dividing. Haunted and aimless, we are now ready for the unfolding of the complicated story of marriage, divorce, and the flow of state fantasy into the outer pockets of the nation that follows. Like the road, marriage is metaphorically overdetermined: a blessed state, a service to God and country, a destiny, a narrative denouement, and an ideological resolution to social conflict. It is also a legal contract adjudicated by the state.

The State of the Marital Union and the Divinity of Divorce

The Woodlanders takes place mainly in the fictional Wessex village of Little Hintock in southern England and centers on Grace's matrimonial possibilities. The daughter of a prosperous, self-made timber merchant, she serves as the crux around which the novel configures the organs of state and mass culture. The newspaper, the courts, and London, the nation's symbolic, as well as political, cultural, and economic center, appear, if only abstractly, in relation to Grace and her crisis. Expensively educated in town and forced to bear the burden of her father's masochistic social ambitions, Grace's destiny can be read as a tiny encapsulation of Hardy's history of England. Her education and urbanization seem to bear out the promises of a progressive liberal ideology that dictates that cultivation is available to all who seek it. Her life takes a new course when, under the direction of her father, she rejects her childhood love, Giles, for Edred Fitzpiers, the newly arrived physician and member of a defunct aristocratic family. The alliance between the upwardly mobile merchant's daughter and the déclassé aristocrat who has sought to survive by latching onto the emergent profession of medicine proves to be humiliating. While enjoying none of the wealth of the landed classes, Fitzpiers has inherited one of its primary vices: philandering. He soon begins a scandalous affair with Felice Charmond, the landowner's capricious widow who now controls the properties and fortunes of the woodlanders. A former actress, she is, like Fitzpiers, an outsider to Little Hintock's insular ways. Their affair mortifies not only Grace but also her father, who had pressured her into marrying the doctor. Meanwhile, Giles is held in a narrative suspension that eventually yields to slow deterioration.

In the preface to the 1896 edition, Hardy suggests that the feeling of love that aspires toward marriage, understood primarily as a legal contract, reveals most powerfully both the inconsistency of the human mind and the limits of the novel form: "In the present novel . . . the immortal puzzle—given the man and woman, how to find a basis for their sexual relation—is left where it stood" (386). It thus makes sense that it is also the feeling that invites the entry of the state. In the preface, and throughout the novel, Hardy implies that this puzzle, "how to find a basis for their sexual relation," comes into existence only when a man and woman, understanding the irrationality of sexuality, seek a rational foundation for it. He goes on to assert that love, once formalized in the marriage bond, exposes how knowing one's mind—a liberal value and imperative—is impossible:

> From the point of view of marriage as a distinct covenant or undertaking, decided on by two people fully cognizant of all its possible issues, and competent to carry them through, this assumption [that it is depraved to be attracted to someone else] is, of course, logical. Yet no thinking person supposes that on the broader ground of how to afford the greatest happiness to the units of human society during their brief transit through this sorry world, there is no more to be said on this covenant; and it is certainly not supposed by the writer of these pages. (368)

Using the dominant Benthamite logic that laws ought to produce the greatest happiness for the greatest number of people, Hardy begins the novel with a bitter interrogation of the utility of marriage. He asserts that it is only when unpredictable, irrational, and contradictory emotions are misrepresented by the uniformity and fixity of the marriage certificate that troubles really begin.

Of all the characters, Fitzpiers is perhaps most explicitly aligned with the state. As a physician and surgeon of the Union, Fitzpiers is required to be state certified and under the review of the Board of Guardians. He thus depends upon the state for his professional identity and livelihood.[14] As a reader of metaphysics, transcendental philosophy, and physiology, he is also the novel's strongest representative of the institution of science and its faith in rationality. But in nothing so much as his attitude toward marriage does Fitzpiers appear as the state's literary envoy. The first fault lines in their romance manifest themselves when Fitzpiers urges Grace to marry him in a registry office instead of in the village church, declaring, "It is a quieter, snugger, and more convenient place in every way" (165). His demand causes deep distress for Grace whose sense of a proper marriage involves friends and family at the church—not signing a certificate in a government office. But Fitzpiers, at times truly sickened at the thought of publicly losing status by marrying beneath him, persists, arguing, "You see, dear, a noisy, bell-ringing marriage at church has this objection in our case; it would be a thing of report a long way round" (165). To clinch his argument, Fitzpiers reports to rationality, equating marriage with other legal arrangements: "Marriage is a civil contract, and the shorter and simpler it is made the better. People don't go to church when they take a house, or even when they make a will" (166).

Fitzpiers emerges as the emblem of a new attitude not only toward marriage but also toward the state. He introduces into Little Hintock a distinctly modern mindset that produces meaning according to the imperatives and rationalities of the state, not the traditional hermeneutic practices of the rural community. Fitzpiers's civil interpretation of marriage was indeed gaining momentum in the latter part of the century as local church courts began to cede power to the common law ones, located mainly in London. In Fitzpiers's fantasy, marriage at a registry office eschews sacred temporality, with all its irrational implications, and deploys a legal one that not only admits it as a property relation, but also incorporates the couple into the simultaneous, synchronic time of the state.[15] While church marriage conscripts the two parties within a specific history, kinship system, and family lore—involving banns, witnesses, and ultimately word-of-mouth stories that weave them into local memory, as well as that of surrounding communities—civil marriage serves a national fantasy of totality. Through civil marriage, they are stripped of their troubling class markers and rendered whole and shiny in national terms: two British subjects now married, equal to other subjects across the country, regardless of place or circumstance.

However, as we have seen, Fitzpiers also seizes upon this rationality out of self-interested desperation. His attachments to other practices of rationality—reading metaphysics and conducting scientific experiments—are similarly not what they seem. The narrator tells us, "Fitzpiers was in a distinct degree scientific . . . but primarily he was an idealist. He believed that behind the imperfect lay the perfect" and "that results in a new and untried case might be different from those in other cases where the material conditions has been precisely similarly" (134). This impractical and ultimately egocentric attitude leads him to pursue Grace, despite their class differences. Having pursued the ideal of Grace, Fitzpiers now instrumentalizes the law, viewing it as a means to privacy, a way of abstracting his social identity from the bespattering, humiliating details of her actual social identity by offering him a virtual sanctuary. He believes that the law will encase him, converting him into an anonymous number in the national registry, whereby he might elude the fate of being planted in the garden bed of local history. In this way, Fitzpiers ironically seizes upon the modern bureaucratic and administrative logic of classificatory knowledge to maintain his archaic social pedigree.

Even though Grace is horrified at the idea of a state-stamped marriage (she eventually does get her church wedding), over time, as she suffers the indignities of Fitzpiers's transgressions, she and her father both become religiously ecstatic about the possibility of a state-granted divorce. As the plot takes this turn, the language of the novel enforces the sense that the secularization of society, represented by Fitzpiers, is met with a persistent sacralization of the state and its laws on the part of those woodlanders who aspire toward bourgeois or even genteel status. The myths that the Enlightenment thinkers thought they dispelled thus return with a vengeance in the political dream work of the modern nation-state.[16]

Divorce enters the narrative through the tainted vessel of Beaucock, a local Hintocker who was once a promising law clerk in a big town. Given to drinking too much, Beaucock lost his job and now conducts unofficial legal business in Little Hintock. Happening upon a depressed Melbury, Beaucock, the false prophet of the state, informs him of a cure for Grace's "sad case": "A new court was established last year, and under the new statute, twenty and twenty-one Vic., cap. eighty-five, unmarrying is as easy as marrying. No more Acts of Parliament necessary: no longer one law for the rich and another for the poor" (271). Dangling this enticing bait before Melbury, Beaucock lures him into a tavern to hear more. Considering the possibilities of this law unhinges Melbury's morality and reason, in part because he is only rarely exposed to newspapers: "The intelligence amazed Melbury, who saw little of newspapers. And though he was a severely correct man . . . such fascination lay in the idea of delivering his poor girl from bondage, that it deprived him of the critical faculty" (271). Hardy describes the effects of Beaucock's "intelligence" on Melbury as both intoxicating and religious: "irradiated with the project and though he scarcely wetted his lips, Melbury never knew how he came out of the inn, or when or where he mounted his gig to pursue his way homeward" (272). When Giles runs into him, he finds Melbury's face "shining as if he had, like the Lawgiver, conversed with an angel" (272). Melbury then exclaims to him, ". . . there's a new law in the land! Grace can be free quite easily. . . . She can get rid of him—d'ye hear—get rid of him. Think of that, my friend Giles!" (272).

To win over Giles, the dubious key player upon whom his new plan for his daughter depends, he retroactively builds an account of having indeed seen the law mentioned in the papers: "Melbury said that he had no manner of doubt, for since his talk with Beaucock it had come into his mind that he had seen some time ago in the weekly paper an allusion to such a legal change; but, having no interest in those desperate remedies at the moment, he had passed it over" (272). The stylistic choice to cast Melbury's speech in indirect discourse links it to the earlier passage and returns our attention to the narrator who is telling the story. It signals to us Hardy's own theory that it is through the organs of failed professionals and imagined newspaper accounts that political knowledge transmits and installs itself from the center to the periphery. In this way, political knowledge from the imperial center seeps into remote rural pockets, mixing with and combusting individual histories and emotions, inducing political optimism, and borrowing the affects of drunkenness and religious experience, collapsing all three kinds of good feelings into one pathetically false hope.

Not consciously deceitful, Melbury seems really to believe what he in fact ardently desires. His wishful, strategic remembrance fulfills its intention. Giles's doubt eventually turns down a notch, leading even him a few days later to think, "Yet a new law might do anything" (277). The brevity of this sentence in the sweep of big events is striking. It shows a consciousness turning over: "yet" signifying a counter to residual doubts; "might" speaking to potentiality, the future; and "anything" to the limitless possibilities, the blank space a subject might fill with his or her heart's desires, that "a new law" as metonym of a sacred entity could enact. It thus shows Giles himself, the exceptional as well as, paradoxically, representative woodlander, infected with the ecstasy coursing through Melbury's body, which suggests just how quickly belief in the state transmits from person to person.[17]

Giles's private thought uncannily resembles what Victorian thinkers increasingly feared was becoming a common and widespread hope. In *On Liberty* (1859), Mill lamented the surge of a particular kind of optimism in the state that was leading to a breakdown of liberal individuality.[18] In this essay, Mill argued that England's greatness was due to its diversity, which striated the overall population's fields of choice, so that they had to compare, evaluate, and thereby develop themselves as critical liberal individuals. But, he lamented, in a vein similar to Hardy's "The Dorsetshire Labourer," these local differences were starting to disappear. Mill cited familiar mid-century historical forces as the engines of this pernicious homogenization, including technological advances in communication, commerce, and manufacture, but he singled out "the State" as the prime instigator: "[a] more powerful agency than even all these, in bringing about a general similarity among mankind, is the complete establishment, in this and other free countries, of the ascendancy of public opinion in the State" (81–2). Swollen on the collective belief that it represents public opinion, "the State" looms in Mill's essay as a self-generating and demonically animated threshing machine, chewing up the population only to spit out its vital individuality as so much chaff: ". . . a State which dwarfs its men . . . will find that . . . the perfection of machinery to which it has sacrificed everything, will in the end avail it nothing, for want of the vital power which, in order that the machine might work more smoothly, it has preferred to banish" (128). Perhaps most of all, Mill dreaded the increasing power of this structure over its subjects' psychic lives and the enormous range of its potential reach: "Every function superadded to those already exercised by the government, causes its influence over hopes and fears to be more widely diffused . . ." (122).

Spencer also warned against this kind of effect. In keeping with his theories of organicism and hereditary evolution, he feared that state intervention would have an insidious effect on the natural order:

> Indeed the more numerous public instrumentalities become, the more is there generated in citizens the notion that everything is to be done for them, and nothing by them. Each generation is made less familiar with the attainment of desired ends by individual actions or private combinations, and more familiar with the attainment of them by governmental agencies; until, eventually, governmental agencies come to be thought of as the only available agencies. (49–50)

The repetition of the word "agencies" in the last sentence perhaps speaks to Spencer's own anxieties about the very possibility of agency, that it may only exist retroactively as an imagined faculty always already inhibited or disabled. However we read it, the passage expresses a palpable fear that the interventionist state was about to usurp even the weakest versions of self-determination.

Sounding out Mill's and Spencer's nightmare visions, the novel follows the news of the divorce law as it takes on a life of its own: First it spreads from person to person, implanting itself in them and giving forth dreams of the future—primarily to those with middle-class ties or aspirations. But while Mill and Spencer maintain a belief in the autonomous individual who becomes infiltrated by the state, Hardy depicts characters who are always, by nature, in constant flux. His characters come into being anew—in space and time—by virtue of their fantasmatic relations to an idea of the state that resides behind the law. In other words, while Foucault's notions of disciplinary and regulatory power show how institutions, discourses, and practices control both individual bodies and populations, respectively, Hardy's novel shows us how the *idea* of a law is enough to reshape subjects.

Melbury's perception of the egalitarian, mistake-erasing divorce law propels him out of Little Hintock on a pilgrimage to London. Before leaving to deliver his appeal, he transmits his hope to Grace and impetuously encourages her to resume her old ties to Giles. While the law inspires Melbury with patriarchal dreams of kinship and retribution that will make him the virtuous man he thinks and hopes himself to be, it inspires Grace, as I mentioned in the beginning of the chapter, with a vision of a divine restoration of her former self: "The 'new law' was to her a mysterious, beneficent, godlike entity, lately descended upon earth, that would make her as she once had been without trouble or annoyance" (278). For Grace, the law will convert her into an imagined past state of pure potentiality—but one circumscribed by her ability to reenter marriage. Her outlook from this point forward until the bitter dashing of her hopes is guided by this sense of her previous and future ideal selves.

As for the peasants of Little Hintock, their relationship to government is described as improvisational and semi-feudal. Felice Charmond as landlord seems to have more direct power over their lives than local or central government officials (neither of whom are present in the novel). Idiosyncratic, she nevertheless suits the woodlanders' style of subjection: ". . . with that marvellous subtlety of contrivance in steering round odd tempers that is found in sons of the soil and dependents generally, they managed to get along under her government rather better than they would have done beneath a more equable rule" (195). Giles is one of these "sons of the soil," but his relative success has also made him independent and proud, and he consequently wavers back and forth as to whether he should allow himself to have optimism in the state.

A relatively independent farmer, Giles might be considered middle class. However, his regional tastes overpower any abstract class distinctions. Like the peasants and smaller farmers, he cannot wholeheartedly believe in the state's power to undo the religious tie of marriage. He never fully reaches the enlightened rationality of the more bourgeois characters who not only view marriage as a contract, but also turn to the state to relieve their distress. The seduction of state optimism nevertheless appears to operate even on Giles, as it appears to implant what presents itself as a latent tendency toward middle-class aspiration. Assimilating the fantasy of the state as sympathetic can be a painful process. Giles's hope at hearing this news from Melbury is described as a kind of welling up of pressure from within: "'Are you sure—about this new law?' asked Winterborne, so disquieted by a gigantic exultation which loomed alternately with fearful doubt, that he evaded the full acceptance of Melbury's last statement" (272). He thus hovers between marrying a woman whose relative wealth and education make her his social superior and remaining a Little Hintocker who knows his place and is well satisfied with it. That he cannot fully inhabit either position eventually proves fatal.

In Grace's divorce case, native skepticism and the reader's legal knowledge coincide. While the Matrimonial Causes Act wrested divorce from the ecclesiastical courts and reassigned it to those of the common law, the act by no means expunged its traditional moral conditions or masculinism. Religious conservatism, nationalism, and male privilege all converged in its definition. The law dictated that lack of affection alone was not grounds for a divorce because it seemed too close to the passion-driven practices of the French Revolution.[19] Where the law did allow a husband to divorce his wife if he could prove that she had committed adultery, a wife could win a divorce only if she could prove her husband had committed adultery *and* one or more of the following: incest, bigamy, cruelty, or desertion. The act thus not only coerced British subjects into performing respectability when love was lacking, but it also discriminated against women.

No wonder Melbury's appeal on behalf of his daughter fails. He writes to Giles from London, warning him not to compromise Grace's situation: "The news was, in sum, that Fitzpiers's conduct had not been sufficiently cruel to Grace to enable her to snap the bond" (289–90). Unwilling to dispel their dream, Giles withholds this information, unwittingly extending Grace's painful state of suspense: "'Oh, why does not my father come home and explain!' she sobbed, 'and let me know clearly what I am! It is too trying, this, to ask me to—and then to leave me so long in so vague a state that I do not know what to do, and perhaps do wrong!'" (292). Because marriage granted Grace both a precise local identity and an abstract national one, her appeal for divorce forces her to experience an identity crisis. She tries to block and suppress her desire, on the grounds that it is determined by the law and social norms: "'I am almost sure,' she added uncertainly, 'that I ought not to let you hold my hand yet, knowing that the documents—or whatever it may be—have not been signed . . .'" (282). However, it is also Grace's faith in the law that leads her to break it unknowingly and experience new sensations: She touches Giles and professes her love in the belief the divorce will work, while her father and the reader already know it will not.

Giles and Grace's hesitant belief in the divorce law allows them to feel love for each other, to unleash their dreams about being together, and to touch and kiss. Bodies in flux, their libidinal energies course anew, making us feel the injustice of the Matrimonial Causes Act, which thwarts sexual attraction. As in the case of the road, the state fails to deliver Giles and Grace from their lack of liberty. Instead, Hardy transforms their desire for change into signs of their exclusion from it to stress precisely just how far they are from such political deliverance.

Hardy's narrative implicates us in the very same process, eliminating any presumed distance between reader and woodlander. As we saw earlier, the opening epigraph to this essay features a "humane person" reduced to tears by the spectacle of political confusion and sputtering hope. In this way, the novel reminds Victorian readers of their own lingering but foundationless optimism in the Victorian state's capacity to grant plenitude or heal wounds. By first sensitizing and depressing the reader, the novel's opening paragraph also places them in the same affective register as the destined-to-be-crushed woodlanders. Sharing these feelings brings the two parties together, rather than elevating the reader to a height from which to analyze, judge, and bestow feeling. If we keep in mind how the late Victorian state was increasingly appropriating the Christian and philanthropic rhetorics of sympathy, then Hardy's disruption of this social emotion suggests its problematic nature as a principle not only of reading, but also of governing.

Sympathology: The Liberalization of Grace

The development of Grace's fantasies throughout the novel can be read as a historical allegory for England's own liberalization and turn toward a fantasy of the state as sympathetic on both national and individual scales. Early in the novel, the narrator indicates that she is "difficult to describe . . . at any time" and that probably no one else more than she is "in herself more completely a *reductio ad absurdum* of attempts to appraise a woman, even externally, by items of face and figure" (38). Sometimes, the narrator tells us, she is beautiful, sometimes not. He ascribes this aesthetic judgment to factors of her health and spirits, but then contradicts himself by putting the judgment of her "true quality" upon the viewer: "The woman herself was a shadowy conjectural creature . . . a shape in the gloom whose true quality could only be approximated by putting together a movement now and a glance then, in that patient attention which nothing but watchful lovingkindness ever troubles to give" (38–9). Grace is formless, but not quite in the way that Romantic writers like Wordsworth and Victorian ones like Mill and Arnold considered the self-cultivating subject to be. By the time the narrator describes her, Grace has already been educated and urbanized, which ought to have started shaping her into more solid liberal form. Instead, she is formless because, in Hardy's view, she takes shape by virtue of others who frame her through their perception. It must be said, however, that Grace does perform a liberal practice—sympathy—that, if only momentarily, congeals her as an ideal liberal individual, specifically of the kind on which the fantasy of the state as sympathetic liberal subject is modeled.

Grace is the novel's most sympathizing, if not sympathetic, character. In fact, she is not susceptible to falling in love unless she first feels sympathy for her beloved. On returning to Little Hintock, Grace is inclined towards Giles, but when a series of mishaps literally dis-homes him, Melbury orders her to discourage him. As Giles's misfortunes pile up, her affection grows in direct proportion:

> There could not be the least doubt that gentle Grace was warming to more sympathy with, and interest in, Winterborne than ever she had done while he was her promised lover; that since his misfortune those social shortcomings of his, which contrasted so awkwardly with her later experiences of life, had become obscured by the generous revival of an old romantic attachment to him. (108)

Sympathy breeds interest and triggers romantic feelings. No isolated incident, this sympathy-to-love progression happens yet again with Giles's competitor. Nervously excited and repelled by Fitzpiers, Grace is ambivalent about his courtship until she visits the ruins of his family's castle. She is moved when she sees how the farmer next door shelters his calves in its crumbling structure. The scene of straw spread on the ruined castle's floors and the cows "cooling their thirsty tongues by licking the quaint Norman carving, which glistened with the moisture" (161) stimulates Grace's sympathy, interest, and romantic feelings: ". . . for the first time the family of Fitzpiers assumed in her imagination the hues of a melancholy romanticism" (162). It is only after this excursion that she begins to imagine she could marry the man.

In his famous treatise on the subject of sympathy, *The Theory of Moral Sentiments* (1759), Adam Smith describes fellow feeling as an imaginative act that arises within an individual to overcome anxiety about the inaccessibility of another's interiority: "As we have no immediate experience of what other men feel, we can form no idea of the manner in which they are affected, but by conceiving what we ourselves should feel in the like situation" (9). It is not too much of a stretch, I think, to view this model as a paranoid deflection of the unknowability of one's own self projected onto others. This social emotion posits a normative bourgeois subject: he who sympathizes well. To sympathize well means fulfilling aesthetic standards of morality, intensity, and vivacity: ". . . this sentiment, like all the other original passions of human nature, is by no means confined to the virtuous and humane, though they perhaps may feel it with the most exquisite sensibility" (9). This aesthetic capacity to imagine how one would feel in another's situation turns into a moral one: If you feel intensely, it is because you have created an aesthetically superior representation of yourself in a sufferer's situation and you thereby show your virtue and humaneness. Having a fine aesthetic capacity to make a representation to yourself of how you would feel in the situation of another becomes an essential attribute of the liberal subject.

During the nineteenth century, the novel emerged as a medium for testing and disseminating the discourse of sympathy. Elizabeth Gaskell's *Mary Barton* (1848) and Harriet Beecher Stowe's *Uncle Tom's Cabin* (1852) taught middle-class readers how to sympathize by narrating scenes of sympathy between characters and teaching them which kinds of subjects were worthy of it: in the case of Gaskell, respectable English workers, in that of Stowe, respectable black slaves. As my reductive summary of these two novels suggests, worthy objects of sympathy tended to display the qualities valued by the middle classes. They were hardworking, family-oriented, Christian practitioners of sympathy. As Lauren Berlant and others have argued after Smith, sympathy distances and detaches by presuming a superior position from which to judge the moral worthiness of the sufferer and then to imagine his or her pain.[20] Sympathy requires the subject to imagine him or herself as unified, rational, and self-transparent and to enter into a process of selection based on moral standards.

Grace's sympathetic attachments imply that one must first refuse to love an object before one can dispense sympathy to it. Such a move allows Grace to maintain her independence, integrity, and inaccessibility to both Giles and Fitzpiers. While this process would seem to invite a feminist reading, I would like to suggest instead that Grace's withholding, sympathizing, and accepting shed light on Hardy's views of the operations of the modern liberal state and why it could not be the utopic solution that various contemporary socialists had argued. While the emergent modern liberal state of the late Victorian period was dispensing welfare and resources, it was also founded upon an initial refusal to fully incorporate or serve all of its members, agricultural laborers and women among them.[21] It kept some at a distance and then across that distance sought to provide help.

Conclusion

The Woodlanders does not explicitly refer to "the state." Instead, Hardy rewinds to an imagined past, a time before the obviousness of the state as a sympathetic person sank into the popular imaginary. From its indexical references to the Matrimonial Causes Act (1857) and also by the brief appearance of a Southern gentleman who refers to the end of the U.S. Civil War (1865), we know that events depicted in the novel could have occurred as early as the 1860s. Hardy collapses the perception that the rural, in particular, is always lagging behind the rest of the nation into his historical insight that late-1880s England itself was permeated by state fantasy. The idea of state fantasy first appears in the opening scene of the road, displaying the conflicts between the state's promises of inclusion and noninterference and its practices of exclusion and control. Hardy also signals its historical emergence in the adjective "new" that Melbury, Grace, and Giles use to define the divorce law. The "new law" is set off in quotation marks in the narrator's speech, drawing our attention to the woodlanders' ignorance. They are perpetually belated—the old to "us" will always appear new to "them." Even more important, the quotation marks serve the realism of the novel, drawing our attention to public belief in the state's capacity to create new ways to intervene legitimately in its citizens' lives.

But Hardy's characters also thwart realist conventions by appearing as collections of matter, effusing and infused with sensations. For Hardy, characters are constantly in flux, not self-contained, self-transparent, monadic liberal subjects. Their senses of self fluctuate, propelling them in different spatial directions and into different social arrangements (for example, Melbury dashes to London; Grace flees from Fitzpiers, runs to Giles, demurely strolls with Fitzpiers; Giles escapes to the woods; and Grace does not know what she is). This eccentric style of characterization has not gone unnoted. Gilles Deleuze described Hardy's characters as "[i]ndividuation without a subject" and "packets of sensations in the raw" (40). Scarry observed how, for Hardy, man is not an independent, self-contained, discrete unit, but continuous with matter, in which we must include other men. As Hardy rejects the normative mode of subjectivity, he also rejects the fantasy that turns the state into a sympathetic subject: The concentrated, knowable, coherent entity of the state remains beyond the discourse of the narrator and characters. His characters are still realistic only insofar as they inhabit their historical moment: We see them grapple with an everyday increasingly shaped by state power.

As the distinctions between characters' internal and external worlds melt away, it becomes their task, sometimes burden, along with the narrator's, to say something meaningful about it all. He may not have the kind of liberal agency that Mill and Spencer do, but the creation of meaning is still the human's task alone. Created by humans, fantasies of the state are also incorporated by them. Instead of residing within the seam between humans' historical sense of their agency and their historical sense of their own powerlessness, fantasies of the state stitch the two self-perceptions together. In the age of biopower, subjects feel powerful when they project agency away from themselves and onto the state. Hardy stays away from debates about state intervention in order to explore the ways that humans displace agency from themselves to structures imagined as external. He depicts people as "packets of raw sensations" from which the affective force of the idea of the state as a sympathetic subject actually rises.

4   The Space of Optimism

State Fantasy and the Case of Gissing's *The Odd Women*

I now turn to a novel that is mainly set in the gridded center of the nation, London. *The Odd Women* (1893) may not seem like the most obvious of George Gissing's novels to select for an investigation of late Victorian state power. Literary critics have tended to mine this exemplary New Woman novel for its sociological treatments of feminism, the Woman Question, and the plight of unmarried middle-class women forced into menial jobs. Surely, one might argue, Gissing more directly expresses his views on the British state and politics elsewhere, such as in the class-warfare novel, *Demos* (1886), for example. However, what makes *The Odd Women* so compelling to this inquiry is that it features a sophisticated economy of optimism in which a new idea of the state functions alongside two older sites of essentially bourgeois optimism that are made to seem anachronistic: the Arnoldian notion of culture and the traditional institution of marriage. The novel also stresses the central roles that gender and genre, or form, play in the operation of this economy.

The Odd Women shows how middle-class female subjects are particularly vulnerable in the social world of the late Victorian period. Unprepared to enter the workplace established by late-nineteenth-century capitalism, Gissing's characters live unsupported and unevenly managed lives. Gissing shows what happens when you are produced as a statistic, the proverbial "odd woman" of the late nineteenth century, and thus an exemplum of the regulatory, taxonomizing techniques of biopower, which results not in being supported by institutions but instead in being cast out from social norms of reproduction and class status. The odd women are captured into a socio-cultural category that at once encloses them into intelligibility and banishes them to the margins of the thinkable.

Throughout the grinding action of the plot, our focus is directed primarily to the female characters who are inflated by hope, made tremulous and inspirited through its effects and affects, and then, just as spectacularly, deflated by their failures to sustain it. The novel focuses on these women's emotional intensity, which function as surplus to the otherwise sociological, depersonalizing characterization of their situations. This gender asymmetry is linked to another axis on which Gissing judges his characters: an axis running from contented but hopeless to discontented but hopeful. In the novel, contentment seems desirable, but, since it necessarily results in the death of hope, it signals a shrinking of horizons and the harboring of an obnoxious complacency. Hope, for Gissing, must always recede into the distance. This incompatibility of contentment and hope complicates a politics of closure, while shedding some light on Gissing's own commitment to depressing his readers. It also informs his use of "the odd women" to experiment with how potential for change may lie with the discontented who live in society's margins.

In *The Odd Women*, gendered differentiation is due in part to genred differentiation: Various genres, such as poetry, political philosophy, and romance novels, appear throughout the novel, training characters to direct their optimism to specific objects.[1] These assignments emphasize the primacy of reading practices to subjectification, whether gendered, classed, or national. *The Odd Women* takes the idea of genre as pedagogical or formative even further, dramatizing how, in the age of the modern state, public spaces appear to operate like a genre, encoding subjects and carrying out the work of the state in shaping cultured citizens.

In the following sections, I shall attempt to make several points about how *The Odd Women* registers the relation between the statist practices of regulatory power and the fantasies, if not exactly consciously of the state, but unconsciously *around* the state, of its subjects. If the argument seems to veer away from the topic, I would like to suggest that this has something to do with the kinds of problems optimism in the state posed to contemporary thinkers. In Gissing's case, it ultimately leads him to pursue a line of flight outside of the novel's inner economy of optimism.

"Let Us Alone": The Old Man of Culture

By setting optimism in the state alongside optimism in a range of ordinary objects, *The Odd Women* not only questions how the state gets inside subjects, but also betrays a haunting preoccupation with the possibility that the state may actually produce subjects—and not just working- or lower-class ones, either. However, while Gissing is ambivalent about the desirability of an interventionist state, his novel also questions the modern platitude, upheld by contemporary critical theorists like Foucault, Brown, Lloyd, and Thomas, that the state is only ever a punitive, disciplinary force. For, at the kernel of the narrator's hard shell of irony, lies a question Gissing seems to have difficulty avowing: What if being subjectified by the state could involve something other than loss or abjection?

"The State" pulsates beneath the surface of the novel, structuring the public spaces through which the odd women pass, being deflected through Gissing's sharp-elbowed irony, and shown to be appropriating other available objects of optimism. Although the novel includes philanthropy, enterprise, and religion, it subjects the culture concept and marriage to its most intense scrutiny, casting them as fatigued and degraded middle-class institutions. *The Odd Women*, in fact, opens with a meditation on culture and links it to the seemingly banal business of life insurance.

The first scene, set in Clevedon in 1872, introduces us to Dr. Madden and his young daughters, who appear to be living according to the dictates of Arnoldian culture. This short chapter, ironically titled "The Fold and the Shepherd," sets the stage for the unfolding of the plot, which concerns the fates of three of Madden's daughters, Virginia, Alice, and Monica, and their childhood friend Rhoda Nunn as they encounter each other again in London in 1887. The novel begins with Dr. Madden's words to Alice as they walk along the coast-downs: "So to-morrow, Alice . . . I shall take steps for insuring my life for a thousand pounds" (31). This statement ushers the reader into a world of risk and accident, while also pointing to the shaky virtue of Dr. Madden.[2] By the nineteenth century, having one's property insured had become a caretaker's moral duty (Ewald 207).

Next, we learn that Dr. Madden loves Tennyson and Coleridge, in fact establishing his practice in Clevedon because of the former, whose cottage he "never passed . . . without bowing in spirit. From the contact of coarse actualities his nature shrank" (32). As a father, Dr. Madden chooses to bequeath the legacy of culture—not economic security—to his children. The girls, we are told, "had received instruction suitable to their breeding, and the elder ones were disposed to better this education by private study. The atmosphere of the house was intellectual; books, especially the poets, lay in every room" (33). Later, when asked to read aloud, Dr. Madden chooses Tennyson's "The Lotos-Eaters," a poem about the lure of giving up hope in the face of inevitable and endless struggle.

In the poem, Tennyson dramatizes an episode from Homer's *Odyssey* in which Odysseus stops at the land of the Lotos-Eaters, where some of his exhausted men consume the narcotic flowers and give in to increasing weariness and melancholy, refusing to return home. Before being interrupted, Dr. Madden reads the following lines: "Let us alone. Time driveth onward fast,/And in a little while our lips are dumb./Let us alone. What is it that will last? /All things are taken from us—" (35). As a dramatic monologue, "The Lotos-Eaters" both enables its speaker to express the desire to stop desiring and to maintain an ironic distance from this negative desire. In reading it aloud, Dr. Madden appears to own this irony. However, the narrator, having already shown Dr. Madden's reluctance to face economic reality, which involves voluntarily applying for life insurance, and his preference to luxuriate in his own complacency, rather than proper Arnoldian liberal reflection, turns on him. Dr. Madden dies a few days later from a riding accident and his daughters are subsequently plunged into poverty and hardship.

Arnold published *Culture and Anarchy* (1869) in the wake of riots over working-class enfranchisement and printed attacks on his character. Citing critics who had charged him with political apathy and ineffectiveness, Arnold argued that culture was the best and only means available to the British for solving their social and political problems. Culture provided a bulwark against materialism and narrow-mindedness by "enabling ourselves, by getting to know, whether through reading, observing, or thinking, the best that can at present be known in the world" (151). These practices develop "a harmonious perfection, a perfection in which the characters of beauty and intelligence are both present . . ." (66). Through this enabling process, the man of culture can disinterestedly approach the reality that lies behind the smoke screen caused by competing self-interests. While Arnold leaves its contents hazy, perhaps to accommodate a range of appropriative impulses, at the heart of it lies a promised narrative of transformation: "reading, observing, or thinking, the best" can reorganize the mental organism, allowing one to transcend class struggles and misery by virtue of the harmonious and balanced exercise of all of one's faculties. By describing culture as a mental exercise and a religious awakening, Arnold emphasizes its active nature: "Not a having and a resting, but a growing and a becoming . . ." (62).

While attached to a notion of culture, Gissing was also bitterly aware of how social status, education, and wealth constrained the quest for it (Dale 272). *The Odd Women* not only critiques such material constraints, but it also denounces the commercialization of culture into a form of leisure.[3] Dating this process to the 1870s, the novel dramatizes it through Dr. Madden's use of culture to pad and decorate his private life. As borne out by the Madden sisters' adult duress, Dr. Madden's worship of culture is harmful. Such worship warps it from the ideal Arnoldian process, which Gissing seeks to preserve, into a consumable commodity whose external object-ness keeps its distance from the doctor's interiority, shoring up and fixing his ego, but not developing it. Dr. Madden's love of poetry is linked to a general desire to ignore reality and indulge lassitude. His adoration of culture registers a degraded use of it. To adore it, he had first to think of it as an object to be consumed, rather than a process to be undergone. Culture does not inspirit Dr. Madden—it sates and anesthetizes him. His unthinking attachment to it ultimately stands in for virtue, causing him to default on his paternal responsibilities.

This failure to cultivate proper liberal individuality coincides with a failure to manage one's own death in a normative fashion. Culture and nongovernmental biopower fold neatly together here. This opening indicates that the normative pursuit of culture and willing subjection to the moral face of biopower are compatible enterprises for Gissing and Arnold. *The Odd Women* thus casts the miserable fates of the Madden girls as effects of their father's moral weakness. This weakness on his part transforms them from being cozily well-off, loved, middle-class young women to being poor, lonely, redundant women, in excess of the number of available men to marry and a problem to society and state. However, the novel only begins with this observation. We then swiftly enter a world in which culture, along with marriage and liberal citizenship, are threatened anew, this time by an increasingly interventionist state. Such a threat is all the more egregious to Gissing because culture, marriage, and citizenship provide optimism in part because they represent, in a classically liberal sense, sites properly beyond the reach of the state. Gissing expresses the fear that the state was starting to appropriate them in two scenes featuring odd women momentarily inhabiting public spaces in strange and distressing ways.

The State-Produced Everyday

Gissing locates the most intense work of the state in its production of public spaces, which, first of all, are not consciously recognized as state spaces and which, second, scramble the self-coherence of subjects as they pass through them. His London comes concretely into being through street names, tramways, park benches, squares, and apartment buildings, circumscribing the rigid movements of its class- and gender-bound subjects as they circulate between highly variegated public and private sites.[4] This web forms a spatial analogue to the social world in which the odd women must move, a world structured by a web of certificate requirements, exploitative employers, and excruciating penny-pinching that binds and alienates them. By virtue of outnumbering men eligible for marriage, the odd women are forced to work for a living, migrating to whatever jobs are available.

After the opening chapter, the primary action of the novel jumps ahead from 1872 to 1887 and from Clevedon to London. For Rhoda, who dedicates herself to the feminist cause, and Monica, who enjoys aimless wandering, London affords personal opportunities and pleasures. But for Virginia, a lady's companion, and Alice, a governess, while the city represents a temporary respite from employment, it also crams them into one stifling room where their miseries concentrate.

Critics have often interpreted the concrete features of Gissing's descriptions as material signposts of his sociological commitment to representing an urban everyday. For example, Arlene Young argues that "the detailed specificity of Gissing's realism, especially in the setting and in the delineation of the minutiae of everyday life" deepens the artifactual nature of *The Odd Women* (16): "London's streets, its parks, its art galleries, its railway lines and stations constitute an almost palpable world in which the characters move and act. The routes the characters take as they move about London are traced precisely, often demarcated with specific landmarks" (16–17). However, set alongside Webb's and Spencer's lists of state regulations, which I touched upon in the Introduction, Gissing's crafted descriptions, cast by Young as reality-thickening, mimetic details, expose a more specific dimension to the urban everyday, one that inspired both denunciation and celebration.

As I noted in the Introduction, Spencer's *The Man Versus the State* (1884) features furious lists of new state regulations, ranging from Lord Palmerston's Ministry in 1860 to Gladstone's in the 1880s, and unfurl as accretions of Liberal absurdity. Webb's response in "Historic" (1889) confirmed yet celebrated the pervasiveness of what Spencer called the "tacit assumption that the Government should step in whenever anything is not going right" (Spencer 46). His essay also resorted to copious lists, in his case detailing the less obvious state services of which its subjects, including Spencer, were "unconscious."[5]

In this light, Young's strangely similar list adds up not simply to an urban quotidian experience, but rather a state-produced everyday, one shot through with the state's desire to manage the life of its population. Spencer and Webb refer to the several rounds of municipalization that had swept through the country, as the central government increasingly sought both to empower but also to regulate local governments. London represented an anomalous case, subject to reverse initiatives to detach it from the central government. By mid-century, London's rapid growth had caused problems that exceeded its government's capacity, leading to the institution of the Metropolitan Board of Works. Designed to deal with urban issues such as sanitation, drainage, fire protection, and parks, the MBW ultimately represented the victory of Conservative anti-centralizers.[6] By the 1880s, scandals surrounding the Board led politicians and the newspapers to call for a new system of local government and in 1884 the Liberal Home Secretary Sir William Harcourt proposed that the City Corporation ought to be the only municipal authority in London. While municipalism had generally incited little public interest, it now became a heated national issue as Conservatives, who supported local autonomy, and Liberals, who sought to centralize, engaged in fierce debates. In 1888, Lord Salisbury passed the Local Government Act, thus instituting a central body to be directly elected.

Gissing brings these material and symbolic crises into play in his novel. While the otherwise barren narrative descriptions of the city render the state tacit, two scenes break through, serving as irregular points of affective concentration: first, Monica, flushed and ashamed, on a bench in Battersea Park and then, later, Virginia, euphoric and intoxicated, wandering into the middle of Trafalgar Square. These scenes dramatize Gissing's sense of the state's historic appropriation and disabling of culture, marriage, and citizenship. For Gissing, what is most disturbing about this appropriation is that it results in the dissolving and reconstitution of selfhood into one bearing the stamp of the state unawares.

After her father's death, Monica becomes a draper's assistant in London. On her twenty-first birthday, she visits her sisters. They give her Keble's *The Christian Year*, a book of devotional poems, and urge her to go to church, despite the fact that neither of them attend regularly. Acquiescing out of guilt, Monica reluctantly agrees to be their proxy. In Gissing's world, religion, like Dr. Madden's culture, offers no inspiration. It only superficially props up limp, spiritless bodies. Most dramatically, Alice piously reads religious writings, but in a kind of addicted desperation, the narrator describing it as "refuge from the barrenness and bitterness of life" (305). Her religious practice only further isolates her, rather than leading her to join a community or participate in a religious public.

During the service, which Monica performs "mechanically," she luxuriates in a memory: "Sitting, standing, or on her knees, she wore the same preoccupied look, with ever and again a slight smile or movement of the lips, as if she were recalling some conversation of special interest" (58). Here we are given one of the telltale signs of hope: abstraction, or pre-occupation, a rehearsal and rehashing of the past with a view toward the future. Of all the characters, Monica is the most susceptible to such bouts of abstraction. For her, they centrally concern her prospects for marriage.

The memory is of an earlier day. Jilted by a friend at the Battersea Park landing-stage, Monica had proceeded by herself to sit on a bench and watch the passing skiffs which coalesce into a generic scene before her envious spectatorship: "a young man who pulled, and a girl who held the strings of the tiller" (58). As she stewed in agony at the sight, a male stranger sat beside her. Formerly a clerk, he tells her later that an inheritance has recently rendered him independent. Leaving his business card, Widdowson asks to meet her again the following Sunday. Although she assents, Monica later recounts feeling "ashamed and confused." Unsure about her attraction to him, she nevertheless feels compelled to comply with his wishes: "In truth, she had not felt the courage to refuse; in a manner, he had overawed her" (60). She does return, and after several episodes of nervous retreats, she exchanges her odd-woman status for the normative one of wife.

In Monica's situation, the city park is a space of both culture and marriage, but one where the work of the state is unseen. Officially, city parks in the nineteenth century were intended to provide "civilization and comfort to the poor, pleasure to the well-off, and grandeur to the imperial capital" (Inwood 666). Along with churches, schools, libraries, and museums, parks were a spatial ordering of the moralizing project of the state, integral to the task of incubating the respectability of the working classes while maintaining that of the middle classes (Inwood 666). Park proponents argued that these landscaped forms would improve the working classes by replacing their low amusements with the restorative benefits of proximity both to nature and to the respectable middle classes. Forty years before this scene, Battersea Fields had been home to gypsies, vagrants, rowdy fair-goers, drinkers, and pigeon shooting. Converting it to a public park, which occurred shortly thereafter, both flushed out undesirable activity and installed a civilizing project in its place (Inwood 668).

The park thus promotes and facilitates memory, the reproduction of bourgeois culture (in both its anthropological and humanistic senses), and heterosexual romance. Monica and Widdowson share an ambiguous middle-class status, sliding halfway down and shooting halfway up, respectively, that prevents them from pursuing conventional routes toward marriage. Unfixed and aspiring, they eagerly seek contentment within established forms. The city park eventually becomes the setting in which their plastic social identities, personally and politically experienced as distressing, can become fixed into the rigid terms of bourgeois, heterosexual romantic spectacle, thus actively attaching two odd strangers into a meaningful couple form. As a metonym of the municipality, the social whole united in serving the interests of the group, the park thus serves two functions. It acts as schoolroom, diffusing culture, which appears in this case to mean providing not just a meditative setting for self-cultivation, but also the normative spectacle of middle-class couples. It also acts as salon, fostering such marital alliances.

At first glance, by allowing Monica and Widdowson to skip the once necessary step of being introduced through acquaintances, Battersea Park seems to provide a field for unconventional social processes. However, this democratic aspect is overshadowed by its emphasis on romance: All are allowed to fill in the normative couple form. The costs of such a union are given a heightened piquancy: The very bourgeois values Monica and Widdowson wish to embrace require them to disavow the conditions that allowed them to realize these values. As Monica tries to explain the encounter to her roommate Mildred, she becomes nervous and defensive, "[p]ainfully conscious" of how her explanations misrepresent her intentions, exclaiming, "I see your opinion of me has suffered. You don't like this story" (129). Meeting a strange man alone in public suggests that her middle-class, feminine sexuality is not a transcendent symbol of England's moral coherence, but rather a commodity on the public market. Furthermore, Monica and Widdowson are more miserable as a couple than they were as single individuals. As a measure of the social problem they represent, Monica conventionally dies in childbirth at the end of the novel, while Widdowson moves in with a male friend, Newdick.

If the preceding scene expresses Gissing's view that the state has subsumed both culture and marriage, changing them from being individuating processes into forms controlled by the state, then Virginia's scene exposes Gissing's fraught relationship with the promises of political personhood. Virginia's consciousness remains dangerously unfilled and her person does not become the content for established forms. Rather, her brief moment parodies citizenship, expressing Gissing's underlying cynicism about official politics. But Virginia's parody, unintentional on her part, also belies Gissing's wish for a political consciousness both nurtured by the state and capable of being exercised against it.

In June 1888, Virginia leaves her stuffy room, where Alice lies sick, to run an errand. Along the way, she furtively stops for a brandy, a fix that instantly infuses her limp body and mind: "Colour flowed to her cheeks; her eyes lost their frightened glare. Another draught finished the stimulant. She hastily wiped her lips, and walked away with firm step" (47). The somatic effects of increased circulation and confidence foreshadow the signs of resolution and optimism that will occur just a bit later, when Virginia calls upon Rhoda.

The bodily sensations Virginia experiences in this later scene repeat meaningfully throughout the novel. At this rendezvous, when Rhoda suggests that Virginia and Alice should invest their precious capital in starting a school, "Virginia at first shrank in alarm, then trembled deliciously at her friend's bold views" (51). Like Monica, who is similarly infused by her memory of what was at first a disruptive event, Virginia turns her encounter with Rhoda into a memory that invigorates her. Back at home, Virginia moves around with "the recovered step of girlhood, [holds] herself upright, and [can] not steady her hands" as she waits for Monica (56). She then gushes to her younger sister, "She is quite like a *man* in energy and resources. I never imagined that one of our sex could resolve and plan and act as she does!" (57). Virginia's sense of hope and its corresponding bodily tics—the firm step, straight posture, increased circulation—produced by her contact with Rhoda's unconventional views echo the effects of her earlier consumption of alcohol. Imbibing alcohol, being influenced by someone else's resolution or unconventionality, and the possibilities of marriage and enterprise, all result in a similar affective reordering of bodies in *The Odd Women*.

When we return to the earlier scene, we can see these similarities more clearly and add yet another object to the list of affect-inducing fantasies: the state. Virginia finishes her draught of brandy and walks into the streets:

> In the meantime a threatening cloud had passed from the sun; warm rays fell upon the street and its clamorous life. Virginia felt tired in body, but a delightful animation, rarest of boons, gave her new strength. She walked into Trafalgar Square and viewed it like a person who stands there for the first time, smiling, interested. A quarter of an hour passed whilst she merely enjoyed the air, the sunshine, and the scene about her. Such a quarter of an hour—so calm, contented, unconsciously hopeful—as she had not known since Alice's coming to London. (47)

What are we to make of such an anomalous scene, restful yet ludicrous, positive yet pathetic? Why are we given such details as Trafalgar Square and the unconsciousness of Virginia's hope?

Designed in 1830 to unify symbolically the Crown, the political domain, and commerce, connecting Pall Mall, Charing Cross, and St Martin-in-the-Fields, Trafalgar Square was also the site of recent counter-state insurgency (Sexby 544).[7] In December of 1887 (just before the fictional Virginia arrives in London), it was the political stage for repeated riots and violent clashes between, on the one hand, the police and, on the other, the unemployed, defenders of free speech, and critics of the British handling of Ireland. The riots grew out of the most recent economic depression. Lasting until 1887, this depression had caused widespread unemployment among industrial and agricultural workers and insufferable overcrowding in working-class urban neighborhoods, famously publicized in W. T. Stead's 1883 *The Bitter Cry of Outcast London*.

In February 1886, twenty thousand unemployed dock and building workers rallied in the square and then set out on a course of looting throughout the city. In October of the following year, they again occupied Trafalgar Square, but first sent a deputation to the Lord Mayor to ask for governmental action to stem unemployment. The Alderman Sir Henry Knight's curt response that they should apply for relief sent the unemployed angrily marching through London again. The next day, Sir Charles Warren, the Chief Commissioner of Police, cleared the square, provoking public condemnation for bluntly violating the rights to free speech and assembly.[8] Despite such public disapproval, on October 18, the police did it again, but the crowd reconvened in Hyde Park where they denounced the police and rioted anew.

In letters to his brother Algernon and his sister Ellen, Gissing noted the gravity of these violent events. On October 19, 1887, Gissing wrote to his brother, "We have daily riots at present: on Monday in Traf. Square, yesterday in Hyde Park. Things begin to look very serious; the police are now made special object of attack. It is amusing to see how little attention is paid to the matter by the newspapers; in all probability they will wake up before long" (*Collected Letters* 3:157). The newspapers did not in fact hold back for long, especially after Warren issued an edict forbidding assemblies in Trafalgar Square, a formal violation of city code. For example, a reporter for the *Pall Mall Gazette* passionately indicted the police, drawing on Dickens: ". . . the police have given affairs another aspect. 'My name is—Law,' says the policeman in 'Pickwick.' The London police and their chiefs say the same" ("Under the Black Flag"). Later, the *Pall Mall Gazette* again defended both the rioters and Trafalgar Square:

> The right of public meeting is one of the most sacred rights which freemen possess. Together with trial by jury, it is the parent of all our liberties. Yet, although in Central London there is practically but one open space where the poor man can hold a public meeting to give articulate voice to his opinions on matters concerning him most nearly, that one open space is to be now closed against him—not by law, but by the arbitrary edict of a policeman. ("What Must")

On November 13, a protest initially organized in support of William O'Brien, the imprisoned radical Irish M.P., became a defense of the right to hold public meetings. In a letter to Ellen dated the same day, Gissing again notes the ongoing protest: "Tremendous rows in London between police & mobs. Meeting to be held to-day in Trafalgar Sq. in defiance of police prohibition" (*Collected Letters* 3:162). The police broke it up in the brutal confrontation known as "Bloody Sunday." The crowd moved on to Hyde Park, overturning carriages and smashing windows along the way.

Trafalgar Square was thus a concentrated site of social antagonism, political contradictions, and violence the month before Gissing began the main action of his novel. The image of Virginia wading into the middle of the square, drunken and shabby yet genteel and "unconsciously hopeful," would have rung a strange note for his readers. On one level, this scene can be read simply as a sign of Virginia's moral decline. However, such a reading omits a crucial detail: the location of Virginia's hopefulness in her unconscious.

The possibility that Virginia might become a political actor when walking onto this stage is implied. However, it quickly degenerates into her occupying the position of a pleasantly expectant spectator whose hopefulness, first of all, is unknown to her and, secondly, depends upon her not knowing the recent story of protest and state violence. She must view it "like a person who stands there for the first time, smiling, interested." Stumbling onto a national political stage, Virginia can only feel "unconsciously hopeful"—a cheap and fleeting sensation that looks like national optimism in the transformative effects of municipalization but is really a private experience of drunkenness. The scene suggests that the state's provision of public spaces to build community might be limited. Virginia pathetically cannot articulate a program that would help her to achieve the full personhood that is currently denied her.

Gissing thus portrays an odd woman, radically detached from history, politics, and agency, experiencing hope on the unconscious level where it remains locked away from her conscious cognitive processes. The city square, initially designed as a spatial solution to multiple conflicts between the nation and the city, on the one hand, and among the religious, political, and commercial aspects of London, on the other, ultimately emerges as the suppressed repository of a recent history of contradiction, violence, and rage. The "residual effectivity" of this history, a term I borrow from Fredric Jameson, is reproduced in the unconscious form it takes in Virginia (187).

In these brief but intense scenes, the state's hand in shaping lives, psychologies, and desire surfaces in dramatic and incoherent ways. Even though Monica's folding into conventionality is disruptive and ultimately fatal, and Virginia's feelings of national optimism amount to an abject parody of self-expression and freedom, neither initial scene fully deviates from state narratives about parks and squares. However, by locating these characters' breakdowns to their passage through public spaces that strangely privatize them—through marriage and unconsciousness, respectively—*The Odd Women* only heightens the hope that different narratives might in fact attach themselves, reside effectively, within these formal state spaces. In particular, the novel searches for a person who could have a critical relation to the state and forge a collective that does not degrade into mob form.

Where Hope Lies

This hope most explicitly emerges in a dialogue between Rhoda and Everard Barfoot, her business partner's cousin. During one of his frequent visits, Everard amuses Rhoda with an anecdote about his impoverished friend Micklethwaite who has been engaged for seventeen years. "I have a theory," he muses, "that when an engagement has lasted ten years, with constancy on both sides, and poverty still prevents marriage, the State ought to make provision for a man in some way, according to his social standing." Everard rounds off his mock political theory with studied *savoir-faire* and priggishness: "When one thinks of it, a whole socialistic system lies in that suggestion" (118).

Proving herself his match in wit, Rhoda strikes back by applying governmental logic and universalizing his exception: "If . . . it were first provided that no marriage should take place until *after* a ten years' engagement." The suave Everard, "in his smoothest and most graceful tone," concedes her point and extends the joke with reference to England's professionalizing culture: "That completes the system.—Unless you like to add that no engagement is permitted except between people who have passed a certain examination; equivalent, let us say, to that which confers a University degree." Rhoda concludes, "Admirable. And no marriage, except where both, for the whole decennium, have earned their living by work that the State recognizes" (118).

At first glance, we might be struck by how this passage pays homage to Jane Austen and Charles Dickens: Spirited but imperfect hero and heroine spar their way toward self-awareness and marital denouement by satirizing the classificatory logic and bureaucratic rationality that dominated Victorian political, economic, and social life. Indeed, as Gissing channels Dickens through his characters' flirtatious mockery of social taxonomies, moral regulations, and professional examinations, he also carefully sets them up for an Austen-style courtship that will painfully expose the limits of their self-images as cultured freethinkers.

However, two features of the passage also diverge from such literary antecedents and their cultural contexts. First, and most obviously, Everard and Rhoda bat "the State" with a big "S" back and forth. It would be difficult to find this term in the work of Austen or in the early work of Dickens. Austen not only tended to sublimate the political into intersubjective relations, but also wrote during a period when the usage of the term as an agent of life-altering change was not as prevalent as it would be by the 1880s and 1890s. Meanwhile, Dickens often figured the government synecdochically, in policemen, teachers, the Chancery, fog, and so on. Not until the 1860s and 1870s do his writings start to feature "the State" in its capitalized form as a subject of action and with assumed duties.[9]

The second feature concerns the tone of the narrator, which provides us with a unique structure of feeling, one that gives us insight not only into the culture of this period and the specifics of Gissing's style, but also the nature of the modern state.[10] While Austen's narrators might have aridly satirized those who violated social codes and Dickens's exuberantly skewered those intoxicated with bureaucratic power, Gissing's narrator is engaged in satirizing his characters' satire of politics, as well as those other ordinary objects of Victorian optimism, culture and marriage. Through such doubling of irony, Gissing prompts us to consider whether his characters' and ultimately his own sophisticated jockeying and arch adoption of critical distance are really just thinly veiling a cluster of shared desires deemed too humiliating to avow. Perhaps they do wish that culture could provide not just salon wit and cool composure, but rather the Arnoldian capacity to create a better world and that marriage could provide a fulfilling sense of self outside of the compromising domains of the commercial and the political.

But, most strikingly, this passage, taken together with the two scenes in public spaces, also betrays the hope that "the State" could provide legibility and plenitude by recognizing competence through certification and removing obstacles to the good life through the distribution of resources. Gissing does not resolve his ambivalence in *The Odd Women*. Rather, after exposing the failures and contradictions of these ordinary objects of optimism, he attempts to move beyond the dilemma altogether by promoting the idea that hope lies in the conditioning of a critical subject who could navigate these historical conditions. The object to which Gissing cathects his own optimism for achieving such a goal is, perhaps unsurprisingly, the novel the reader holds in his or her hands.

Love, Marriage, and Culture Redux

Marriage is the object of optimism most associated with the genre of the novel. The spectacle of the couple form lies at the heart of marriage in *The Odd Women*, emerging in its social world as a privileged, public form of human organization, both in literary romances and in social practice. It induces different kinds of pain for individuals based on whether they are within it or orbiting around its instantiations. In particular, with Rhoda as mouthpiece, Gissing launches a critique of how popular romances perpetuate the desire for marriage. While claiming to represent this desire on behalf of their readers, the romances, Gissing argues, instill it, formalizing desire in the progression of the love plot.

Rhoda also exemplifies how marriage and its genre produce not only compliant subjects, but also resistant ones whose very insistence on the separateness of institutions and individuals ironically works to uphold the ideological conditions necessary for such devices as romance plots to work. Gissing's optimism eventually alights on the possibility that individuals might use serious literature, like his own, not romance novels, to develop a critical consciousness of both kinds of determinative relations. In other words, for Gissing, novels such as his can foster the recognition that romance novels produce the desire they claim to represent. Rhoda's torturous courting by Everard, which she begins to understand through the novelistic conventions of the love plot, forces her to recognize how this plot already structures her own desire, despite her fiercely reasoned anti-novel and anti-marriage principles, thus producing her surprised sense of belonging after all to a feminine public.

While Monica and Virginia avidly consume romances, Rhoda condemns them as the source of ordinary women's problems. A committed celibate and feminist, Rhoda works for Mary Barfoot, an independently wealthy woman dedicated to saving young middle-class girls from the drudgery of teaching and retail work by training them as secretaries. Rhoda's reaction to a student who runs off with a married man only later to be abandoned by him testifies to her views on love stories and the women who read them. In effect, this plot line amounts to an internal romance story itself, existing only for the reader through the character's, and not the narrator's, references to it.

For Mary, Bella simply fell in love, a common and forgivable enough mistake. But for Rhoda, such an excuse makes the act even more contemptible: " 'Fell in love!' Concentration of scorn was in this echo. 'Oh, for what isn't that phrase responsible!' " (81). As Mary deliberates whether to receive Bella again, Rhoda argues,

> The girl's nature was corrupted with sentimentality, like that of all but every woman who is intelligent enough to read what is called the best fiction, but not intelligent enough to understand its vice. Love—love—love; a sickening sameness of vulgarity. What is more vulgar than the ideal of novelists? They won't represent the actual world; it would be too dull for their readers. In real life, how many men and women *fall in love*? (82)

In a later fight, Mary responds, "You have hardened your heart with theory. Guard yourself, Rhoda! To work for women one must keep one's womanhood" (150). While, for Mary, "theory" and "womanhood" are incompatible, for the narrator, "theory" does not threaten Rhoda's "womanhood" so much as her ideal of herself as cultured and critical. This story line ends, typically enough, in the student's anguished suicide.

Upon being courted by Everard, and thus positioned as an object of male desire and inserted into a marriage plot, Rhoda finds herself alienated yet pleased, the sensation rerouting her sense of self and causing what feels like a transformative moment: "It made her feel as if she had to learn herself anew, to form a fresh conception of her personality. She the object of a man's passion!" (164). As for Everard, he understands himself to be conducting an experiment, not a courtship: "His concern with her was purely intellectual; she had no sensual attraction for him, but he longed to see further into her mind . . . to understand her mechanism, her process of growth" (121). As their relationship progresses, Everard decides to test the hypothesis that her feminist side would always dominate her "womanly" side by proposing a free union, "to share his life . . . without sanction of forms which neither for her nor him were sanction at all" (148).

Rhoda at first refuses on the grounds that its social risks are too high. She then conducts her own experiment, testing the sincerity of his love by holding out for marriage, all the while fearing that Everard's love may depend upon her contempt for formalities. Eventually, Rhoda changes her mind, favoring the free union as a sensational political act that would leave her feminist reputation intact. Rhoda's assent, however, only activates Everard's underlying conventionality, which erupts through his unconventional veneer. Pretending elation, he is quick to express his desire to privatize their radicalism: "I am no Quixote, hoping to convert the world. It is between you and me—our own sense of what is reasonable and dignified" (270). He even slips a marriage ring upon Rhoda's finger, which she draws off, exclaiming, "No—that proves to me I can't! What should we gain? You see, you dare not be quite consistent. It's only deceiving the people who don't know us" (271). Everard replies, "The consistency is in our selves, our own minds" (271). Understanding that his radical stance is not based on a political program that seeks to externalize internal analysis but is instead founded on his sexual attraction to her unconventionality, she tells him, "Custom is too strong for us. We should only play at defying it" (271). When Everard asks her if she still wants "that old, idle form," she replies, "Not the religious form, which has no meaning for either of us. But—" (272). The chapter ends with their plan to go to the registrar's to obtain a marriage license, while the next chapter begins, "And neither was content" (273).

Joseph Allen Boone has argued that Rhoda and Everard's struggles reveal the contradictions underlying marriage fictions "that attempt to reconcile the desires of the individual with the very institutions regulating and proscribing those desires" (66). For Boone, the most difficult task for the novelist who wants to write stable marriage fiction is to reconcile "the contradictory pull between the protagonist's independent identity and sexual marital-role" (12). While Boone convincingly represents this distinction between the individual and the institution as one located in the fiction, his work also reproduces it, obscuring how this distinction is an underlying presumption of Victorian liberal individualism and an ideological effect of governmental processes.

In *The Odd Women*, the individual/institution distinction is in a constant state of erosion. At this point it is useful to turn to Timothy Mitchell, who argues that the appearance of the modern state as "an apparatus that stands apart from the rest of the social world," including individuals, is merely the overall effect of disciplinary techniques (1999, 89). Thus, for Mitchell, the modern state as coherent and separate, or autonomous, is "the counterpart of the production of modern individuality" (1999, 89). A similar claim informs *The Odd Women*: Much of the novel's irony comes from its portrayal of the dependence of Rhoda's self-image (a radical individual whose unconventional desires signal her authentic identity) upon the institution of marriage itself: Only through the possibility of marriage can Rhoda understand herself as an individual whose autonomy is in danger.

Moreover, these problems are local manifestations of the problem of the state-citizen relationship. Adrian Poole has argued that Gissing's work is primarily motivated by the desire for a romantic relationship that is not based on dependence or domination and that "will redeem the sterility of singleness without precluding its independence . . ." (191). In this formulation, we hear the echo of the problem of the late Victorian liberal state: How does one create a state that is not based on dependence and domination? How does the liberal individual exercise agency and will and also submit to state authority? For Arnold, the solution was culture. However, in *The Odd Women*, as we have already seen, the culture concept has been evacuated of potential.

Having linked the degradation of culture to its commodification and to its provision by the state, *The Odd Women* now links it to a commodification of politics. Gissing releases most of his bile on Everard, who initially appears to use culture to develop a critical discontent with forms. That is, unlike Dr. Madden, he seems to use culture to develop a political stance—a capacity that Arnold was at pains to assert. However, in a discussion with Mary, Everard debases Arnold's argument, by flippantly asserting that his "idea of enjoyment" is "an infinite series of modes of living. A ceaseless exercise of all one's faculties of pleasure" (105). While Arnold argued that culture requires the cultivation of others as well as oneself, Everard freely admits to Mary that he embraces a self-interest that does not require him to have either a "theory" or feel socially responsible: "The only thing clear to me is that I have a right to make the most of my life" (106). Everard's appropriation of culture thus does not lead to inner cultivation, but rather to a set of aesthetic sensations and evaluations. He approaches political views and culture as ready-made objects to consume and display, not as processes that he must shape and undergo himself.

Assuming the position of viewer/consumer whose restlessness causes him to pursue various needs, whether cultural, political, or romantic, Everard occupies what Rachel Bowlby has called "the structures of experience in urban consumer society" (14). Indeed, in *The Odd Women*, women and political positions form related fields of choice for the male consumer. In the novel, people become physically excited by radical views and by unconventionality in ways that recall the rhythms of consumer desire. Unconventional framings of life offer new visions of how things might be, reordering the body and producing deliciously new sensations.

Everard quickly leaves such heady heights, spurning Rhoda and finding an endpoint to his "infinite series of living" by making friends in a different world, one with which he retroactively claims natural affinity: "wealthy and cultured people who seek no prominence, who shrink from contact with the circles known as 'smart,' who possess their souls in quiet freedom" (317). The Brissendens create for him a "new atmosphere" that has a "soothing and bracing quality" (317). The women "were not in declared revolt against the order of things, religious, ethical, or social; that is to say, they did not think it worth while to identify themselves with any 'movement'; they were content with the unopposed right of liberal criticism" (317). In this setting, he comes to observe himself contentedly: "at times, as he sat conversing in one of these drawing-rooms, he broke off to marvel at himself, to appreciate the perfection of his own suavity, the vast advance he had been making in polished humanism" (317–18). The narrator's tone is ironic, mocking Everard's privileged capacity to abstract from himself without conflict or pain. His union with the Brissendens seals not only his marital fate, but also his cultural and political containment. Signaling neither a becoming nor a processing, his alliance represents contentment with static forms of culture and politics that contrasts brilliantly with Rhoda's discontent.

The Novelization of Rhoda

Through Rhoda, *The Odd Women* ultimately suggests that the high-realist social novel might fill the critical void left by culture, marriage, and the state. It is perhaps not surprising that Gissing ultimately vaunts the novel as the genre most fit for producing ethical citizens who can critique the state and its attempts to "plot" them. While *The Odd Women* narrates how poetry, religious writings, the romance novel, and even parks and squares engender subjects who are literate in their conventions but passive in their conscription within them, it claims for its own species the capacity to objectify the social and thereby condition a critical reading subject. In particular, as Rhoda agonizingly comes to recognize her unconscious attachment to the marriage plot, she becomes, in Gissing's view, a more critically astute political thinker, one who understands how subjects are taught to desire and that hope must exist but only if it is not attached to existing forms. In this sense, Gissing's novel suggests that state culture can be resisted by virtue of its own novelization, a term that I am adapting from Mikhail Bakhtin to refer to the process by which modern individuals come to a conscious understanding of their world and themselves as fictional constructs that are bound by normative plots.[11]

By forcing Rhoda, who has only been critical of love and who sees it purely as an invention of novelists, to occupy the position of sexual object, the novel teaches her how it feels to be an actor in a love plot, to identify with a position that has value in her society—the courted woman, the woman who is desired as a future wife. This experience enables her to abstract from herself, understand how she has already been forcedly determined, and thus to sympathize with other women "in love." I call this process novelization, rather than Rhoda's humanization, because she so vividly perceives romantic love as a scripted set of conventions that she finds herself strangely living out in ways that are beyond her control. If the term "novelization" seems to position her as a genre, this may in fact be the effect of the version of society that Gissing constructs in *The Odd Women*. Once Rhoda has been novelized, she can, like a novel, represent at least to herself other social positions with compassion. Novelization, because it claims the capacity to represent other points of view in an objective way, entails what we may call "ethicization." In this way, Gissing seeks to revitalize the notion of Arnoldian culture. Sullied by its degraded form as a commodity, the culture concept as process re-emerges as novel reading.

However, unlike Arnold, who explicitly advocates a stratified society, novelization in *The Odd Women* tenuously affords a possibility for hope only by positing an unknown and as yet unfixed conclusion. Toward the end, a pregnant and estranged Monica visits Rhoda. After a terrible marriage to Widdowson and an unconsummated flirtation with Bevis, a wine-merchant with longings to be a musician, Monica lives now with her sisters. Rhoda, having suspected Monica and Everard of carrying on an affair, at first receives her ungraciously. Monica assures Rhoda that her suspicions are groundless, and after securing her trust, relates her hopelessness over her own position. Rhoda finds herself feeling a new power and tells Monica,

"Life seems so bitter to you that you are in despair. Yet isn't it your duty to live as though some hope were before you?" (314). To advocate that a formerly despised enemy live as though hope were "before" her—a hope that positions the subject in time (on the verge of) and space (in front of)—represents a new experience for Rhoda: "Herself strongly moved, Rhoda had never spoken so impressively, had never given counsel of such earnest significance" (314).

Unlike her earlier political principles, which the narrator liberally douses in irony, this simple dictum "to live as though some hope were before you" appears to be articulated without any kind of overarching tonal implication: "She felt her power in quite a new way, without touch of vanity, without posing or any trivial self-consciousness" (314). The moment most calling for her composure thus occasions a new sense of self: "When she least expected it, an opportunity had come for exerting the moral influence on which she prided herself . . . the combative soul in her became stronger when faced by such conditions" (314). A kind of secularized version of faith, this "living as though hope were before you" offers a model of optimism in which desire has not yet attached itself to a form or a norm. However, narratorial irony does seep in around the edges of this free indirect discourse, linking Rhoda's delighted self-abstraction to Everard's. Even the novelized subject, aware of her own partial determination by outside forces, does not fully escape the narrator's irony, an irony that, as we have seen, simultaneously deflates and indexes a desire.

Conclusion

I have attempted to show how *The Odd Women* shifts from a familiar narrative about the late Victorian Woman Question into an unfamiliar exploration of the mechanics of optimism and desire at a moment when the state was felt to be defining the parameters of the imaginable and the unconscious. In this way, a novel that investigates the economic and emotional effects of oddness begins to rub up against the paradoxes of liberal individualism. Gissing strikes out into new territory in some ways while, in what appears to be a gesture of renunciation and failure, repeating some of the novel's most familiar conventions by the end. Ultimately, however, the novel form itself emerges as a qualified site of optimism. By teaching the reader how state forms such as marriage and culture shape subjectivities, Gissing suggests that the novel can in turn transform the reader into a critical, ethical subject. This resort to a determinative and formalizing role for the novel paradoxically renders his novel partially complicit in the reifying, privatizing state culture he critiques, which perhaps accounts for the irony that ultimately affects this option. However, it also suggests that open-ended hope, despite exposing one to irony, may powerfully register a refusal to be merely contented.

5   *Hysterical Citizenship in Grand's*
    The Heavenly Twins

With their independent views about marriage, Lyndall, Grace, and Rhoda typify the New Woman, that late Victorian social and sexual icon. While they suffer excruciating disappointments and, in the case of Lyndall, even death, their narrators nevertheless represent them as complex characters and render their struggles with varying degrees of compassion. Often, however, this social and literary figure of emancipated womanhood received far less sympathetic treatment in the late Victorian print world. As many scholars have noted, the New Woman was its own incitement to discourse, giving rise to numerous essays, editorials, literary reviews, and cartoons, mostly negative and often contradictory. Some contemporary critics claimed that the New Woman, whether in real life or as a literary character, was sexless and, because she violated the edicts of traditional femininity, unnatural, while others argued that she was too sexual and excessively feminine in her lack of self-discipline. However she was figured, the New Woman was often rendered both symbol and cause of all that was wrong in the fin-de-siècle— the degeneration of British masculinity across the social spectrum, from peasants to aristocrats, and the consequent erosions of traditional gender relations, the empire, and homeland security, rendering the unmanned mainland vulnerable to incoming native hordes. In the symbolic economy of late Victorian England, the figure of the New Woman was busy indeed.

In this chapter, I examine Sarah Grand's *The Heavenly Twins* (1893), a landmark New Woman novel, in the context of what I have identified as late Victorian state fantasy: the fantasy of the state as a heroic actor, imaginatively personified and endowed with the capacity to intervene in individuals' lives to help them achieve the good life. A bestseller, *The Heavenly Twins* was wildly popular in both England and the United States. It presented its readers with lurid spectacles of female injury, rage, and rebellion, setting off a steady stream of damning reviews that pronounced it not only obscene and unwomanly, but also badly written. Unlike *The Odd Women*, which was published the same year, *The Heavenly Twins* is not interested in the economic deprivations of middle-class women. Instead, it attacks the social and political structures that endanger the physical and moral health of privileged women. Of all the novels I have discussed in this book, *The Heavenly Twins* is most explicitly a feminist protest novel. It self-consciously stakes out a critique of gender relations and provides a dramatic justification for what Grand advocated in her nonfiction journal articles: state regulation of male sexuality. In these writings, Grand argued that men ought to be subjected to physical examinations and certification requirements to make sure they are fit to marry and reproduce, in effect reversing the mode of state biopower sanctioned against prostitutes by the Contagious Diseases Acts.

In my reading, the novel's explicit desire to engage in a politics configured around a certain mode of state intervention accounts for the many contradictions that it has generated for contemporary and recent readers. Rather than locating these contradictions within the specific politics or aesthetics of *The Heavenly Twins*, I argue that they point to the complexity of this historical moment in liberalism: It is the very claim toward freedom achieved through the means of a masculinist and governmentalized state that constrains the liberal subject. Despite the novel's statist sympathies, it nevertheless reveals how the more the liberal subject fights to be free through the aegis of state biopower, the more she upholds the structures that subordinate her.

In what follows, I examine three primary contradictions in *The Heavenly Twins*. The first contradiction concerns the novel's relation to publicity. Historically, because it exposes injustice and is credited with transforming ignorance into knowledge, publicity is liberalism's antidote to abuses of power. *The Heavenly Twins* attests to the confidence that reform-minded, liberal Victorians placed in the power of publicity to eradicate social injury. It details the hardships faced by three women from Britain's upper class: Evadne, daughter of the gentry and the novel's failed feminist heroine whose self-repression results in insanity; Angelica, daughter of the aristocracy and one of the rebellious twins of the title; and Edith, daughter of the church and the novel's primary example of how religious serenity anesthetizes women, placing them in harm's way. Although the form of the novel would seem to publicize women's oppression, the narrative actually chronicles the failure of public protests, whether in print (such as political treatises and novels) or in speech (such as conversations with politicized thinkers), to reform the late Victorian sexual regime. In a range of scenarios, the novel asks repeatedly how socially privileged female subjects, despite their own personal experience of injustice and their exposure to feminist critique, remain tenaciously attached to the Victorian gender ideology that dehumanizes them.

The second contradiction emerges from the novel's proposed solution to this quandary. As I mentioned, in her journalistic writings, Grand argued that men, with their sexual waywardness and dramatic self-absorption, ought to be subject to state regulation and control. She proposed that marriage be professionalized and its male participants certified by the state in order to ensure the collective health of society. Strikingly, however, in *The Heavenly Twins*, no mention of the state with a capital S appears. The novel includes some quasi-political references—a mysterious group known only as "the New Order" and a brief mention of Angelica writing Parliamentary speeches for her husband to deliver—but they are empty of content. We never learn exactly what the New Order believes or the argument of Angelica's speeches. If Grand so adamantly advocated state intervention in her nonfiction writings and so graphically depicted the social injustices that such intervention was supposed to cure in her novel, why does her novel lack explicit references to the state? As I shall elaborate in the discussion that follows, the novel leaves out mention of the state as a means of shaping a normative state subject.

However, the novel ultimately troubles what it means to turn to the state to protect women, which leads to the third contradiction. At the conclusion, Evadne, the failed feminist heroine, descends into hysteria, silence, and the care of her doctor/baronet husband. Professional and landed, Galbraith combines the scientific disinterest of the specialist with the virtuous disinterest of the aristocrat. In this way, he embodies two state-related formations, one emergent and the other residual.[1] As husband and father, he is also, of course, a patriarchal figure. In my reading, Galbraith stands in for the kind of state Grand imagined would guide a collective society by providing the proper conditions in which the public good and liberal individuality could flourish. However, the version of female citizenship imagined in relation to such a patriarchal state is, perhaps even despite the intentions of the text, hysterical and masochistic: This subject knows that she is conscripted within institutional forms of authority, but she must disavow the debilitating effects of such conscription in order to hold on to even an admittedly attenuated sense of self.

The Heavenly Twins uses the late-nineteenth-century, feminized condition of hysteria as a trope to describe more generally the historical shift that I have outlined earlier and explored in specific contexts in the preceding chapters: the late-nineteenth-century citizen's psychic experience of a change in the mode of governance from, as David Lloyd and Paul Thomas have broadly termed it, coercion to hegemony (115). The key link between hysteria and this shift in the citizen's psyche becomes clearer when we keep in mind that hysteria for Freud would later become evidence for the universal existence of the unconscious. Thus, the "hysterical citizenship" in my title refers to what I would like to suggest is the more general condition of modern state citizenship: The subject knows that the state is not coherent, animated, or wholly benevolent and ethical, and yet we do not know. As Jacqueline Rose points out, Freud first encountered this split between knowing and not knowing in a hysterical patient, but later theorized it as the general condition of consciousness itself (109). *The Heavenly Twins* suggests that this split partially accounts for how the modern state is able to uphold its power.

In the conclusion, readers are invited to identify both with Evadne, the wounded subject, and Galbraith, the heroic savior. To complicate our relationship to this scene even further, the painfulness of Evadne's psychic state, as she hovers between the conscious and the unconscious, is eroticized. These two formal aspects of the scene work to maintain state biopower. Power, vulnerability, and sexual pleasure, which has been excised elsewhere by the bourgeois moral economy of the novel, converge at the end in the spectacle of the heroine's hysterical submission to the hero.

These contradictions forcefully reveal the complexity of the kind of subject shaped by state biopower at the end of the nineteenth century. *The Heavenly Twins* presumes that the reader is a liberal humanist subject who will be persuaded by the key ingredients of rational argument—reasons and evidence—to act ethically in the future. But Grand's repetitive account of the characters' fierce attachment to oppressive forms in the face of feminist critique, her choice not to name the state directly as a solution, and the narrative's suggestion that a patriarchal state produces hysterical citizens indicate that another kind of subject is operating in her text. This subject is formed through subjection, that is, through external power relations that become internalized and in fact necessary for the subject to exist as such. As Judith Butler has argued in *The Psychic Life of Power* and elsewhere, this subject is compelled to maintain the very power relations that oppress her because her self-identity exists only inasmuch as those relations do. In liberal culture, subjects regard their subjectivity as originating in themselves and disavow how external forces of power have shaped it. In this conception, denial, repression, and sublimation, therefore, do the work of maintaining the subject's sense of self.

Liberalism, Knowledge, and Publicity

Despite inspiring a copious amount of periodical pages in the 1880s and 1890s, New Woman fictions were largely neglected in scholarly studies until the 1970s and '80s. According to Ann Ardis, critics during these years only continued the tradition of degrading them, dismissing such works as crippled by "hysterical feminist fervor" and denigrating their authors as "a pool of mediocre talents out of which the great female modernists emerged" (3). In her key 1990 recovery of New Woman fictions, Ardis reclaimed their subversive qualities, arguing that works such as *The Heavenly Twins* made substantive political and formal interventions. In her readings, New Woman fictions rewrote the marriage plot so fundamental to nineteenth-century realist novels and challenged the masculinist norms governing literary realism.

Since Ardis, *The Heavenly Twins* has received at least two more waves of feminist readings. The first wave continues Ardis's positive reclamation of the novel. For example, Marilyn Bonnell uses the work of Carol Gilligan to argue that *The Heavenly Twins* challenged masculinist notions of detachment and objectivity in favor of an ethic of care. John Kucich contends that the supposed failures of Grand's realist method were actually calculated aesthetic attempts to resolve the ideological contradictions facing late-nineteenth-century feminism. Teresa Mangum argues that Grand challenged normative femininity and heterosexism in *The Heavenly Twins* not only by representing female desire, but also by insisting that it should be directed toward collective projects of emancipation, instead of toward marriage. For Demetris Bogiatzis, the novel demonstrates the social constructedness of gender identity. Finally, Ann Heilmann asserts that the novel rejects the view that hysteria could offer a politically emancipatory stance for women. Instead, Heilmann argues, *The Heavenly Twins* indicts the medical complex for Evadne's debilitation.

Taking a different approach, a second wave of critics has situated the novel within a liberal bourgeois tradition of feminism, one that is exclusive and complicit with capitalism. These critics either argue that Grand's novel features containment strategies that maintain the status quo of gender, class, sexuality, and racial norms or they implicate its feminist rage within a market economy where scandal and sensation sell. For example, Angelique Richardson draws attention to Grand's eugenic principles and her narrative's incorporation of biologically essentialist notions of heredity and reproduction. Meegan Kennedy argues that *The Heavenly Twins* critiques the "pathological realism" of French naturalist fiction, displacing unsavory, physical descriptions of male syphilitic bodies with mental/emotional descriptions of diseased female minds. In Kennedy's reading, *The Heavenly Twins* ultimately reinforces the conservative cultural myth of women's emotional instability. Andrea L. Broomfield examines the journalistic rivalry between Grand and the anti–New Woman writer Eliza Lynn Linton.[2] She proposes that the current feminist recovery and celebration of nineteenth-century women's voices—what Amanda Anderson might call the production of their "aggrandized agency"—prevents us from evaluating how economic imperatives may have at times carried more weight than ideological ones in the content and style of their publications. Pointing to the marketplace of the print sphere and the pressure on editors to deliver sensation and scandal, Broomfield maintains that current feminist literary critics overemphasize the political, as opposed to the commercial, imperatives of New Woman fiction and prose.

In addition to the concerns that this second wave of feminist critics raise, we can also point to the novel's commitment to imperialism and class politics as a troubling constraint on its feminist vision. In one particularly vivid scene, the novel showcases its feminist heroine Evadne as a queen to native workers in Malta, while expelling awareness of any violence that attended such imperial power. *The Heavenly Twins* also exclusively addresses middle- and upper-class women. Working-class women appear only as instruments of the plot. They serve as silent signs of male degeneracy and as occasions for the well-to-do female characters to contemplate the suffering of the world and experience their interiority as a theater of flooding pain and soothing sympathy. Finally, in keeping with Grand's social purity principles, the novel promotes a version of bourgeois bodily discipline that marks all expressions of sexual desire or passion as morally degrading and politically pernicious.

In these ways, *The Heavenly Twins* mobilizes what Lauren Berlant, in the context of American sentimental fiction, has termed "the female complaint," a testifying and critical exposition of women's problems that at once registers a desire for freedom and full human expression, but lapses into the conservative norms of "womanhood." These female-centered works contest the limits of gendered standards, but redeploy feminine and bourgeois ideals. Such literature, in its desire to produce political alliances, tends to homogenize women, asserting womanhood as fundamental to identity and thereby disregarding socially constructed yet powerfully politicized and experienced differences, such as race, nationality, and class. This version of liberal bourgeois feminism seeks to address political inequality in public discourse and in public spaces. However, it often does so through asserting privatizing solutions or revalorizing the domestic, the maternal, and the subjective at the cost of rethinking the public/private divide in ways that do not entail inhibition, coercion, and prohibition. Berlant approaches this genre of women's culture quizzically. Instead of concluding with a pronouncement of the conservative aspects of contemporary women's culture, she asks, why do women passionately consume fictions that, in claiming to represent their real lives, thoughts, and feelings, also confirm and maintain their suffering?

The Heavenly Twins represents a twist on the genre of the female complaint, because, while it testifies to women's suffering and offers conservative solutions, it asks similar questions. In fact, questions about female agency punctuate the novel. These questions are shaded by discourses of evolution and biology: Are some women born with the desire to know about sexual injustice and thereby gain a critical purchase on what is taken for granted? Can the desire to know be acquired in life? If so, how? And what can those who see through the myths of sexual difference do to awaken other women? These questions define the women and men in the novel according to an axis of seeing or not seeing the "truth" that women are just as rational as men. This axis in turn generates a range of scenarios and specifications, which lead to another set of questions: What makes some women who see the truth still act as if they do not? Why do they keep returning to the cold comfort of ideology? Do women in fact choose their subjection? If so, how does such a self-defeating act happen? How can it be remedied? If exposing them to the truth does not change their minds, what will?

In a *North American Review* essay, "The New Aspect of the Woman Question" (1894), Grand referred to women who do not want to know as "the cow-kind of woman" (Heilmann, ed., *Journalistic Writings*, 270). She wrote that they cultivate a religiosity, gentleness, and goodness. In "The Modern Girl" (1894), Grand suggested that "the cow-kind of woman" may actually know the truth of her situation, but professes and reproduces ignorance out of a profoundly annihilating lack of optimism and oppressive sense of the inevitable: "[Elder married women] cannot believe that the world will ever be any better than it is, and they can think of no other way of serving girls than by keeping them in ignorance as long as possible" (Heilmann, ed., *Journalistic Writings*, 36). The bovine metaphor suggests a more domesticated quality than the female characters in *The Heavenly Twins* display. Neither weak nor passive, these characters are instead fiercely attached to their "ignorance" and aggressive when confronted with "the truth" of women's suffering.

For example, after Evadne runs away from her husband once she suspects that he may carry a sexual disease, she visits her beloved aunt, Mrs. Orton Beg. Evadne criticizes her and others who have allowed men to engage in depraved behavior that endangers future generations. Evadne's parents and aunt expect her to give up her foolish principles and return to her husband, even helping him to repent, if she likes. Evadne explains her case to Mrs. Orton Beg:

> You think I should act as women have been always advised to act in such cases, that I should sacrifice myself to save that one man's soul . . . I see that the world is not a bit the better for centuries of self-sacrifice on the woman's part and therefore I think it is time we tried a more effectual plan. And I propose now to sacrifice the man instead of the woman. (80)

Her aunt hears Evadne's declaration with excruciating pain: "Every word you say seems to banish something—something from this room—something from my life to which I cling. I think it is my faith in love—and loving" (80). Mrs. Orton Beg goes on to say,

> If I ever let myself dwell on the horrible depravity that goes on unchecked, the depravity which you say we women license by ignoring it when we should face and unmask it, I should go out of my mind. I do know—we all know; how can we live and not know? But we don't think about it—we can't—we daren't. (80–1)

The breaks in her speech indicate the fissures in her thought process, as her conscious knowledge of injustice fights against her unconscious desire to adhere to normative femininity.

The Heavenly Twins primarily unfolds as a failed Bildungsroman. As a young woman, Evadne displays exceptional intellect and personality. Sounding like a celebrity biographer, the narrator assumes the interest of its audience in how Evadne developed over time. For example, a journal from her early years becomes an artifact, "an interesting record still in existence of her course of reading between the ages of twelve and nineteen" (13). Although we never see her holding forth on a platform or publishing political treatises, we learn that Evadne split an undefined public. Again, assuming the voice of a celebrity biographer discussing his subject posthumously, the narrator tells us, "Some people in after life, who liked her views, said they saw the guiding hand of Providence directing her course from the first; but those who opposed her said it was the devil; and others again, in idleness or charity, or the calm neutrality of indifference, set it all down to the Inevitable . . ." (20–1). Despite such promising beginnings, Evadne does not develop into a revolutionary leader. Her story appears as a tragedy: She was a great woman who did not fulfill her destiny or the expectations of those who knew her. A traumatic event associated with her marriage renders her not simply apolitical but reactionary. At the conclusion of the novel, the tone of the narrator switches to the detached stance of a scientist observing the growth of a pathology.

The self-cultivating principle that drives so much of liberal thinking in the period can be found in Grand's description of Evadne. An autodidact, Evadne evolves by constantly questioning the platitudes around her. One can hear the echo of Mill in the narrator's glowing account of how Evadne seizes the materials at hand and recovers them as her own intellectual resources. Like other ladies of her station, Evadne's formal education stops early, but her natural inquisitiveness turns her daily life, in particular, her conversations with her father, into a classroom. A magistrate with houses in both the country and the town, prosperous and educated, Evadne's father is a moderate Churchman described in terms of his bigotry and prejudice. He represents an older form of government, not a newer one, like Schreiner's stranger.

The novel thus participates in the liberal fantasy of a coherent, unified subject, distinct from an objective world and capable of exercising rationality and thereby penetrating the mists of delusion. Evadne converts her father's irrational, contradictory speeches into material for her own development. By absorbing his conservative arguments and forming her own counterarguments in dialectical fashion, she learns to reason:

> She had never to fight a daily and exhausting battle for her private opinions as talkative people have, simply because she rarely if ever expressed an opinion; but her father stood ready always, a post of resistance to innovation, upon which she could sharpen the claws of her conclusion silently whenever they required it. (16)

Her father's constant assertions of women's inferiority "set [Evadne's] mind off on a long and patient inquiry into the condition and capacity of women, and made her, in the end of the nineteenth century, essentially herself" (13).

The novel also endorses a theory of voluntarism and self-actualization. Evadne concludes one journal entry with the assessment that "women had originally no congenital defect of inferiority and that, although they have still much way to make up, it now rests with themselves to be inferior or not, as they choose" (13). Now that women know what they know, they have no excuse not to act on it and become the equals of men. The other side of such a claim is, of course, blame. The youthful Evadne also writes in her journal that it takes moral strength, not just critical consciousness, to break the chains of what we might call ideology:

> The daily life into which people are born, and into which they are absorbed before they are aware, forms chains which only one in a hundred has moral strength enough to despise, and to break when the right time comes—when an inward necessity for independent action arises, which is superior to all outward conventionalities. (33)

Written after Karl Marx and Friedrich Engel's *Communist Manifesto* (1848), this excerpt echoes the metaphor of ideology as chains that must be broken. Unlike that text, however, Grand's proclamation rests upon moral strength and a sense of an autonomous self, acting independently when it can no longer accept conditions as they are. This self does not seek to produce a common identity known as "woman" that would provide the material to form a global alliance, but rather perpetuates the myth of modern individuality, fanning an imagined inner flame that demands freedom.

In keeping with its liberal investments, writing emerges as the most politically urgent act in the novel, at pain of death, both psychic and physical. In this act, a performance that is at once private but audience-oriented and potentially public, the subject writes herself in a dynamic relation with a reader. Grand's feminist fictional world confirms a belief in writing as the expression of an a priori unique, monadic, and agential individual. This belief in the ontology of the subject extends to the novel's version of realism. The novel adheres to the notion of an absolute truth that transcends particular material attributes, thus displaying a conviction that a certain kind of literary style can represent or reflect truthfully an outside "real." As George Levine has argued about Victorian realists, professing to such a notion does not exclude the self-conscious goal of teaching a moral lesson. In the service of a particular social message, the novel seems both critical of aesthetics, yet caught up in its conventions, as well.

The novel reveals its contradictory theory of representation when the narrator, describing the young Evadne's notebook, praises its style as a nonstyle:

> There are few erasures or mistakes of grammar or spelling, even from the first, and little tautology; but she makes no attempt at literary style or elegance of expression. Still all that she says is impressive, and probably on that account. She chooses the words best calculated to express her meaning clearly and concisely, and undoubtedly her meaning is always either a settled conviction or an honest endeavour to arrive at one. (13)

This rhetoric of "honesty" and suspicion of style, understood in terms of "elegance," "poetry," and "romance," as somehow dishonest appears again in the description of Mrs. Malcomson, the closest author surrogate in the novel. A military wife, Mrs. Malcomson explicitly voices the novel's implied critique of the church and the subjection of women, dismissing an older clergyman's ideal of suffering womanhood as "the poetry of the pulpit" (179). Grand's discourse, the reader is to understand, is not "poetry," which here comes to mean a kind of manipulative, misty, ideological fantasy-bribe. Sermons produce bodily sensations of ecstasy that compensate women for suffering.

Mrs. Malcomson most perfectly exemplifies the writer of the "nonstyle" endorsed by the novel. When describing her, the narrator theorizes how publishing can wash out toxins from the body, functioning as a therapy for built-up pathogens: "She was thirty years of age, and had been married to a military man for ten, and in that time she had seen some things which had made a painful impression upon her, and suggested ideas that were only to be got rid of by publishing them" (333). Unsurprisingly, her virtue lies in literary method: "Out of everyday experiences everyday thoughts had come to her, and when she began to embody such thoughts in words she did not suppose that their everyday character would be altered by the process" (333). Her realism, like Grand's, combines a commitment to representing life "truthfully" *and* morally, a contradiction that only registers in the structure, not the statements, of the novel:

> She was a simple artist, educated in the lifeschool of the world, and desiring above everything to be honest—a naturalist, in fact, with positive ideas of right and wrong, and incapable of the confusion of mind or laxity of

conscience which denies, on the one hand, that wrong may be pleasant in the doing, or claims, on the other, with equal untruth, that because it is pleasant it must be, if not exactly right, at all events, excusable. (333–4)

An implicit critique of French naturalism, represented by Émile Zola and the Goncourts, and notorious for its representations of the sick, the sexual, bodily passions, and the lower orders of society, the narrator here reappropriates the term in the service of extolling Mrs. Malcomson's version of "natural" representation as unstylized, "honest," and moral.

In this way, *The Heavenly Twins* levies a novel-length argument for publicity in the carefully rendered realist style of "nonstyle" as the means for consciousness-changing, which in turn will lead to social change. However, the novel, in seeking to represent "the real," also narrates the persistence of ideology and the seductive compensations offered by social and psychic conformity. In this way, it complicates its own confidence in the power of publicity to eradicate social injury. Not written in a realist mode, but actually quite poetical and allegorical, the opening prose poem establishes this complication at once.

Three bars of Felix Mendelssohn's "Elijah" ring in the prose poem, or "proem." Resounding from a high Cathedral tower in the "old fashioned city" of Morningquest, this popular oratorio and its accompanying line, "He, watching over Israel, slumbers not, nor sleeps," identify the novel's geoliterary center, its range of social actors, and its overarching moral economy. In these first paragraphs of the novel, the narrator informs us that the chimes radiate over village, heath, and city, inspiring hope and pleasure in the full-hearted and punctuating the heaven-turned thoughts of the pious. The chimes reach their limit, however, with those laboring in the fields and those rushing through city streets. In the case of agricultural laborers, their crudity and exhaustion block their receptivity: "when it spread in another direction over the fields, it meant nothing to the yawning ploughman, either musical or poetical, had no significance whatever for him if it were not of the time of day, gathered, however, with the help of sundry other sensations of which hunger and fatigue were chief" (xliv). But to explain the imperviousness of the urban dwellers to the power of the chimes, the narrator turns to another culprit: "Doubtless, the majority of those who had ears to hear in the big old fashioned city heard not, use having dulled their faculties; or if, perchance, the music reached them it conveyed no idea to their minds, and passed unheeded" (xliii). For these urban dwellers, the chimes have fallen prey to the pernicious process of habituation—the bugbear of liberals such as Matthew Arnold. In the novel, this process familiarizes and immunizes insufficiently individualized subjects to the beautiful and uplifting, but also compensates them with an experiential plenitude: "It was but an accustomed measure, one more added to the myriad other sounds that make up the buzz of life, and help, like each separate note of a chord, to complete the varied murmur which is the voice of 'a whole city full'" (xliii).

Operating in the medium of sound, the chimes function as a self-conscious analogy for the novel as it moves in the medium of print. The novel's obsession with knowledge and education as the route toward women's emancipation makes it fall in line with liberal values, but the novel also suggests that one must be born with the desire—a claim that would contradict the drive to expose the truth. These contradictions point to the problem of protest and a de-normativizing politics in a liberal culture that has subsumed evolutionary principles within it, as well. A tangle of contradictions concerning whether one must be born wanting to know or whether one can be exposed to truth and then work for change, the novel is finally coherent about one thing at least: Ignorance is not a passive state, but one that is actively held on to because it offers its own pleasures.

Good Mechanism: Governmentality, Liberalism, and Novel-Reading

Grand gave lectures and published articles in which she advocated the vote for women and reform of the marriage law, often relying on a collective, as well as eugenic, rhetoric of national interest. She argued that if one part of the whole suffered, the entire social organism suffered and that the effects of this suffering extended from the scale of an individual life to future generations of British citizens. If *The Heavenly Twins* suggested that publicity fails to effect change for women, Grand's nonfiction deployed the fantasy, specific to the 1880s and 1890s, that appealing to the state could.

Grand advocated what amounted to the professionalization of marriage, which would require that the state regulate marriage by granting certificates to those individuals who passed a medical examination and a training course. Thus, Grand literalizes into a political program the state mandates on marriage that Everard, Rhoda, and Gissing's narrator in *The Odd Women* mock and yet also seem to want. She also offers a solution to the problem of marriage that Hardy posed in his preface to *The Woodlanders*. Here, as I discussed earlier, Hardy focused on the idea of marriage as a legal contract, which implied, he argued, that its participants were fully aware of all it entails. In practice, however, he caustically remarked, very few people fully understand into what kind of contract they were permanently entering.

In "The Modern Girl," Grand defends marriage as "the holiest and most perfect state for both men and women" and decries the ease with which anyone may contract it, asking, ". . . in what way are our young men and maidens taught to qualify themselves for it?" (Heilmann, ed., *Journalistic Writings*, 36). In an 1896 interview with Sarah A. Tooley, Grand maintains the controversial logic of the Contagious Diseases Acts, but reverses it, to protect women's health and safety, as well as men's:

> Men endeavour to protect themselves from disease by restrictive laws bearing on women, but nothing has yet been done to protect the married women from contagion. I hope that we shall soon see the marriage of certain men made a criminal offense. (Heilmann, ed., *Journalistic Writings*, 222)

Grand, in effect, posits marriage not only as a sacred institution, but also explicitly as a state institution.

In her exploration of what she terms "eugenic love," Richardson draws on the work of Francis Galton, who defined eugenics as "the science of improving stock" (Bland 222). Found among the ranks of late-nineteenth-century social purity feminists, eugenicists encouraged the morally and physically "fit" to reproduce in the service of maximizing the health of the following generation and of the nation at large. For Grand, the choice of marriage partner requires the sacrifice of one's passions for the good of the community: ". . . individuals should suffer—they should glory in suffering and self-sacrifice for the good of the community" (Heilmann, ed., *Journalistic Writings*, 86). This imperative demands that women carefully choose their mates on the basis of health and morality, not love or sexual passion. Because these two qualities were considered hereditary, it became the woman's responsibility to ensure that bad health and immorality did not get passed down into future British generations. Richardson calls Grand's formulation of the intersubjective bond between two people who strike such a balance "eugenic love." This form of love, Richardson writes, requires that "the flesh should submit to the spirit in order to contribute to racial progress; pleasure is overshadowed and undercut by the imperative of (re)production" (233). The act of judging whom to marry, which immediately translates to the question of with whom to reproduce, constitutes for Grand the practice of female citizenship. Sexual desire based on passion was therefore an act of treason: "It would lead not only to the leisurely repentance of hasty marriages but, ultimately, to the degeneration of the British race" (Richardson 234).

Given her commitment to "eugenic love," it is perhaps not surprising that female sexual desire holds no place in Grand's moral economy. Throughout *The Heavenly Twins*, the narrator emphasizes sexual passion's ephemerality and uselessness. Angelica's passionless marriage to an old family friend, Mr. Kilroy, receives lengthy praise from the narrator:

> She was not in love with him, but she probably liked him all the better on that account, for she must have been disappointed in him sooner or later had she ever discovered in him those marvellous fascinations which passion projects from itself on to the personality of the most commonplace person. . . . Nothing so vulgar and violent as passion entered into [her ideal of pleasure], and nothing so transient, so enervating, corroding, and damaging both to the intellectual powers and the capacity for permanent enjoyment; and nothing so repulsive either in its details, its self-centred egotistical exaltation, and the self-abasement which arrives with that final sense of satiety which she perceived to be inevitable. That part of her nature had never been roused into active life, partly because it was not naturally strong, but also because the more refined and delicately sensuous appreciation of beauty in life, which is so much a characteristic of capable women nowadays, dominated such animalism as she was equal to, and made all coarser pleasures repugnant. (467)

Angelica's marriage thereby confirms the eugenic logic that codes Grand's representation of all three of her main female characters.

Despite the pedagogical implications of her text, the novel was accused of not having a clear program. For example, in an 1894 article in the *Quarterly Review*, William Barry faulted *The Heavenly Twins* for being awash in the melodramatic conventions of lachrymose scenes and didactic protest, while skirting the clear statement of any plan of action:

> Of feeling, passionate or tearful, rebellious, unmanageable, and seeking relief in paroxysms, every other page bears the tokens; but sublime thought, a religion which may be construed, or even a distinct policy in the question wherewith this author professes to busy herself, are not matters of feeling, and we lay the volume down as we took it up, still wondering that the woman, in a Hansard-like flood of eloquence, can nowhere state her case clearly enough for the jury of reason to decide upon it. (Heilmann, ed., *Journalistic Writings*, 452)

Barry's denunciation of Grand's work is in keeping with nineteenth-century devaluations of melodramatic and sentimental women's fiction. Here he positions philosophy ("sublime thought"), religion, and public policy as domains of rationality and "not matters of feeling."

And, in fact, the state does not appear explicitly in the action of the novel. What the novel does offer in the way of the explicitly political is a mysterious, cultish organization, referred to as a "clique" and a "set" by its critics. The narrator calls it the "New Order" and tells us that the best men and women belong to it and that they are working, in unspecified ways, to improve society by liberating women. Its own members appear to have a sixth sense in detecting future adherents. When Ideala, one of the luminaries of the New Order, witnesses the struggles of Angelica, she whispers to the latter's uncle, an enlightened man himself, that the young woman will be "one of us." He responds in suitably cryptic terms that Angelica and her brother "will both be of us eventually; only we must make no move, but wait in patience, 'Until the day break, and the shadows flee away'" (268). The New Order remains remarkably unexplained and, in effect, empty of political content. Neither the narrator nor its members explicitly state its program. Instead, non-members refer to it with vague disparagements of its belief in women's equality and their role in saving the nation from degeneration.

The only other plot development that gestures toward the explicitly political also fails to state a program and furthermore implicitly condones women's exclusion from official politics. After Angelica's conversion at the syphilis sickbed of Edith, she becomes involved in the New Order, which ultimately leads to her writing speeches for her M.P. husband to deliver on the Parliamentary floor. As with the New Order, however, we are never given the political content of these speeches. Furthermore, their mediatory nature—Angelica's physical exclusion from Parliament and her use of her less bright husband as mouthpiece—appears acceptable and proper within the novel's moral system.

Ironically, the state makes less of an appearance in the polemical *The Heavenly Twins* than it does in the high-realist novels I examined earlier because of the nature of the power it is interested in harnessing. For Barry, Grand's displays of feeling are excessive and crowd out rational argument, bewildering her reading audience, "the jury of reason," who wish to deliberate her case and the evidence she has marshaled. But, for Grand, feeling is the unacknowledged spur that turns knowledge into action. Knowledge is abstract. The subject might recognize it, but also protect herself from it. But feelings incorporate knowledge within the subject and lead to action. To name the solution as turning to the state would be authoritarian and counterproductive for the kind of state and type of citizen Grand envisioned. Her text serves as a kind of feeling preface to the conscious, rational appeal to the state. In this sense, her proximity to New Liberals such as L. T. Hobhouse starts to emerge in ways other than explicit political beliefs, that is, through formal methodological tactics of feeling.

In her journalistic writings and fictions, Grand was invested in a liberal-collective model of society over which a benevolent state would hover at a distance, while ensuring that relations among individuals were equitable. Collectivism as a movement rested theoretically upon an organic notion of society, which in turn grew out of biologistic accounts. In the organic notion, a whole is made up of parts that are distinct from each other but which are significantly changed or even vanquished by their removal from the whole. On the political level, Stuart Hall and Bill Schwarz define collectivism as a relationship between the citizen and the state, whereby the citizen identifies his interests with others, forming a class or body, and then appeals to the state to operate according to corporate rather than individual interests (16).

As a set of ideas and a process, collectivism gained ground during the latter part of the nineteenth century, underwriting the late Victorian period's mass political culture and profoundly unsettling the assumptions and operations of mid-century liberalism. It emerged alongside recent political developments that promoted democracy and its expansion: the Reform Act, which extended the franchise to working-class men; an organized feminist demand for the female franchise; and trade union and labor group demands for political representation. These developments constituted a new understanding of what one could rightfully demand of the state, who could make these demands, and also ultimately a new theory of citizenship that extended proper activity from the law and official politics to the issues of economic and social well-being. Hall and Schwarz write, "What the democratic challenge carried was nothing more nor less than a new set of claims on the state by the unenfranchised masses, a new conception of citizenship and, indeed, an expansion of the rights of citizenship from the sphere of legal and political to economic and social rights" (21). While theoretically resting on an organic notion of society, collectivism thus also practically rested upon the notion of a regulating, maintaining state, which, by expressing the ethical conscience and will of the people, could most effectively and legitimately carry out the goals of a progressive society.

As society became charged with the sense of collective relations, the state as solution to social ills began to assume the mantle of inevitability, defying the laissez-faire creed of the mid-Victorian period in new ways. Pointing to the state's status as the expression of a consensus, Michael Freeden writes, "Government, by this view, could not be alien or external to society, being a manifestation of human rationality. To this extent, liberalism eschewed its nineteenth-century prejudices" (96–7). Hall and Schwarz also note how the state was invested with the role of articulating what Hobhouse calls the common will: "Thus, within the collectivist perspective, the state was seen as representing particular collective interests, and thereby required to intervene positively in civil society on behalf of these, rather than holding the ring within which individual interests compete" (16).

In the New Liberal model of collectivism, this power-bearing entity theoretically does not directly intervene in the lives of its subjects. Instead, as Hobhouse put it,

> The heart of Liberalism is the understanding that progress is not a matter of mechanical contrivance, but of the liberation of living spiritual energy. Good mechanism is that which provides the channels wherein such energy can flow unimpeded, unobstructed by its own exuberance of output, vivifying the social structure, expanding and ennobling the life of mind. (66)

The New Liberals combined a socialist belief that the state should dispense welfare with a liberal belief that individuality must be fostered. In other words, while they maintained a collective view of society as the evolutionary telos of human progress, they by no means abandoned an individualist model of the self. For them, it was only within a collectively organized society that individuality could thrive. While supposedly ruling from a distance, the state was necessary to this social schema and positioned as the primary agency that could work to improve society. In Hobhouse's language, the state did not pursue the public good by forcing itself upon individuals. Instead, it sought to "ennobl[e]" them. Foucault's model of governmentality—biopower practiced by the state—and Grand's contradiction-riddled feminist novel allow us to see that the governmental stance of ennobling the population was neither benign nor neutral. It was rather the rhetorical face of "the power to *foster* life or *disallow* it to the point of death" (Foucault, 1978, 138).

In *Liberalism*, Hobhouse argued that an interventionist state was increasingly becoming the inevitable "choice" for England as a progressive nation.

Because they were the results of the evolutionary development of consciousness, state interventionism and collectivism could only by rights be forced upon resistant individuals if they violated the norms of society and sought to coerce others. His ideal state would only exercise force in restrictive ways on those individuals whose negative actions affected all of society. Hobhouse extended this logic to the moral development that the state should ethically provide. Seeking to assuage anti-statists who feared that the state was seeking to undermine individuals by engineering and standardizing them, Hobhouse asserted that all the intervening state could ethically do was to provide the conditions in which personality and character could develop to their fullest potential:

> To try to form character by coercion is to destroy it in the making. Personality is not built up from without but grows from within, and the function of the outer order is not to create it, but to provide for it the most suitable conditions of growth. Thus, to the common question whether it is possible to make men good by Act of Parliament, the reply is that it is not possible to compel morality because morality is the act or character of a free agent, but that it is possible to create the conditions under which morality can develop, and among these not the least important is freedom from compulsion by others. (69)

By separating character and circumstances and claiming simply to provide the proper environment for character to grow "from within," proponents of state intervention found a way to fit their policies within classical liberalism, while denying the charge that the state was involved in the project of undercutting liberal agency by engineering homogeneous, compliant subjects.

This separation of character and circumstances and the denial of the charge of coercion can also be found in the work that Grand's novel claims to perform: her emphasis on feeling as opposed to argument. In this way, both Grand's novel and Hobhouse's political philosophy bear out Foucault's theory of disciplinary individualism and biopower, the management of the population. The novel conditions readers into understanding the state as an appropriate site to which to turn for social problems. In keeping with a liberal model of education, the text works to condition the reader into appealing to the state for marriage reform, votes for women, and equal access to education and the professions. It refuses to articulate a policy or solution to the problems it spells out because it wishes to circumvent accusations of authoritativeness or coercion. The collective feeling and fantasy of the state has to be reached through individual awareness—one that organically grows from within because external conditions for growth have been provided and not through external argument, coercion, or demand. In this way, Grand's novel appears analogous to Hobhouse's intervening liberal state: It, too, claims not to tell the subject what to do, but instead only to provide the conditions for the subject to grow from within.

In other words, Grand's novel imagined itself to be shaping a liberal subject for whom appealing to an ethical state to transform society constituted an unconscious, natural, and logical step in England's progress. To participate in the pedagogical project of shaping such a complicit state subject, Grand had to grapple with a set of contradictions that provoked many of her contemporaries: mainly the clash between, on the one hand, earlier notions of the classical liberal individual as one who preexisted the state and whose autonomy and self-reliance were defined over and against an interfering state and, on the other, the emerging sense that a new kind of subject was forming, one who relied upon the state to transform his circumstances, and in turn, his character. For those commentators who advocated state intervention, this subject understood her interdependence with other members of the national social and achieved her ethical expression in the state. Meanwhile, for the anxious and anti-statist, this subject's freedom and individuality were being radically undercut by an interfering state, which was bent on homogenizing and bullying subjects until they were rendered dependent and needy. For Grand, at the core of the conflict between the theoretical classical liberal individual and the historical encroachment of the intervening state lay the keystone institutions of marriage and education, which she identified as the causes of women's suffering. However, in both her fiction and nonfiction, she also theorized how they could potentially function as primary sources of national political optimism, but only if their relations to the state were expanded tacitly and indirectly.

Sexing the State

Grand's utopic vision expunges bourgeois sexuality, but still needs to acknowledge some kind of pleasure for its bourgeois women. *The Heavenly Twins* seems to acknowledge that practicing female citizenship through sensible matings is a hard sell. Its first solution is to deflect female sexuality from heterosexual passion to more inward forms of libidinal intensity that take place around the spectacle of the lower classes and colonized subjects. If women's passion for romance leads them to death and decay, then it can be redirected toward helping the poor. Such a move maintains traditional class relations, allowing the upper-class women in the novel to fashion themselves as symbols of the empire.

As the novel's plot unfolds, the problem of the working classes, first introduced in the pastoral image of the "yawning ploughman," vanishes. It returns only in two sensationalist depictions of working-class and downtrodden women who serve as figures of economic and sexual exploitation. Dotting the landscape, they produce opportunities for the novel's main upper-class female characters to experience heightened consciousness, while confirming Grand's moral case that upper- and middle-class male immorality, understood in sexual-economic terms, weakens society universally. The novel links the upper-class women to lower-class and typically French women through the contagion of sexually transmitted disease, the metaphorical displacement of masculine failure and weakness. Syphilis is, in the logic of the novel, simply the physical form of male sexual desire.

Angelica and Edith each participate as witnesses in spectacles of suffering women. In both cases, they are in carriages when they view women in the footpaths alongside the main road. The suffering women are doubly exposed, since they function in the novel mainly as repressed symptoms of a corrupt social system. Angelica, caught in the jaws of boredom, goes out for a ride:

> "But what should she do with the rest of her day?" Her handsome horses were prancing through Morningquest as she asked herself the question; and there was a little milliner on the footway looking up with kindly envy at the lady no older than herself, sitting alone in her splendid carriage with her coachman and footman and everything—nothing to do included, very much included, being, in fact, the principal item. (487)

Angelica theorizes the limits of individual aid and sees the need for collective action, but while she reasons, she loses her chance:

> "I should be helping her," thought Angelica. "She is ill-fed, overworked, and weakly, while I am pampered and strong; but there is no rational way for me to do it. If I took her home with me and kept her in luxurious idleness for the rest of her days, as I could very well afford to do, I should only have dragged her down from the dignity of her own honest exertions into the slough of self-indulgence in which I find myself, and made bad worse. She should have more and I should have less; but how to arrive at that? Isolated efforts seem to be abortive—yet—" she stopped the carriage, and looked back. The girl had disappeared. (487)

In her long contemplation, she loses her chance to help the girl. Angelica commands the coachman to return and she drives up and down to find her, but they do not recover a trace of her:

> "Another opportunity lost," thought Angelica. "A few pounds in her pocket would have been a few weeks' rest for her, a few good meals, a few innocent pleasures—she would have been strengthened and refreshed; and I should have been the better too for the recollection of a good deed done." (487)

For Angelica, one performs good deeds because it makes for a pleasant memory and leads to a feeling of self-satisfaction.

As a young maiden, Edith also encounters a poor woman on the road. She is with her mother in a carriage, going to the country to pay a call:

> On the way back Edith noticed a beggar, a young slender, very delicate-looking girl, lying across the footpath with her feet toward the road. A tiny baby lay on her lap. Her head and shoulders were pillowed upon the high bank which flanked the path, her face was raised as if her last look had been up at the sky above her, her hands had slipped helplessly on to the ground on either side of her, releasing the child, which had rolled over on to its face and so continued inertly. (160)

Edith says nothing until a bit later and then asks her mother if she saw the young woman. Mrs. Beale did not but commands her driver to turn around. The footman knows who she is, a French dressmaker who had come to England with her sister: ". . . but they got to know some of the gentry—" (160). Mrs. Beale is horrified and stops him. He suggests that they could tell the workhouse, an idea that relieves Mrs. Beale: "It had not occurred to either of the two ladies, gentle, tender, and good as they were, to take the poor dusty disgraced tramp into their carriage, and restore her to 'life and use and name and fame' as they might have done" (160). She discovers later that the gentry that the footman was referring to was actually Menteith, the betrothed of Edith, and that had they spoken with the sick woman, they might have prevented Edith's own impending syphilitic death and the ill health of her child.

The instrumentality of the poor in Grand's novel extends to the imperial context, specifically Malta, where much of the action occurs. Stationed in Malta, Evadne's husband introduces his wife to the sights of the place and we encounter an idyllic spot through her senses:

> Colonel Colquhoun pointed out the lighthouses of St. Elmo, patron saint of sailors, on the right, and Ricasoli on the left. Then they were met by a

rainbow fleet of dghaisas, gorgeous in color, and propelled by oarsmen who stood to their work, and were also brightly clad—both boats and boatmen, clothed by the sun, as it were, having blossomed into color unconsciously as the flowers do in genial atmospheres. (174)

The British controlled Malta, a small island south of Sicily in the Mediterranean, throughout the nineteenth century because of its strategic location (Hobsbawm 67). The inhabitants, a mix of different ethnicities, including Arab, Sicilian, French, Spanish, Italian, and British, are not given a voice in the narrative. They remain inscrutable aspects of the landscape over which Evadne exerts a sense of mastery:

> The boats, carrying fruits, flowers, tobacco, cheap jewelry, and coarse clothing for sailors, each cargo adding something of picturesqueness to the scene, formed a gay flotilla about the steamer and accompanied her, she towering majestically above them, and appearing to attract them and hold them to her sides as a great cork in the water does a handful of chopped straw. The boatmen held up their wares, chattering and gesticulating, their sun-browned faces all animation and changeful as children's. One moment they would be smiling up and speaking in wheedling tones to the passengers, and the next they would be frowning round at each other, and resenting some offense with torrents of abuse. (174)

A classic example of late-nineteenth-century colonial discourse, the narrator infantilizes the natives, rendering them child-like and irrational. The white British woman offers the only image of peace and unity. For Evadne, the scene not only gives her a feeling of majesty, but also heightened sensations and pleasure. She feels "herself suddenly aglow with warmth and color, a part of the marvellous beauty and brightness, and uplifted in spirit out of the everyday world above all thought and care into regions of the purest pleasure" (174).

The lower classes and the imperialized subjects of the British Empire thus serve the function of fostering intense feelings within the main female characters. Feelings of sympathy for the poor and downtrodden and feelings of superiority and paternalism over the infantilized natives become sanctioned moments of libidinal and inward intensity in the novel. If sexuality in the form of attraction, passion, and romance for another person is only ever presented as immoral, weak, and dangerous to the bodily integrity of the individual and of the British nation, then exalted self-understandings in relation to minor subjects compensates while maintaining the racialized hegemony of the middle classes over those within the nation and those outside of it. Thus, the racism of these two scenes, in which the two under-class women and the Maltese natives appear as essentially different categories from the white upper-class English women who regard them, is impossible to separate from the sexuality of the ones in power. By figuring them as racial others, our heroines find a channel for their sexual drives and impulses that also upholds the workings of a state that increasingly dedicates itself to managing the lives of the population.

But it is the story of Evadne that most dramatically seeks to rewire the sexuality of the readers. Evadne's hysteria allows Grand an opportunity to teach the reader to eroticize a relation of dependence and helplessness. Evadne's tragedy, after all, is far more *romantic* than Mrs. Malcomson's level-headed sensibleness.

Evadne's marriage provides the main opportunity for the novel to explore the consequences of male immorality and the possibilities for feminist critique. While they manage to produce a livable, if sexless marriage in Malta, Colonel Colquhoun eventually exacts a damaging promise from Evadne:

> Will you promise me that during my lifetime you will not mix yourself up publicly—will not join societies, make speeches, or publish books, which people would know you had written, on the social subjects you are so fond of. (342)

Evadne agrees to this condition and suffers in consequence. Her actual downfall is linked explicitly to this promise to remove herself from the public sphere, which she ultimately comes to interpret as a removal from the circuit of knowledge. Her life cut down to "objectless contemplation" (349), she returns to church and switches images of suffering on her walls to images of peace: ". . . she would listen to nothing that might move her to indignation and reawaken the futile impulse to resist . . ." (350). She falls sick and ceases to write in her journal.

In the final section of the novel, Grand tries to imagine a romance that extends past individuals to a national body. Dr. Galbraith, a specialist in nervous disorders, takes over the narratorial perspective from the earlier omniscient, enraged narrator. He provides a medical and personal account of the effects of Evadne's promise to her husband Colquhoun not to "mix [herself] up publicly" during his lifetime, which results in her gradual breakdown.

Once Colquhoun dies of a heart attack, Dr. Galbraith proposes to her. She accepts and they begin to have children. However, her illness does not subside and she contemplates suicide. Upon seeing Edith's syphilitic child, which brings home again "the awful needless suffering!" Evadne suffers another attack, falling even more ill (677). Dr. Galbraith is forced to conclude that her withdrawal from public life might have had permanent, negative effects. The novel ends with Dr. Galbraith pleading with her to allow him to comfort and assure her:

> . . . if at any time you will not listen to my words, if nothing I can do or say strengthens or helps you, if I cannot keep you from the evil that it may not grieve you, then I shall know that I have lost all that makes life worth having, and I shall not care how soon this lamp of mine goes out. (679)

His final speech expresses the collective sentiment that regulates the novel and Grand's political theory: The health of the whole organism depends on the health of its individual parts. It is couched in the rhetoric of heterosexual romance and the claim that one's life is not worth living if the love object suffers. In the very last scene of the novel, Dr. Galbraith self-consciously tries to find meaning. Drawing the reader's attention to the limits of his subjectivity and to the fact that he is interpreting Evadne's gestures, he writes, "She looked up at me in a strange startled way, and then she clung closer; and I thought she meant that, if she could help it, I should not lose the little I ask for now—the power to make her life endurable" (679).

Heilmann interprets Evadne's life course as the dramatization of Grand's critical intervention into the two historically prevalent views of women's hysteria. Medical professionals in the mid-Victorian period, most notably Sir William Acton, located the source of women's hysteria in their sexual overactivity. Meanwhile, Freud and his followers claimed that it was precisely the lack of sex that rendered women hysterical. Heilmann contends that Grand countered their claims with her own view that while hysteria did indeed result from the suppression of women's desire, this desire was not sexual, but rather professional: the desire to have a career. I would like to refine Heilmann's point further by suggesting Grand not only uses hysteria as a dramatic effect of women's oppression, but she also promotes it as an affective compensation for turning to the state to redress injustice.

Heilmann notes that Dr. Galbraith appears to be a positive character, but compares his role in Evadne's decline to that of the husband in Charlotte Perkins Gilman's "The Yellow Wallpaper," which appeared the year before (236). Heilmann analyzes this last book as Grand's critique of the medical establishment and, in particular, the male scientific gaze. This final section's opening lines, in which Dr. Galbraith approaches Evadne as a case, a mystery to be explored and analyzed, support aspects of Heilmann's argument:

> Evadne puzzled me. As a rule, men of my profession, and more particularly specialists like myself, can class a woman's character and gauge her propensities for good or evil while he is diagnosing her disease if she consult him, or more easily still during half an hour's ordinary conversation if he happens to be alone with her. But even after I had seen Evadne many times, and felt broadly that I knew her salient points as well as such tricks of manner or habitual turns of expression as distinguished her from other ladies, I was puzzled. (555)

While Heilmann readily allows that Grand does not totally vilify Dr. Galbraith, in my reading he in fact emerges as a figure of Grand's optimism in the state and the collectivist view of society.

First of all, his view coincides with the omniscient narrator, who has the tone of the celebrity biographer:

> In looking back now, I am inclined to ask why we, Evadne's intimate friends, should always have expected more of her than we did of other people. That certainly was the case, and she disappointed us. We felt that she should have been a representative woman such as the world wants at this period of its progress, making a name for herself and an impression on the age; and it was probably her objection, expressed with quite passionate earnestness, to play a part in which we gathered from many chance indications that she was eminently qualified to have excelled, that constituted the puzzle. Her natural bent was certainly in that direction, but something had changed it; and here in particular the external tormenting difficulty with regard to her occurred with full force. At a very early period of our acquaintance, however, I discovered that her attitude in this respect was not inherent, but deliberately chosen. (555)

"Natural bent" and "choice" collide in his account of Evadne and constitute the puzzle that the whole novel takes up regarding women's adherence to normative gender ideology. Dr. Galbraith's surprised disappointment that Evadne does not emerge as a feminist heroine mirrors the narrator's.

His politics are not under question in the novel and he is a paragon of masculine and political virtue. While he is undoubtedly guilty of the appropriating gaze of the male scientist, Grand upholds the objectivity of science as a tool for women's liberation. Other kinds of scientific cures are discounted in the novel and Dr. Galbraith and his mentor Sir Shadwell Rock emerge as women's champions. Heilmann's claim that he upholds motherhood as an ideal and therefore seeks to dominate Evadne does not take into account Grand's own belief that an unsentimentalized motherhood marks the highest duty of women, in particular their duties as citizen-makers. Furthermore, Dr. Galbraith endorses the view that women need to experience themselves both privately and publicly:

> The natural bent of the average woman is devotion to home and husband and children; but there are many women to whom domestic duties are distasteful, and these are now making life tolerable for themselves by finding more congenial spheres of action. (645)

Dr. Galbraith combines two kinds of virtuous disinterest: the objective, scientific kind and the traditional, economically based kind. In earlier parts of the novel, when the omniscient narrator has control of the perspective, Dr. Galbraith enters a room after attending to the syphilitic French dressmaker, the very same one that Edith and her mother passed by but whom Dr. Galbraith places in the charge of a nurse and tends to himself: ". . . there was a shade of weariness or depression on his strong pale face; but his deep gray kindly eyes—the redeeming feature—were as sympathetically penetrating as usual" (163). He is part of the New Order, along with Ideala and Lord Dawne, who all share the characteristic of "giving the whole of their attention to the person with whom they were conversing for the moment" (164). His scientific virtue is enhanced only when he inherits a baronetcy. Now his disinterest is buttressed by economic independence. He uses the fortune to expand a small private hospital for the poor that he had already established.

Heilmann's argument rests on the multiple layering that she sees in the editorial note framing the chapter. This note is written from the perspective of the omniscient narrator:

> The fact that Dr. Galbraith had not the advantage of knowing Evadne's early history when they first became acquainted adds a certain piquancy to the flavour of his impressions, and the reader, better informed than himself with regard to the antecedents of his "subject," will find it interesting to note both the accuracy of his insight and the curious mistakes which it is possible even for a trained observer like himself to make by the half light of such imperfect knowledge as he was able to collect under the circumstances. (554)

According to Heilmann, the emphasis on Dr. Galbraith's fallibility establishes the unreliability of his narrative and the superiority of the reader's vantage point: "In the guise of commending Galbraith, the text points to the gaps in his knowledge, suggesting that his incomplete understanding of the case and his personal bias led to diagnostic errors, and advising readers to approach the first-person narrative with caution . . ." (2001, 129).

But the narrator's remarks on the limits of Dr. Galbraith's impression in fact legitimate and humanize him, casting him as the real interest of the piece:

> But more interesting still [than the representation of how much Evadne has changed], perhaps, are the glimpses we get of Dr. Galbraith himself in the narrative, throughout which it is easy to decipher the simple earnestness of the man, the cautious professionalism and integrity, the touches of tender sentiment held in check, the dash of egotism, the healthy-minded human nature, the capacity for enjoyment and sorrow, the love of life, and, above all, the perfect unconsciousness with which he shows himself to have been a man of fastidious refinement and exemplary moral strength and delicacy: of the highest possible character; and most lovable in spite of a somewhat irascible temper and manner which were apt to be abrupt at times. (554)

His moments of arrogance not only point to the inescapable power dynamics of male science, but also render him a romantic figure in the Victorian tradition of Jane Austen's Darcy and Charlotte Brontë's Rochester: irascible, yet human and harmless through the mellowing and sanctifying practice of bourgeois marriage.

Dr. Galbraith's interest in Evadne is both scientific and romantic. As the narrator eroticizes Evadne's powerlessness, we are introduced to one of the more disturbing aspects of the intervening state: its dependence upon wounded, needy state subjects and its role in producing them as such. Thus, while I disagree with Heilmann's claim that Grand intentionally critiques Dr. Galbraith as a figure of masculinist objectivity, I do agree that Grand's portrayal unwittingly suggests how the intervening state does reimpose relations of power. The final section encourages the reader to identify with Dr. Galbraith as a figure of the state and the collective: We, too, mourn Evadne's broken state and are shown many instances of her suffering and fragility. In this way, the rationale of an ethical state appears clear and persuasive. The reader merges with Dr. Galbraith, who by extension is associated with the state and the collective will, and feels the pleasure and the necessity of providing care for those who suffer. However, the reader also, through the circulation of erotics in this section, is encouraged to identify with Evadne. The reader identifies not only with her sense of helplessness and impotence to change the world, but also with her own erotic desire for a caring, concerned, interested, and regulating state/husband.

Conclusion

The Heavenly Twins is both invested in liberal models of agency—the female subject must morally choose to break away from the chains of subjection—and frustrated by it. Liberal philosophy presumes that the subject has willpower and that her thoughts are transparent to herself. However, daily experience of social injustice endangers the liberal subject's belief in her own agency. The idea of agency is so appealing, however, that it then becomes necessary to do whatever it takes to maintain it, even if that means handing it over to an imagined authority for safe keeping. *The Heavenly Twins* reveals how the fantasy of the state as a heroic actor relieves the subject's internal struggle with the social order, but the fantasy simultaneously indexes the extent to which the liberal subject has projected her agency away from herself in order to keep it.

Coda

While literary critics from Georg Lukács to George Levine tend to view late Victorian realist novels in terms of breakdown—the breakdown of realism, the breakdown of the liberal subject, and the breakdown of knowledge—I have suggested that we see them instead as producing something new. In his classic article, "The Realist Floor-Plan," Fredric Jameson argued that realist novels programmed readers who could navigate a new, secularizing culture. In this book, I have argued that late Victorian realist novels shaped readers who could navigate a new, sacralizing state culture. They represented the late Victorian everyday as saturated materially by state intervention and symbolically by state fantasy. On the one hand, late Victorian realism sought to teach readers to take the state's shaping of everyday life for granted, and, on the other hand, to defamiliarize their own unconscious optimism in the state's capacity to change their lives.

By drawing attention to British subjects' unconscious conflicts about political authority, these novels helped to cultivate the subject of psychoanalytic discourse. The modern liberal interventionist state and the discipline of psychoanalysis formed nearly simultaneously in the closing decades of the nineteenth century, a convergence that was not, I suggest, coincidental. Late Victorian state intervention and the neurotic symptoms that interested the emerging set of psychoanalysts were deeply intertwined. My readings of key novels reveal that a psychic split lay at the heart of late Victorian state subjectivity. This split might be expressed in the first-person plural as, "We know that the state is not a coherent, animated agent, and yet we do not know." Not knowing served a range of functions, including hiding from one's own agency and seeking to repress political optimism. As I mentioned in the beginning of Chapter 5, Freud first encountered the split between knowing and not knowing in a hysterical patient and later theorized it as the general condition of consciousness itself (Rose 109).

Lest this sound totalizing, let me emphasize that these novels also expose the inadequacy of the profile of the ideal liberal individual. This profile could not accommodate the emotional and political experiences of late-nineteenth-century British subjects looking out across a crumbling empire abroad and an unstable social order at home. In this way, inasmuch as the twenty-first century has inherited the ideals and problems of Victorian liberalism, they point to the necessity of reducing the hold that certain liberal abstractions have over us. For instance, the compulsive attention to freedom, understood as the freedom to possess, and independence, understood as the impossible state of operating without any institutional support whatsoever, have been associated with the misery of many.

Late Victorian realist novels thus constitute an important genealogical episode in the ongoing project of thinking about the political. What is state fantasy today? Future work might explore the different meanings attached to "state" versus "government" in political thought. Recent critical theory tends to favor the word "state" when discussing centralized political authority. For example, Michael Taussig, Wendy Brown, Judith Butler, and Gayatri Spivak use the term "state" to theorize official forms of power. This choice of terminology may have to do with the traditions of eighteenth- and nineteenth-century philosophy that inform their work. But in non-academic contexts in the United States, critics of state power often critique "Big Government." This divergence of nomenclature is not without meaning that a genealogy could uncover.

The scholars I mention in the previous paragraph, whose work has informed my own, also speak of the state mainly as a site of discipline and repression. In this book, I too have tracked the disabling effects of the state and its perpetuation of social inequality. However, the project began out of my attraction to a historical moment that imagined the state as a site of optimism and as a resource with the capacity to cohere a disparate population through both symbolic and material means. In fact, my project was inspired by the exchange between Rhoda and Everard in *The Odd Women*. The style of their banter about the state struck me as strange for the Victorian period, but intensely familiar to the present moment. It is how we talk about the state now: wearily. This weariness, as I hope to have shown, belies an optimism that the state could be able to protect everyone from the brutalities of capitalism and to achieve social justice. If nations, as scholars have shown, are premised on exclusion, could the state form be premised on something other than an inclusion/exclusion model? If the state knows that we love it, can it act responsibly to us and safeguard our love? After all, as I hope that my readings of novels show, the state needs the love of its subjects to exist.

Notes

Introduction: The Lyricism of the State

1. Notable exceptions include Aretxaga's "Maddening States," Taussig's notion of the state maleficium in *The Nervous System*, and Mbembe's consideration of the banality of Cameroonian state power in *On the Postcolony*.

2. Timothy Mitchell provides a historical account of how the state lost favor as an object of study in the social sciences. In the 1950s, he notes, U.S. social scientists rejected the term "state" because they could not agree upon its definition. Focusing on the state, they argued, also often resulted in casting other political processes outside the critical lens. Mitchell argues that this turn away from the state was also a question of disciplinary survival. The relation between political science and political power had shifted in the 1950s and political scientists had to reassert their indispensability to government policy officials. They turned from the study of the state to the study of society, expanding its field of inquiry to incorporate questions traditionally asked by anthropologists, "pushing [their] investigation into the meticulous examination of the activities of political groups, the behavior of social actors, even the motivations of individual psyches" (Mitchell 1999, 78). This politically motivated shift in method resulted in the obscuring of the limits of the political system. As social scientists' field of inquiry expanded, seemingly without boundaries, it became increasingly difficult to distinguish among politics, society, the economy, and culture.

In the following decades, this border confusion led in part to the reclamation of the state as not only an object of study, but also as the central entity of any analysis of power. This shift also marked a change in strategic thinking. Within the field of political science, many prominent thinkers held that the United States could not exercise its influence in the third world without fostering statist cultures. Additionally, in most Western countries, the state had endured in mainstream politics: despite the shift away from the state in 1950s academia, political speech had continued to feature the state and debate its proper role in the economy and society. Because of these renewed disciplinary and strategic emphases, the state and its conceptual aspects reemerged as a legitimate problem in the 1970s. This new generation of political scientists and sociologists considered the state as not only the central site of power, but also an autonomous entity, distinct from society, the economy, and culture. Two challenges to this schema then emerged. First, Foucault argued that power did not emanate from the centralized site of the state but rather was dispersed throughout society, working on the micrological level. Second, attention to globalization and transnational flows of capital resulted in the downgrading of the state's power. These latter studies cast nation-states as shells of their former selves. In the 1980s and '90s, sociologists and political scientists, such as Mitchell, began to resituate the state within their studies of modern power. Their works have demonstrated the enduring hold that the state form has over the ways societies organize themselves and the ways that state practices produce hegemonic identities and senses of belonging that are felt by individuals to be uniquely theirs. To paraphrase Mitchell, as an object of study, the state refuses to disappear (1991, 77).

3. I rely on the term "fantasy," rather than imagination, because I wish to connote the creation of both conscious as well as unconscious scenarios.

4. Inspired by Foucault, Mitchell argues that the separation between the individual and the institution is an effect. However, like other political-science approaches, Mitchell's analysis ignores a crucial aspect of state power: how it feels and how it functions on the level of fantasy. While nimbly framing the complex nature of modern power, Mitchell does not consider state subjects' interiority. That is, he does not take into account subjects' experience of the state nor the ways that they imagine it.

1. An Imperial Origin Story: Aloof Rule in Schreiner's The Story of an African Farm

1. J. A. Hobson, Hannah Arendt, Eric Hobsbawm, and Elleke Boehmer have identified this period as the era of high imperialism. This era starts with the Berlin Conference and ends in 1914 with the start of World War I.

2. In *King Solomon's Mines*, Haggard's narrator Allan Quatermain self-consciously aestheticizes the South African coastal landscape from the side of a ship as he approaches, fixing it as a scene to analyze, absorb, and enjoy:

> It is a lovely coast all along from East London, with its red sandhills and wide sweeps of vivid green, dotted here and there with Kafir kraals, and bordered by a ribbon of white surf, which spouts up in pillars of foam where it hits the rocks. (32)

As Mary Louise Pratt famously established, these ways of freezing and abstracting the landscape provided ideological justification for acquisition, casting the land as rich, desirable, and appropriable. Haggard's novel responds to increasing criticism of the cost of Britain's imperial adventures. We can thus read this representation as an attempt to defend and justify the continued possession of South Africa.

3. In *King Solomon's Mines*, the moon is a benevolent, approving source. In the midst of a long, trial-filled trek through the desert, Quatermain waxes poetical, "... at last the full and glorious moon peeps above the plain and shoots its gleaming arrows far and wide, filling the earth with a faint refulgence, as the glow of a good man's deeds shines for a while upon his little world after his sun has set, lighting the fainthearted travellers who follow on towards a fuller dawn" (Haggard 123).

4. Schreiner to Havelock Ellis, St. Leonards, March 28, 1884, *Letters 1871–99*, 36.
   5. Rive, ed., *Letters 1871–99*, fn. 5, 36.

2. *"Rather a Geographical Expression Than a Country": State Fantasy and the Production of Victorian Afghanistan*

   1. Andrew, 28.
   2. Afghanistan is not the only country to have been described this way. Prince Metternich famously used this expression earlier in the century to describe Italy (Sandeman 168).
   3. Two examples of studies that do focus on imperialized sites are Lauren Berlant's "Poor Eliza" from *The Female Complaint*, and Robert Aguirre's *Informal Empire: Mexico and Central America in Victorian Culture*.
   4. See Jennifer Hill and Joseph Bristow.
   5. As Gail Clark among others have noted, boys' adventure novels sought to correct for what was imagined to be a softening, feminized, degenerating culture in England.
   6. See Arata, 140, and McLaughlin, 28.
   7. In *On Liberty* (1859), Mill writes, "[The liberal individual] must use observation to see, reasoning and judgement to foresee, activity to gather materials for decision, discrimination to decide, and when he has decided, firmness and self-control to hold to his deliberate decision" (65).
   8. See Daniel Hack.
   9. In his reading of Wilkie Collins's novel *Basil* (1852), Hack argues that the narrative assignation of revenge to the putative man of modernity, Mannion, soothes anxiety about the kind of modern "drive and discipline" he represents, thus transforming the threatening modern man into the obsolete man of the past (283).
   10. Describing the main character Perowne in Ian McEwan's *Saturday*, Hadley notes the particular combination of social incoherence and subjective harmoniousness that Matthew Arnold's "Dover Beach" (1867) also tries to craft. As Perowne observes a range of disconnected social actors in the park from his bedroom window, he entertains a subjective train of thought: "In the face of the inscrutable, McEwan privileges Perowne's habit of narration, his meditative attribution of agency, his thoughts about the social sublime that are more nearly alert to their status as thought than as anything else. This is, in fact, a classic Victorian liberal response to the world without—what I call a cognitive formalism that makes beautiful thought about humanity taken as a social whole, as when Arnold identifies with Sophocles, who 'brought/Into his mind the turbid ebb and flow/Of human misery' (16–18)" (2005, 95).
   11. Ultimately, Rothfield argues that detective fiction "turns realism to perverse ends" (147). This subgenre of fiction, he argues, upon the historical subordination of clinical science by specialized sciences, that is, the rise of detection over diagnosis, but it does not then expel the clinical, the diagnostic, or the embodied person from

its pages. Rather, detective fiction needs the clinical mode, with its diagnostic approach to the body, both to humiliate and incite sadomasochistic pleasure in characters and readers.

3. The Rise of the State as a Sympathetic Liberal Subject in Hardy's The Woodlanders

1. Hardy, 282.
2. The conditionality of this phrasing is, of course, intentional: the scene would make a humane person cry if he or she could have access to the psychic lives of these geographically and culturally remote woodlanders. See Barrell.
3. See Jordan, Wardley, and Woollard.
4. See Hindley, 67–8.
5. A place becomes a space by virtue of the "operations that orient it, situate it, temporalize it, and make it function in a polyvalent unity of conflictual programs or contractual proximities" (De Certeau 117).
6. For Chambers, the loiterer troubles distinctions between social order and disorder: "Loitering tends to blur the distinctions on which social order depends—between innocence and guilt, between the good citizen enjoying a moment's respite and the seedy character who may just be taking the sun on this bench or idling in that shady doorway, or who may be a prostitute angling to catch a john or a two-bit criminal looking for an easy mark" (8).
7. Formally introduced in 1706, turnpikes were promoted by the popular idea that those who used the roads ought to pay for them. Turnpike trusts then took responsibility for collecting tolls and maintaining the roads, and despite corruption and inefficient management, they continued to flourish across England until the Highway Act of 1862. This act altered the existing system, authorizing the partitioning of parishes into Highway Districts, each empowered to coordinate road administration, thereby diminishing the authority of both the turnpike trusts and the parishes. For the history of the road, see Gregory, McCord, Clapham, Finer, Hindley, and Webb and Webb (1913).
8. In *The Anatomy of National Fantasy: Hawthorne, Utopia, and Everyday Life*, Lauren Berlant explains this totalizing promise of the nation as a feature of all nations and one exchanged for the maintenance of an abstract idea of "the people" (25).
9. Hardy's disruption of what Rick Rylance calls the "associationist romance" also disturbs the conventions of the British regional novel (66). Liz Bellamy has noted how eighteenth-century regional novels that focus on the "backward" cultures of Ireland and Scotland not only represented these foreign communities as unique and colorful but also participated in constructing a counter-notion of what constituted British national identity (55). Bellamy argues that regional novels show how marginalized cultures could be written about and consumed with pleasure only when they no longer threatened national legitimacy and economic domination. Through its representational strategies, eighteenth-century regional literature

instrumentalized and "sanitised" recalcitrant cultures "into a romantic ideal which could challenge the values of the present, instead of being a dangerous and destabilising force" (57).

10. A General Report on the Census of 1881 reported that, between the years 1871 and 1881, the overall number of agricultural laborers had decreased, while the number of general laborers had increased. Confirming general fears that traditional farming was failing in the face of new mass farming techniques, the report also announced decreases in the acreage of arable land, the number of laborers per hundred acres, and the number of farmers overall and increases in the acreage of permanent pasture, the number of owners and operators of agricultural machines, foremen, and bailiffs. See Hasbach 296.

11. In 1887, the M.P. Jesse Collings drafted such a bill. Designed to buttress the vanishing peasant class through land distribution, it was eventually passed in a much milder version as the Allotments Act of 1887. Its policy makes clear connections between small farmers and English nationalism, on the one hand, and home and virtue, on the other.

12. Another example is the 1890 Report of the Parliamentary Committee, assembled to investigate Small Holdings and chaired by Joseph Chamberlain. Hasbach quotes from it to highlight how its rhetoric positioned peasant farmers who owned or rented property as the suppliers of good character for the entire nation:

> A numerous and well-to-do peasantry must, it was said, be considered beneficial to any country from a national, social, and economic standpoint. From a national standpoint, because they provide an important element in national defence, and valuable elements of character, and mean security of property and a contented population. From a social standpoint, because small holders, "whether as owners or tenants," are distinguished by industry and economy; the small holding gives heart and hope to the ordinary laborer; he sees a possibility of setting his foot on the first rung of the social ladder. Without this hope, "he is only a bird of passage; there is no national sentiment in his heart. In the absence of a home a man has very little to work for." (qtd. in Hasbach, 317)

13. See Dames for his insightful genealogy of nostalgia in the nineteenth century.

14. Goodlad has helpfully elaborated the split in the British nineteenth-century middle classes between a dominant entrepreneurial set and an emergent professional one. Drawing on Harold Perkin's work, Goodlad elaborates how the entrepreneurial class, aligning itself with concepts of self-interest, free enterprise, laissez-faire, and competition, assumed an essentially antagonistic position toward the state. In contrast, the professional class, defining itself in terms of specialization and service, looked to the state to recognize and valorize its worth through certifications and regulations. Underlying their essential conflict, Goodlad argues, was competition over whose occupation could lay claim to gentility (2003, 148–9).

15. Here I refer to Anderson's famous application of Walter Benjamin to describe the temporality of the modern nation form (24). As my larger argument

maintains, in the closing decades of the nineteenth century, the state emerges as the more forcefully charged symbolic construct.

16. See Horkheimer and Adorno for the classic Frankfurt School argument about the return of the sacred in an aggressively secular modern time.

17. For a fascinating psychoanalytic account of this process, see Teresa Brennan's *The Transmission of Affect*.

18. This form of personhood is the foundation for Mill's liberal political philosophy, set forth in *On Liberty*, for it counters custom and conformity through the act of asking oneself, as Mill writes, "what do I prefer?" or, "what would suit my character and disposition?" or, "what would allow the best and highest in me to have fair play, and enable it to grow and thrive?" (68)

19. See Horstman, 80–1.

20. See Berlant, 2004, 4.

21. For example, the central government played a part in actively creating the free market that it claimed simply to protect retroactively and it barred most women from voting in parliamentary elections until 1928.

4. The Space of Optimism: State Fantasy and the Case of Gissing's The Odd Women

1. Lauren Berlant argues that genres provide maps for how to live in the world, each one tracing out different desires and entailing its own notions of probability and agency, thereby formally shaping different kinds of social subjects (2004, 227).

2. For Foucault, let us remember, life insurance is a primary instance of biopower, a "sub-State institution," that regulates the population by seeking to manage life and death (2003, 250).

3. In a letter of March 20, 1893, on the occasion of Tennyson's death, Gissing writes to Edmund Gosse that, "Even an honest liking for verse, without discernment, depends upon complex conditions of birth, breeding, education" (*Collected Letters* 5:98).

4. For more on nineteenth-century literary representations of the city, see Choi and Poole (31–2).

5. See pages 11–14 in the Introduction.

6. For histories of municipalization, see Clifton, Inwood, Sheppard, and McCord.

7. Another symbolic dimension was added in 1843 when Sir Charles Barry finished installing the Nelson Column, an ode to British naval power.

8. For example, see "Occasional Notes."

9. I am grateful to the reviewer who referred me to the "Hyper-Concordance" function at the Victorian Literary Studies website (http://victorian.lang.nagoya-u.ac.jp/concordance).

10. Williams defines "structure of feeling" as "a kind of feeling and thinking which is indeed social and material, but each in an embryonic phase before it can become fully articulate and defined exchange" (1977, 131).

11. Michael McKeon notes that for Mikhail Bakhtin, novelization, the historical process by which other genres became free to change with history, along the lines of the novel, takes on the positive role of providing historical change itself (320).

5. *Hysterical Citizenship in Grand's* The Heavenly Twins

1. Drawing on the work of Harold Perkin, Lauren Goodlad has argued that the professional class was strongly associated with the state. See Ch. 3, n. 14.

2. Grand and Linton exchanged vitriolic attacks in periodicals, the former defending the New Woman and chastising those who accepted gender norms, the latter dismissing Grand and other feminist writers as "Wild Women" or "odd." As Broomfield points out, it matters that the two women, as they jousted in vitriolic "political" print debates over the Woman Question, also vied for journalistic success and longevity at a time when editors, ever anxious for readers, turned scandal into publishing policy and explicitly sought out and promoted controversy.

Bibliography

Abrams, Philip. "Notes on the Difficulty of Studying the State (1977)." *Journal of Historical Sociology* 1 (March 1988): 58–89.
Aguirre, Robert. *Informal Empire: Mexico and Central America in Victorian Culture.* Minneapolis: University of Minnesota Press, 1995.
Althusser, Louis. "Ideology and Ideological State Apparatuses (Notes towards an Investigation)." In *Mapping Ideology*, ed. Slavoj Žižek, 100–40. New York: Verso, 1994.
Anderson, Amanda. "The Temptations of Aggrandized Agency: Feminist Histories and the Horizon of Modernity." *Victorian Studies* 43 (Autumn 2000): 43–65.
Anderson, Benedict. *Imagined Communities: Reflections on the Origin and Spread of Nationalism.* New York: Verso, 1991.
Andrew, W. P. *Our Scientific Frontier.* London: W. H. Allen & Co., 1880.
Arata, Stephen. *Fictions of Loss in the Victorian Fin de Siècle.* New York: Cambridge University Press, 1996.
———. "Realism." In *The Cambridge Companion to the Fin de Siècle*, ed. Gail Marshall, 169–87. New York: Cambridge University Press, 2007.
Ardis, Ann L. *New Women, New Novels: Feminism and Early Modernism.* New Brunswick, N.J.: Rutgers University Press, 1990.
Arendt, Hannah. *The Origins of Totalitarianism.* 1951. New York: Harcourt Brace Jovanovich, 1973.
Aretxaga, Begoña. "Maddening States." *Annual Review of Anthropology* 32 (2003): 393–410.
Armstrong, Nancy. *Desire and Domestic Fiction: A Political History of the Novel.* New York: Oxford University Press, 1987.
———. *How Novels Think: The Limits of Individualism from 1719–1900.* New York: Columbia University Press, 2005.
Arnold, Matthew. *Culture and Anarchy and Other Writings.* New York: Cambridge University Press, 1993.
"The Avuncular State." *The Economist* (April 8, 2006): 67–9.
Barrell, John. "Geographies of Hardy's Wessex." In *The Regional Novel in Britain and Ireland, 1800–1990*, ed. K. D. M. Snell, 99–118. New York: Cambridge University Press, 1998.
Barry, William. "The Strike of a Sex." 1894. Reprint in *Journalistic Writings and Contemporary Reception*, ed. Ann Heilmann. Vol. 1 of *Sex, Social Purity and Sarah*

Grand, ed. Heilmann and Stephanie Forward, 443–53. New York: Routledge, 2000.

Beer, Gillian. "Finding a Scale for the Human: Plot and Writing in Hardy's Novels." In *Critical Essays on Thomas Hardy: The Novels*, ed. Dale Kramer, 54–73. Boston, Mass.: G. K. Hall & Co., 1990.

Bellamy, Liz. "Regionalism and Nationalism: Maria Edgeworth, Walter Scott, and the Definition of Britishness." In *The Regional Novel in Britain and Ireland, 1800–1990*, ed. Snell, 54–77. New York: Cambridge University Press, 1998.

Berlant, Lauren. *The Anatomy of National Fantasy*. Chicago: University of Chicago Press, 1991.

———. "Pax Americana: The Case of *Show Boat*." In *Cultural Institutions of the Novel*, ed. Deidre Lynch and William B. Warner, 399–422. Durham, N.C.: Duke University Press, 1996.

———. *The Queen of America Goes to Washington City: Essays on Sex and Citizenship*. Durham, N.C.: Duke University Press, 1997.

———. "The Compulsion to Repeat Femininity." In *Giving Ground: The Politics of Propinquity*, ed. Joan Copjec and Michael Sorkin, 207–32. New York: Verso, 1999.

———. "Introduction: Compassion (and Withholding)." In *Compassion: The Culture and Politics of an Emotion*, ed. Berlant, 1–13. New York: Routledge, 2004.

———. "Slow Death (Sovereignty, Obesity, Lateral Agency)." *Critical Inquiry* 33 (Summer 2007): 754–80.

———. *The Female Complaint: The Unfinished Business of Sentimentality in American Culture*. Durham, N.C.: Duke University Press, 2008.

Bhabhba, Homi K. *The Location of Culture*. New York: Routledge, 1994.

Bland, Lucy. *Banishing the Beast: English Feminism and Sexual Morality, 1885–1914*. New York: Penguin Books, 1995.

Boehmer, Elleke. "Introduction." In *Empire Writing: An Anthology of Colonial Literature, 1870–1918*, ed. Boehmer, xv–xxxvi. New York: Oxford University Press, 1998.

Bogiatzis, Demetris. "Sexuality and Gender: 'The Interlude' of Sarah Grand's *The Heavenly Twins*." *English Literature in Transition: 1880–1920* 44:1 (2001): 46–63.

Bonnell, Marilyn. "Sarah Grand and the Critical Establishment: Art for [W]oman's Sake." *Tulsa Studies in Women's Literature* 14 (Spring 1995): 123–48.

Bonnell, Victoria E. and Lynn Hunt, eds. *Beyond the Cultural Turn*. Berkeley: University of California Press, 1999.

Boone, Joseph Allen. *Tradition Counter Tradition: Love and the Form of Fiction*. Chicago: University of Chicago Press, 1987.

Bowlby, Rachel. *Just Looking: Consumer Culture in Dreiser, Gissing and Zola*. New York: Methuen, 1985.

Brantlinger, Patrick. *Rule of Darkness: British Literature and Imperialism, 1830–1914*. Ithaca, N.Y.: Cornell University Press, 1988.

Brennan, Teresa. *The Transmission of Affect*. Ithaca, N.Y.: Cornell University Press, 2004.

Bristow, Joseph. *Empire Boys: Adventures in a Man's World*. London: HarperCollins Academic, 1991.
Broomfield, Andrea L. "Eliza Lynn Linton, Sarah Grand and the spectacle of the Victorian Woman Question: catch phrases, buzz words and sound bites." *English Literature in Transition: 1880–1920* 47:3 (Summer 2004): 251–72.
Brown, Bill. *The Material Unconscious: American Amusement, Stephen Crane, and the Economics of Play*. Cambridge, Mass.: Harvard University Press, 1996.
Brown, Wendy. *States of Injury: Power and Freedom in Late Modernity*. Princeton, N.J.: Princeton University Press, 1995.
Butler, Judith. *The Psychic Life of Power: Theories in Subjection*. Stanford, Calif.: Stanford University Press, 1997.
Butler, Judith, and Gayatri Chakravorty Spivak. *Who Sings the Nation-State? Language, Politics, Belonging*. New York: Seagull Books, 2007.
Caird, Mona. *The Morality of Marriage and Other Essays on the Status and Destiny of Woman*. London: George Redway, 1897.
Cannadine, David. *Ornamentalism: How the British Saw Their Empire*. New York: Oxford University Press, 2001.
Carter, Harold. "William Ewart Gladstone." In *The Oxford Companion to British History*, ed. John Cannon, 415–17. New York: Oxford University Press, 2002.
Chakrabarty, Dipesh. "Reconstructing Liberalism? Notes toward a Conversation between Area Studies and Diasporic Studies." *Public Culture* 10 (Winter 1998): 457–81.
Chambers, Ross. *Loiterature*. Lincoln: University of Nebraska Press, 1999.
Choi, Tina Young. "Writing the Victorian City: Discourses of Risk, Connection, and Inevitability." *Victorian Studies* 43 (2001): 561–89.
Chrisman, Laura. *Rereading the Imperial Romance: British Imperialism and South African Resistance in Haggard, Schreiner, and Plaatje*. New York: Oxford University Press, 2000.
Clapham, Sir John. *An Economic History of Modern Britain, Free Trade and Steel, 1850–1886*. New York: Cambridge University Press, 1952.
Clark, Gail S. "Imperial Stereotypes: G. A. Henty and the Boys' Own Empire." *Journal of Popular Culture* 18:4 (Spring 1985): 43–51.
Clifton, Gloria C. *Professionalism, Patronage and Public Service in Victorian London: The Staff of the Metropolitan Board of Works, 1856–1889*. Atlantic Highlands, N.J.: Athlone Press, 1992.
Comitini, Patricia. "A Feminist Fantasy: Conflicting Ideologies in *The Odd Women*." *Studies in the Novel* 27 (Winter 1995): 529–43.
Corrigan, Philip, and Derek Sayer. *The Great Arch: English State Formation as Cultural Revolution*. Oxford: Basil Blackwell, 1985.
Cuddon, J. A., ed. *The Penguin Dictionary of Literary Terms and Literary Theory*. New York: Penguin Books, 1991.
Dale, Peter Allan. "Gissing and Bosanquet: Culture Unhoused." In *Homes and Homelessness in the Victorian Imagination*, ed. Murray Baumgarten and H. M. Daleski, 269–80. New York: AMS Press, 1998.

Dames, Nicholas. *Amnesiac Selves: Nostalgia, Forgetting, and British Fiction, 1810–1870.* New York: Oxford University Press, 2001.

Daston, Lorraine. "Historical Epistemology." In *Questions of Evidence: Proof, Practice, and Persuasion across the Disciplines,* ed. James Chandler, Arnold I. Davidson, and Harry Harootunian, 282–9. Chicago: University of Chicago Press, 1994.

De Certeau, Michel. *The Practice of Everyday Life.* Translated by Steven Rendall. Berkeley: University of California Press, 1984.

De Laura, David J. "The Ache of Modernism in Hardy's Later Novels." *ELH* 34:3 (September 1967): 380–99.

Deleuze, Gilles, and Claire Parnet. *Dialogues II.* Translated by Hugh Tomlinson and Barbara Habberjam. New York: Columbia University Press, 2002.

Dickens, Charles. *Bleak House.* 1853. New York: Penguin, 1985.

Dilke, Sir Charles Wentworth. *Problems of Greater Britain.* New York: Macmillan, 1890.

Doyle, Arthur Conan. *A Study in Scarlet.* 1887. New York: Random House, 2003.

Duncan, Ian. *Scott's Shadow: The Novel in Romantic Edinburgh.* Princeton, N.J.: Princeton University Press, 2007.

Eagleton, Terry. "The Flight to the Real." In *Cultural Politics at the Fin de Siècle,* ed. Sally Ledger and Scott McCracken, 11–21. New York: Cambridge University Press, 1995.

Elphinstone, Mountstuart. *An Account of the Kingdom of Caubul, and Its Dependencies, in Persia, Tartary, and India.* London: Longman, Hurst, Rees, Orme and Brown, 1815. Accessed January 1, 2009. http://tiny.cc/Elphinstone

Ermarth, Elizabeth Deeds. *Realism and Consensus in the English Novel.* Princeton, N.J.: Princeton University Press, 1983.

———. "George Eliot's Conception of Sympathy." *Nineteenth-Century Fiction* 40:1 (June 1985): 23–42.

Esty, Jed. "The Colonial Bildungsroman: *The Story of an African Farm* and the Ghost of Goethe." *Victorian Studies* 49:3 (Spring 2007): 407–30.

Ewald, François. "Insurance and Risk." In *The Foucault Effect: Studies in Governmentality,* ed. Graham Burchell, Colin Gordon, and Peter Miller, 197–210. Chicago: University of Chicago Press, 1991.

Fillingham, Lydia. "'The Colorless Skein of Life': Threats to the Private Sphere in Conan Doyle's *A Study in Scarlet.*" *ELH* 56:3 (Autumn 1989): 667–88.

Finer, Herman. *English Local Government.* London: Methuen & Co., Ltd., 1946.

Foucault, Michel. *The History of Sexuality, Volume I: An Introduction.* New York: Random House, 1978.

———. "The Subject and Power." *Critical Inquiry* 8 (Summer 1982): 777–95.

———. "Two Lectures." In *Power/Knowledge: Selected Interviews and Other Writings 1972–1977,* ed. Colin Gordon, trans. Gordon et al., 78–108. New York: Pantheon Books, 1980.

———. "Governmentality." In *The Foucault Effect: Studies in Governmentality,* ed. Graham Burchell, Colin Gordon, and Peter Miller.

———. "Society Must Be Defended": Lectures at the Collège de France, 1975–1976, ed. Mauro Bertani and Alessandro Fontana, trans. David Macey. New York: Picador, 2003.
Freeden, Michael. *The New Liberalism: An Ideology of Social Reform*. Oxford: Clarendon Press, 1978.
Frierson, William C. *The English Novel in Transition, 1885–1940*. New York: Cooper Square Publishers, Inc., 1965.
Gissing, George. *New Grub Street*. 1891. New York: Penguin Books, 1985.
———. *The Odd Women*. 1893. Orchard Park, N.Y.: Broadview Press, 1998.
———. *Charles Dickens*. 1898. Port Washington, N.Y.: Kennikat Press, Inc., 1924.
———. *George Gissing on Fiction*, ed. Jacob and Cynthia Korg. London: Enitharmon Press, 1978.
———. *The Collected Letters of George Gissing*. Vol. 3, ed. Paul F. Mattheisen, Arthur C. Young, and Pierre Coustillas. Athens: Ohio University Press, 1992.
———. *The Collected Letters of George Gissing*. Vol. 5, ed. Mattheisen, Young, and Coustillas. Athens: Ohio University Press, 1992.
Gladstone, W. E. *Political Speeches in Scotland, November and December 1879*. Edinburgh: Andrew Elliot, 1880. Accessed December 20, 2008. http://tiny.cc/Gladstone
Goode, John. *George Gissing: Ideology and Fiction*. London: Clarke, Doble, & Brendon Ltd., 1978.
———. *Thomas Hardy: The Offensive Truth*. New York: Basil Blackwell, 1988.
Goodlad, Lauren M. E. "'A Middle Class Cut into Two': Historiography and Victorian National Character." *ELH* 67 (Spring 2000): 143–78.
———. *Victorian Literature and the Victorian State: Character and Governance in a Liberal Society*. Baltimore: The Johns Hopkins University Press, 2003.
Gramsci, Antonio. *Selections from the Prison Notebooks*, ed. and trans. Quinton Hoare and Geoffrey Nowell Smith. New York: International Publishers, 1989.
Grand, Sarah. *The Heavenly Twins*. 1893. Ann Arbor: University of Michigan Press, 1992.
———. "The Morals of Manner and Appearance." 1893. Reprint in *Journalistic Writings and Contemporary Reception*, ed. Ann Heilmann, 21–8. Vol. 1 of *Sex, Social Purity and Sarah Grand*, ed. Heilmann and Stephanie Forward. New York: Routledge, 2000.
———. "The Modern Girl." 1894. Reprint in *Journalistic Writings and Contemporary Reception*, ed. Heilmann, 36–44. Vol. 1 of *Sex, Social Purity and Sarah Grand*, ed. Heilmann and Forward. New York: Routledge, 2000.
———. "The New Aspect of the Woman Question." 1894. Reprint in *Journalistic Writings and Contemporary Reception*, ed. Heilmann, 29–35. Vol. 1 of *Sex, Social Purity and Sarah Grand*, ed. Heilmann and Forward. New York: Routledge, 2000.
———. "The Tree of Knowledge." 1894. Reprint in *Journalistic Writings and Contemporary Reception*, ed. Heilmann. Vol. 1 of *Sex, Social Purity and Sarah Grand*, ed. Heilmann and Forward, 65–6. New York: Routledge, 2000.

———. "What to Aim At." 1894. Reprint in *Journalistic Writings and Contemporary Reception*, ed. Heilmann. Vol. 1 of *Sex, Social Purity and Sarah Grand*, ed. Heilmann and Forward, 149–53. New York: Routledge, 2000.

———. "The Woman's Question: An Interview with Madame Sarah Grand." Interview by Sarah A. Tooley. 1896. Reprint in *Journalistic Writings and Contemporary Reception*, ed. Heilmann. Vol. 1 of *Sex, Social Purity and Sarah Grand*, ed. Heilmann and Forward, 220–9. New York: Routledge, 2000.

———. "Marriage Questions in Fiction: The Standpoint of a Typical Modern Woman." 1898. Reprint in *Journalistic Writings and Contemporary Reception*, ed. Heilmann. Vol. 1 of *Sex, Social Purity and Sarah Grand*, ed. Heilmann and Forward, 77–91. New York: Routledge, 2000.

Gregory, J. W. *The Story of the Road: From the Beginning down to A.D. 1931*. London: Maclehose & Co., 1931.

Hack, Daniel. "Revenge Stories of Modern Life." *Victorian Studies* 48:2 (Winter 2006): 277–86.

Hadley, Elaine. *Melodramatic Tactics: Theatricalized Dissent in the English Marketplace, 1800–1885*. Stanford, Calif.: Stanford University Press, 1995.

———. "On a Darkling Plain: Victorian Liberalism and the Fantasy of Agency." *Victorian Studies* 48:1 (Autumn 2005): 92–102.

Haggard, H. Rider. *King Solomon's Mines*. 1885. New York: Puffin Books, 1994.

Hall, Stuart, and Bill Schwarz. "State and Society, 1880–1930." In *Crises in the British State, 1880–1930*, ed. Mary Langan and Schwarz, 7–32. London: Hutchinson, 1985.

Hardy, Florence Emily. *The Life of Thomas Hardy, 1840–1928*. New York: St. Martin's Press, 1962.

Hardy, Thomas. "The Dorsetshire Labourer." 1883. Reprint in *Thomas Hardy's Personal Writings: Prefaces, Literary Opinions, Reminiscences*, ed. Harold Orel, 168–91. Lawrence: University Press of Kansas, 1966.

———. *The Woodlanders*. 1887. New York: Penguin Books, 1998.

———. "Candour in English Fiction." 1890. Reprint in *Thomas Hardy's Personal Writings: Prefaces, Literary Opinions, Reminiscences*, ed. Orel, 125–33. Lawrence: University Press of Kansas, 1966.

———. Preface from *Far from the Madding Crowd*. 1912. Reprint in *Thomas Hardy's Personal Writings: Prefaces, Literary Opinions, Reminiscences*, ed. Orel, 8–11. Lawrence: University Press of Kansas, 1966.

Harris, Jose. *Private Lives, Public Spirit: Britain, 1870–1914*. New York: Penguin Books, 1994.

Hasbach, W. *A History of the English Agricultural Labourer*. London: P. S. King & Son, 1908.

Heilmann, Ann. *New Woman Fiction: Women Writing First-Wave Feminism*. New York: St. Martin's Press, 2000.

———. "Narrating the Hysteric: *Fin-de-Siècle* Medical Discourse and Sarah Grand's *The Heavenly Twins* (1893)." In *The New Woman in Fiction and in Fact: Fin-de-Siècle Feminisms*, ed. Angelique Richardson and Chris Willis, 123–35. New York: Palgrave, 2001.

Heilmann, Ann, ed. *Journalistic Writings and Contemporary Reception.* Vol. 1 of *Sex, Social Purity, and Sarah Grand*, ed. Heilmann and Stephanie Forward. New York: Routledge, 2000.
Henty, G. A. *For Name and Fame, or Through Afghan Passes.* London: Blackie & Son, 1886. Accessed January 5, 2009. http://tiny.cc/Blackie
Hill, Jennifer. *White Horizon: The Arctic in the Nineteenth-Century British Imagination.* Albany: State University of New York Press, 2008.
Hindley, Geoffrey. *A History of Roads.* London: Peter Davies, 1971.
Hobhouse, L. T. *Liberalism and Other Writings*, ed. James Meadowcroft. New York: Cambridge University Press, 1994.
Hobsbawm, E. J. *The Age of Empire, 1875–1914.* New York: Vintage Books, 1987.
———. "Mass-Producing Traditions: Europe, 1870–1914." In *The Invention of Tradition*, ed. Hobsbawm and Terence Ranger, 263–307. New York: Cambridge University Press, 1992.
Horkheimer, Max, and Theodor W. Adorno. *Dialectic of Enlightenment*, trans. John Cumming. New York: Continuum, 1994.
Horstman, Allen. *Victorian Divorce.* New York: St. Martin's Press, 1985.
Hutcheon, Linda. *Irony's Edge: The Theory and Politics of Irony.* New York: Routledge, 1994.
Ingham, Patricia. *Thomas Hardy.* New York: Oxford University Press, 2003.
Inwood, Stephen. *A History of London.* New York: Carroll & Graf Publishers, Inc., 1998.
Jalland, Pat. *Women Marriage and Politics, 1860–1914.* New York: Clarendon Press, 1986.
Jameson, Fredric. "Reification and Utopia in Mass Culture." *Social Text* 1 (Winter 1979): 130–48.
———. *The Political Unconscious: Narrative as a Socially Symbolic Act.* Ithaca, N.Y.: Cornell University Press, 1981.
———. "The Realist Floor-Plan." In *On Signs*, ed. Marshall Blonsky, 373–83. Baltimore: Johns Hopkins University Press, 1985.
Jay, Elisabeth. *The Religion of the Heart: Anglican Evangelicalism and the Nineteenth-Century Novel.* Oxford: Clarendon Press, 1979.
Jordan, Spencer, Peter Wardley, and Matthew Woollard. "Emerging Modernity in an Urban Setting: Nineteenth-Century Bristol Revealed in Property Surveys." *Urban History* 26:2 (August 1999): 191–210.
Kennedy, Meegan. "Syphilis and the Hysterical Female: The Limits of Realism in Sarah Grand's *The Heavenly Twins.*" *Women's Writing* 11:2 (2004): 259–80.
Kucich, John. "Curious Dualities: *The Heavenly Twins* (1893) and Sarah Grand's Belated Modernist Aesthetics." In *The New Nineteenth Century: Feminist Readings of Underread Victorian Fiction*, ed. Barbara Leah Harman and Susan Meyer, 195–204. New York: Garland Publishing, Inc., 1996.
Laplanche, Jean, and Jean-Bertrand Pontalis. *The Languages of Psycho-Analysis*, trans. Donald Nicholson-Smith. New York: Norton, 1973.

———. "Fantasy and the Origins of Sexuality." In *Formations of Fantasy*, ed. Victor Burgin, James Donald, and Cora Kaplan, 6–35. New York: Routledge, 1986.
Levine, George. *The Realistic Imagination: English Fiction from Frankenstein to Lady Chatterley*. Chicago: University of Chicago Press, 1981.
Lloyd, David, and Paul Thomas. *Culture and the State*. New York: Routledge, 1998.
Loomba, Ania. *Colonialism/Postcolonialism*. New York: Routledge, 1998.
Mangum, Teresa. *Married, Middlebrow, and Militant: Sarah Grand and the New Woman Novel*. Ann Arbor: University of Michigan Press, 1998.
Mbembe, Achille. *On the Postcolony*. Berkeley: University of California Press, 2001.
McClintock, Anne. *Imperial Leather: Race, Gender, and Sexuality in the Colonial Contest*. New York: Routledge, 1995.
McCord, Norman. *British History, 1815–1906*. New York: Oxford University Press, 1991.
McCracken, Donal P., and Patricia McCracken. *Natal, the Garden Colony: Victorian Natal and the Royal Botanical Gardens, Kew*. Sandton: Frandsen Publishers, 1990.
McCracken, J. L. *The Cape Parliament, 1854–1910*. Oxford: Clarendon Press, 1967.
McKeon, Michael. "Grand Theory III." In *Theory of the Novel: A Historical Approach*, ed. McKeon, 317–20. Baltimore: Johns Hopkins University Press, 2000.
McLaughlin, Joseph. *Writing the Urban Jungle: Reading Empire in London from Doyle to Eliot*. Charlottesville: University Press of Virginia, 2000.
Mill, John Stuart. "On Liberty." 1859. In *On Liberty and Other Essays*, ed. John Gray. New York: Oxford University Press, 1998.
———. *Considerations on Representative Government*. Indianapolis: Bobbs-Merrill, 1958.
Miller, D. A. *The Novel and the Police*. Berkeley: University of California Press, 1988.
Miller, Jane Eldridge. *Rebel Women: Feminism, Modernism and the Edwardian Novel*. Chicago: University of Chicago Press, 1997.
Mitchell, Timothy. "The Limits of the State: Beyond Statist Approaches and Their Critics." *American Political Science Review* 85 (March 1991): 77–96.
———. "Society, Economy, and the State Effect." In *State/Culture: State-Formation after the Cultural Turn*, ed. George Steinmetz, 76–97. Ithaca, N.Y.: Cornell University Press, 1999.
Murphy, Patricia. *Time Is of the Essence: Temporality, Gender, and the New Woman*. Albany: State University of New York Press, 2001.
"Occasional Notes." *Pall Mall Gazette*. October 18, 1887: 4.
Pateman, Carole. "The Patriarchal Welfare State." In *Feminism, the Public and the Private*, ed. Joan B. Landes, 241–74. New York: Oxford University Press, 1998.
Perkin, Harold. *The Rise of Professional Society: England since 1880*. New York: Routledge, 1989.
Poole, Adrian. *Gissing in Context*. New York: Macmillan, 1975.
Poovey, Mary. *Making a Social Body: British Cultural Formation, 1830–1864*. Chicago: University of Chicago Press, 1995.

Porter, Andrew, ed. *Oxford History of the British Empire*. Vol. III. New York: Oxford University Press, 1999.

Pratt, Mary Louise. *Imperial Eyes: Travel Writing and Transculturation*. New York: Routledge, 1992.

Pykett, Lyn. *The "Improper" Feminine: The Women's Sensation Novel and the New Woman Writing*. New York: Routledge, 1992.

———. ed. *Reading Fin de Siècle Fictions*. New York: Longman, 1996.

Quinault, Roland. "Afghanistan and Gladstone's Moral Foreign Policy." *History Today* 52:12 (December 2002): 28–34.

Rabine, Leslie W. *Reading the Romantic Heroine: Text, History, Ideology*. Ann Arbor: University of Michigan Press, 1985.

Review of *The Heavenly Twins* by Grand. 1893. Reprint in *Journalistic Writings and Contemporary Reception*, ed. Heilmann, 411–13. Vol. 1 of *Sex, Social Purity and Sarah Grand*, ed. Heilmann and Forward. New York: Routledge, 2000.

Rich, Eric E. *The Education Act of 1870: A Study of Public Opinion*. London: Longmans, Green and Co. Ltd., 1970.

Richardson, Angelique. "The Eugenization of Love: Sarah Grand and the Morality of Genealogy." *Victorian Studies* 42 (Winter 1999/2000): 230–55.

Ritchie, David G. *The Principles of State Interference: Four Essays on the Political Philosophy of Mr. Herbert Spencer, J. S. Mill, and T. H. Green*. London: Swan Sonnenschein & Co., 1891.

Roberts, David. *Victorian Origins of the British Welfare State*. New Haven: Yale University Press, 1960.

Rose, Jacqueline. *Sexuality in the Field of Vision*. London: Verso, 2005.

Rothfield, Lawrence. *Vital Signs: Medical Realism in Nineteenth-Century Fiction*. Princeton, N.J.: Princeton University Press, 1992.

Rylance, Rick. *Victorian Psychology and British Culture, 1850–1880*. New York: Oxford University Press, 2000.

Said, Edward W. *Culture and Imperialism*. New York: Vintage Books, 1993.

Sandeman, George Amelius Crawshay. *Metternich*. New York: Brentano, 1911. Accessed September 22, 2011. http://catalog.hathitrust.org/Record/009669356.

Saunders, Christopher, and Iain R. Smith. "Southern Africa, 1795–1910." In *The Oxford History of the British Empire, Volume III: The Nineteenth Century*, ed. Andrew Porter, 597–623. New York: Oxford University Press, 1999.

Scarry, Elaine. "Work and the Body in Hardy and Other Nineteenth-Century Novelists." *Representations* 3 (Summer 1983): 90–123.

Schreiner, Olive. *The Story of an African Farm*. 1883. Orchard Park, N.Y.: Broadview, 2003.

———. *Letters 1871–99*, ed. Richard Rive. Cape Town: David Philip, 1987.

Scott, Walter. *Waverley*. 1814. New York: Penguin Books, 1985.

———. "Culloden Papers." *The Quarterly Review* 14:28 (January 1816): 283–333.

Sedgwick, Eve Kosofsky. *Epistemology of the Closet*. Berkeley: University of California Press, 1990.

———. *Touching Feeling: Affect, Pedagogy, Performativity*. Durham, N.C.: Duke University Press, 2003.

Sexby, J. J. *The Municipal Parks, Gardens, and Open Spaces of London: Their History and Associations*. London: Elliot Stock, 1905.

Shapple, Deborah L. "Artful Tales of Origination in Olive Schreiner's *The Story of an African Farm*." *Nineteenth-Century Literature* 59:1 (2004): 78–114.

Sheppard, Francis. *London: A History*. New York: Oxford University Press, 1998.

Smith, Adam. *The Theory of Moral Sentiments*. 1759. Indianapolis: Liberty Fund, 1984.

Spencer, Herbert. *The Man versus the State*. 1884. Indianapolis: Liberty Classics, 1981.

Steedman, Carolyn Kay. *Landscape for a Good Woman: A Story of Two Lives*. New Brunswick, N.J.: Rutgers University Press, 1994.

Steinmetz, George. "Culture and the State." Introduction to *State/Culture: State-Formation after the Cultural Turn*, ed. Steinmetz, 1–49. Ithaca, N.Y.: Cornell University Press, 1999.

Stewart, Kathleen. *A Space on the Side of the Road: Cultural Poetics in an "Other" America*. Princeton, N.J.: Princeton University Press, 1996.

Stoler, Ann Laura. *Race and the Education of Desire: Foucault's History of Sexuality and the Colonial Order of Things*. Durham, N.C.: Duke University Press, 1995.

Stott, Rebecca. "'Scaping the Body: Of Cannibal Mothers and Colonial Landscapes." In *The New Woman in Fiction and in Fact: Fin-de-Siècle Feminisms*, ed. Richardson and Willis, 150–66. New York: Palgrave, 2001.

Taussig, Michael. *The Nervous System*. New York: Routledge, 1992.

Tennyson, Alfred. "The Lotos-Eaters." 1842. Reprint in *The Norton Anthology of English Literature*. Vol. 2, ed. M. H. Abrams, 1063–7. New York: Norton, 1993.

Thane, Pat. *Foundations of the Welfare State*. New York: Longman, 1982.

Tucker, Irene. *A Probable State: The Novel, the Contract, and the Jews*. Chicago: University of Chicago Press, 2000.

"Under the Black Flag: Who the Men Are That Follow It, and Why." *Pall Mall Gazette*. October 19, 1887: 5.

Van Drenth, Annemieke, and Francisca de Haan. *The Rise of Caring Power: Elizabeth Fry and Josephine Butler in Britain and the Netherlands*. Amsterdam: Amsterdam University Press, 1999.

Webb, Sidney. "Historic." In *Fabian Essays in Socialism*, ed. G. Bernard Shaw, 30–61. London: The Fabian Society, 1889.

———. *The London Programme*. London: Swan Sonnenschein & Co., 1891.

———. Preface to *A History of the English Agricultural Labourer* by W. Hasbach, vii–xi. London: P. S. King & Son, 1908.

Webb, Sidney, and Beatrice Webb. *English Local Government: The Story of the King's Highway*. New York: Longmans, Green and Co., 1913.

"What Must Be Done at Once." *Pall Mall Gazette*. November 10, 1887: 1.

Williams, Merryn. *Thomas Hardy and Rural England*. New York: Columbia University Press, 1972.

Williams, Raymond. *The Country and the City.* New York: Oxford University Press, 1973.
———. *Marxism and Literature.* New York: Oxford University Press, 1977.
———. *Culture and Society, 1780–1950.* New York: Columbia University Press, 1983.
Windscheffel, Ruth Clayton. "Gladstone and Scott: Family, Identity, and Nation." *The Scottish Historical Review* LXXXVI, 1: No. 221 (April 2007): 69–95. Accessed December 26, 2008. http://tiny.cc/Windscheffel
Winter, Sarah. "Curiosity as Didacticism in *The Old Curiosity Shop.*" *Novel: A Forum on Fiction* 34 (Fall 2000): 28–55.
Young, Arlene. Introduction to *The Odd Women* by Gissing, 9–21. Orchard Park, N.Y.: Broadview Press, 1998.
Žižek, Slavoj. "The Spectre of Ideology." Introduction to *Mapping Ideology*, ed. Žižek, 1–33. New York: Verso, 1994.
———. *The Plague of Fantasies.* New York: Verso, 1997.

Index

administrative rationality, Bonaparte (*The Story of an African Farm*), 37
Adorno, Theodor, 168
Afghanistan, 15, 22
   Elphinstone experience, 58–60
   as geographical expression, 45
   Great Britain and, 46, 47, 49
   imperialism *versus* colonialism, 46
   India and, 47–48, 59–60
   pre-nationhood, 45
   Scottish Highlands and, 49, 50–51, 54, 56–58, 60–61
   Second Anglo-Afghan War, 45, 47, 50, 51–52, 61, 68, 72, 75, 81
   Sherlock Holmes, 48
   vagueness in description, 48
   Victorian period, 46
Afghans
   changeability, *For Name and Fame,* 63, 69, 70
   Gladstone description, 53–55
   Indians and, Elphinstone, 59–60
   For Name and Fame, other colonized subjects and, 69
   Scottish Highlanders, Sir Walter Scott and, 58
   sovereignty, individual, 45–46
agricultural laborers, peasants as, 94
agricultural capitalism, 85–86
Aguirre, Robert, 165
Allotments Act of 1887, 167
aloof rule, 22, 34, 35, 39, 44
An Account of the Kingdom of Caubul (Elphinstone), Culloden Papers and, 57–58

Anderson, Amanda, 136
Anderson, Benedict, 1, 31, 90, 167–68
Andrew, W. P., 45, 48
Anglo-Afghan War. *See* Second Anglo-Afghan War
anti-romance method of Olive Schreiner, 27
Arata, Stephen, 18, 71, 72, 165
Ardis, Ann, New Woman fictions, 18, 135
Arendt, Hannah, 22, 34–35, 40–41, 164
Aretxaga, Begoña, 163
Arnold, Matthew, 41, 67, 105, 109, 111–13, 123, 126, 128, 142–43, 165
associationist romance, 166
Austen, Jane, 122

Bakhtin, Mikhail, novelization, 128, 169
Barrell, John, 92, 166
Barry, Sir Charles, Nelson Column, 168
Barry, William, 145–46
Basil (Collins), 165
Battersea Park, 116–17
Beer, Gillian, 92
Beerbohm, Max, 18
Bellamy, Liz, backward cultures, 166–67
Berlant, Lauren, 24, 107, 136–37, 165, 166, 168
Bhabha, Homi, 47
Bildungsroman of *The Heavenly Twins,* 138–39

183

184 Index

biopower, 14–15, 35, 44, 108, 109, 113, 132, 134, 148, 149, 168
Bleak House (Dickens), 4–5, 7
"Bloody Sunday," Trafalgar Square, 120
Boehmer, Elleke, 164
Bogiatzis, Demetris, 135
Bonnell, Marilyn, 135
Boone, Joseph Allen, 125
Bowlby, Rachel, 18, 127
boys' adventure novels, 165
Brantlinger, Patrick, 46
breakdown and realist novels, 18, 89, 161
Brennan, Teresa, 17, 168
Bristow, Joseph, 165
British Empire, imperialized sites, 46–47
British realist novels, 18
Broomfield, Andrea L., 136, 169
Butler, Judith, 134

Cannadine, David, 46
Chambers, Ross, 166
Chandler, James, 56
character, 6, 52, 58, 59, 63, 70, 94, 112, 149–50, 156, 158, 167, 168
Choi, Tina, 168
Chrisman, Laura, 18
citizens, 12, 87, 134
citizenship, Hobhouse, 16
city parks, 116–17
Clapham, John, 166
Clark, Gail, boys' adventure novels, 165
class hierarchy, 62–63, 94, 109, 167
Clifton, Gloria C., municipalization, 168
collectivism, 9, 147–49
Collings, Jesse (M.P.), Allotments Act of 1887, 167
Collins, Wilkie, *Basil,* 165
colonial life, *The Story of an African Farm,* 27
Communist Manifesto (Marx and Engel), *The Heavenly Twins* and, 140

Considerations on Representative Government (Mill), 86
Contagious Diseases Acts, 132
Corrigan, Phillip, 9–10
cow-kind of woman, 137–38
Culloden Papers (Scott), 22, 49, 56, 57–58
culture, 19, 23, 57, 111–13, 115, 116–17, 122–23, 126–27, 128, 129
Culture and Anarchy (Arnold), 41, 112

Dames, Nicholas, 57, 167
De Certeau, Michel, 90–91, 166
De Laura, David J., 88
Deleuze, Gilles, 108
Demos (Gissing), 109
dependence and domination, 126
Dicey, A. V., shift from individualism to collectivism, 9
Dickens, Charles, 4–5, 7, 63, 119, 122
disciplinary individualism, 2–3
discipline, 14, 162
Discipline and Punish (Foucault), 14
"The Dorsetshire Labourer" (Hardy), 85–86
Doyle, Arthur Conan, 48, 71, 72. See also *A Study in Scarlet*
Duncan, Ian, and Sir Walter Scott, 57–58

education, state and, 6
Education Act of 1870, 9
Elphinstone, Sir Mountstuart, 49, 57–58, 59–60
emotional attachments of women, *For Name and Fame,* 63–64
English Local Government: The Story of the King's Highway (Webb and Webb), 92–93, 166
Enlightenment, myths returned, 99
Ermarth, Elizabeth, 18
Esty, Jed, 26
ethic of care, 135
ethical state, 5, 9, 150, 158

eugenic love, 144–45
eugenics, 136, 144
everyday, the (and everyday life), 8, 13, 20, 23, 89, 90, 108, 113–14, 161

Fabian Socialists, 5, 92
fantasy, 1, 20, 39, 44, 47, 49, 88, 164
feminine, 61–62, 63–64
feminism, capitalism and, 135–36
fictions and suffering of women, 137
fin de siècle, 18, 88, 131
Finer, Herman, 166
For Name and Fame, or Through Afghan Passes (Henty), 45, 48
   Afghans, 63, 69, 70
   Amir Sheer-Ali, Gladstone's Liberal government, 69–70
   birthmark as signature, class hierarchy and, 65–66
   Captain Ripon, 63–64, 65
   character depth, 62
   class hierarchy, 62–63
   England's domestic scene, 63
   family structure, 66
   femininity, emotional attachments, 63–64
   gypsies, 64
   masculinity, 61–62, 63
   orphan of high birth, 66
   racism, 62
   Ripons, 64, 65
   Second Anglo-Afghan War, 61
   self-development and, 71
   Tom's abduction, 65–66
   William Gale, 61, 67–69, 70–71
   Yakoob Khan, 70
   Yossouf, 70
Foucault, Michel
   biopower, 14–15, 35, 149
   Discipline and Punish, 14
   "Governmentality," 2, 14
   life insurance, 168
   sovereignty, 14, 35
Frankfurt School, 168

Freeden, Michael, 148
French naturalism, *The Heavenly Twins*, 142
Frierson, William, 18

Gaskell, Elizabeth, *Mary Barton*, 106–7
General Highway Act of 1862, 93
geographical expression of Afghanistan, 45
Gissing, George. See also *The Odd Women*
   Austen, Jane and, 122
   culture and, 112–13
   Demos, 109
   Dickens, Charles and, 122
   hope and contentment, 110
   love plot, 123
   The Odd Women, 7–8, 17, 18, 23, 109–30
   political personhood, 117
   realism, Young, Arlene on, 114
   state and, 113–14, 115
   Tennyson's death, 168
   Trafalgar Square riots, 119–20
Gladstone, William
   Afghans, 50–51, 53–54, 56, 57, 60
   India, repressive laws, 58–59
   Jacobite rebellion, 55–56
   Liberal government, 52–53
   Midlothian speeches, 48, 50, 54–56
   political background, 50
   Second Anglo-Afghan War, 51–52
   Tory government, 52, 54
Goode, John, 88
Goodlad, Lauren, 3, 16, 167, 169
governmentality, 3, 14, 76, 143, 148
Gramsci, Antonio
   ethical state, 5–6, 9
   hegemony, 9
Grand, Sarah. See also *The Heavenly Twins*
   abstractness of knowledge, 146–47
   cow-kind of woman, 137–38
   eugenic principles, 136

The Heavenly Twins, 16, 23–24,
  131–59
  marriage, 143–45
  men, 132, 133
  New Liberals and, 147
  optimism, 156
  rivalry with Eliza Lynn Linton, 136,
    169
Gregory, J. W., 166

Hack, Daniel, 80, 165
Hadley, Elaine, 82, 165
Haggard, H. Rider, *King Solomon's
  Mines*, 30, 164
Hall, Stuart, 9, 147–48
Hardy, Thomas. See also *The
  Woodlanders*
  Arcadian innocents, 86
  associationist romance, 166
  characters, as collections of matter,
    108
  characters in flux, 102
  "The Dorsetshire Labourer," 85–86
  historical conditions of works, 88
  Jude the Obscure, 94
  landowning peasant class, 94
  post-Romantic culture, 95
  sensations and, 89
  state fantasy and humans, 108
  Tess of the D'Urbervilles, 94
Harris, Jose, 10
Hasbach, W., 167
The Heavenly Twins (Grand), 16, 23–24
  Angelica, 132, 145, 151–53
  attachment to ignorance, 138
  Bildungsroman, 138–39
  bodily discipline, 136
  chimes from cathedral, 142–43
  church and clergy, 141
  Colonel Colquhoun, Evadne's
    promise, 154
  Communist Manifesto and, 140
  contradictions, 132–33, 141
  Dr. Galbraith, 156, 157–58

  Edith, 132, 151–53
  ethic of care, 135
  Evadne, 132, 138, 139–40, 154
  the female complaint (Berlant), 136
  female desire, 135
  feminism, capitalism and, 135–36
  femininity, normative, 135
  fighting for freedom and upholding
    structures, 132
  French naturalism, 142
  Galbraith, as stand-in for state, 133
  gender identity, 135
  health of organism and individual
    parts, 155
  heterosexism, 135
  hysteria, 133–34, 135, 154
  Ideala, 146
  Malta, 152–53
  medical establishment critique,
    155–56
  men, 133, 151, 155–56
  Mrs. Malcomson, 141–42
  Mrs. Orton Beg, 138
  New Order, 146
  New Woman and, 131
  publicity, 132–33
  self-actualization, 140
  sexual passion, 145, 149–50
  sexually transmitted disease, 151
  state, protection of women, 133
  State references, 133
  syphilis and male sexual desire, 151
  version of realism, 140–41
  voluntarism, 140
  women, 132, 133, 136, 137
Heilmann, Ann, 135
Henty, G. A., 45, 48, 61. See also *For
  Name and Fame, or Through Afghan
  Passes*
Hill, Jennifer, 165
Hindley, Geoffrey, 166
"Historic" (Webb), 11, 12–14, 114
Hobhouse, L. T., 5–6, 16, 148–49
Hobsbawm, Eric, 46, 164

Hobson, J. A., 5, 164
Horkheimer, Max, 168
Horstman, Allen, 168
Hyper-Concordance (Victorian Literary Studies website), 168
hysteria, 133, 134, 135, 154, 155

ideal individual, John Stuart Mill and, 74
identity, womanhood and, 137
ideology, 1, 5, 21, 137, 140, 142, 152
imagination, state fantasy and, 164
imagined community, 31
imperialized sites of British Empire, 46–47, 81
India, 47–48, 58–60
individualism shift to collectivism, 9
Ingham, Patricia, 88
insurance, 111, 168
interventionist state, 61–62, 96, 149, 158
Inwood, Stephen, 116, 168

Jacobite rebellion, 55–56
Jameson, Fredric, 89, 161
Jordan, Spencer, Peter Wardley, and Matthew Woollard, 166
Jude the Obscure (Hardy), 94

Kennedy, Meegan, 136
King Solomon's Mines (Haggard), 30, 164
Koselleck, Reinhart, 57
Kucich, John, 135

landowning peasant class. *See* peasant class
Langbauer, Laurie, 72
legal-political knowledge, 87
Levine, George, Victorian realists, 18, 140–41, 161
liberal governance, 28, 61–62
Liberal government, Gladstone, 52–53
liberal individuality, 23, 46, 51, 67, 82, 83, 101, 113, 133, 161, 165
Liberal Party, Spencer and, 12

liberal-realist classification, 20
liberal state, rhetoric of sympathy, 88
liberal subject, 18, 24, 28, 78, 81, 89, 105, 106, 108, 132, 150, 159, 161
liberal theory, 4, 5, 95
liberalism, 16, 82, 149
Liberalism (Hobhouse), 5–6, 148–49
Linton, Eliza Lynn, 136, 169
Livesey, Ruth, 21
Lloyd, David, 9, 133–34
Local Government Act, 115
Locke, John, *Two Treatises on Government*, 4
loitering, 166
London, municipalism, 115
Loomba, Ania, 46
"The Lotos-Eaters" (Tennyson), 111–12
love plot of romances, 123
Lukács, Georg, 19, 161

Maiwand, Battle of, 71, 72, 74, 75, 77, 79, 81
male romance genre, Sherlock Holmes, 72
Malta, 136, 152–53
Maltz, Diana, 21
The Man versus the State (Spencer), 6, 12–15, 16, 101–2, 114
Mangum, Teresa, 135
manhood, *For Name and Fame*, 61, 62
manual laborers, political discussions, 86
marginalized persons, 43, 86
marriage
    Grand, Sarah on, 143–45
    as legal arrangement, 98
    love plot of romances, 123
    New Woman fictions, 135
    optimism and, 123–27
    provisions for, 121–22
    self-image and, 126
    sexual relation and, 97
    state and, 19
    utility of, Hardy on, 97

Marxism and Literature (Williams), 8
Mary Barton (Gaskell), 106–7
masculinity, 61–62, 63, 131
Matrimonial Causes Act of 1857, 86, 87, 103, 104, 107
Mbembe, Achille, 163
McCord, Norman, 166, 168
McEwan, Ian, *Saturday,* Perowne's social incoherence and subjective harmoniousness, 165
McKeon, Michael, novelization, 169
McLaughlin, Joseph, 71, 72
melodramas, 36, 39
men, immorality and weakening of society, 151
Metropolitan Board of Works (London), 115
Mill, John Stuart, 74, 86, 101, 139, 165, 168
Miller, D. A., 72
Mitchell, Timothy, 3, 24, 126, 163–64
Mormons, British authors on, 72–73
municipalism, 115

naming, and ownership, 33
nation, 1–2, 33
nation building, British in Afghanistan, 47
national fantasy, 1, 3, 94–95, 98
nationalism, 1
Nelson Column, 168
New Liberals, 5, 6, 147, 148–49
New Woman, 18, 131, 135
novelization, 127–28, 169
novels, 1, 7, 8, 11, 15–21, 24–25, 36, 123, 132, 161–62

The Odd Women (Gissing), 7–8, 23
  Alice Madden, 111
  Bella, 124
  city park, 116–17
  contentment and hope, 110
  culture, degradation, 126
  Dr. Madden, 111, 112–13
  emotional intensity of the women, 110
  Everard Barfoot, 7–8, 121–22, 125, 126, 127
  feminism and, 109
  gender, genre and, 110
  hope, 121–23
  insurance, 111
  London, 114
  Monica Madden, 111, 115–16, 117, 121
  optimism, 109, 110
  political personhood, 117
  politics, commodification of, 126
  religion, 115–16
  reordering of bodies, 118
  Rhoda Nunn, 7–8, 111, 121–22, 124–25, 126, 127–29
  romance reading, 124
  satirization of characters' satire of politics, 122–23
  state, 110, 111
  Trafalgar Square, 118–19
  unconventionality, 127
  Virginia Madden, 111, 117–20, 121
  Widdowson, meeting with Monica, 116, 117
  womanhood and theory, 124
  women, vulnerability, 109
  women's detachment, 121
Oliver Twist (Dickens), masculinity and, 63
On Liberty (Mill), 101, 165, 168
optimism, 101, 109, 110, 123–27
ownership, naming and, 33

paternal government, Dr. John Watson, 76
peasant class, 94, 167
Perkin, Harold, 167, 169
political authority, 38, 161
political discussions of disenfranchised classes, 86
political knowledge, acquisition, 100

politics, 87, 122–23, 126
Poole, Adrian,
　nineteenth-century representations of London, 168
　romantic relationships of Gissing, 126
Poovey, Mary, disciplinary individualism, 2–3
Porter, Andrew, 46
power, 2–5, 11–12, 14, 15–17, 22, 24–28, 35–37, 39, 43, 44, 49, 102, 132, 134, 148–49, 158, 159, 162
Pratt, Mary Louise, 164

racism, *For Name and Fame* (Henty), 62
realism, 18, 39, 140–42, 161
Reform Act of 1884, 94
Reform Bill of 1867, 9
religion, isolation of Monica Madden, 115–16
reproduction, 33–34
revenge, 80–81, 165
rhetoric of sympathy, liberal state and, 88
Richardson, Angelique, eugenic love, 18, 136, 144
Ritchie, D. G., 5
road, 89–90, 91, 92–93, 96, 166
romance plots, 123–24, 166
Rose, Jacqueline, 17, 134, 161
Rothfield, Lawrence, detective fiction, 74, 83, 165–66
rural working class, 85–86, 94
Rylance, Rick, 166

Said, Edward, 46
Saturday (McEwan), Perowne, social incoherence and subjective harmoniousness, 165
Sayer, Derek, 9–10
Scarry, Elaine, 89, 108
Schreiner, Olive, 21–22, 24, 27, 30–31, 32–33. See also *The Story of an African Farm*
Schwarz, Bill, 9, 147–48

Scott, Sir Walter, 49, 56–58
Scottish Enlightenment, Sir Walter Scott, 56–57
Scottish Highlanders, 49, 50–51, 57, 58, 60
Scramble for Africa, 29
Second Anglo-Afghan War, 45, 51–52, 61, 68–69, 72, 80–81
self, liberal personhood and, 28
sexual difference, 17
sexuality, 38, 97, 145
Shapple, Deborah, 26
Sheppard, Francis, 168
Sherlock Holmes, 48, 71, 72, 81–83
Smith, Adam, *The Theory of Moral Sentiments*, 106
socialism, Sidney Webb, 13
socialist-feminist realist fiction, 20
socialist utopic novels, 20
South Africa, Hannah Arendt, 34
sovereignty, 14, 35, 44, 45–46
Spencer, Herbert, 6, 11, 12–13, 27, 101–2, 114
state
　as agent of transformation, 5
　appropriations, 115
　burden of, 6
　as character, Dickens, 4
　city parks and, 116–17
　dependence and domination, 126
　Dickens, Charles, 122
　and education, 6
　effect on natural order, 101
　ethical state, 9
　evils and, 6
　interventionist, 61–62, 96, 149, 158
　marriage, 19, 121–22, 144–45
　Mitchell, Timothy on, 126
　nation and, 1–2
　New Liberals, standards set by state, 6
　as origin of power, 2
　power, fantasies of marginalized and, 43
　production of subjects, 110

psychoanalytic inquiry, 1–2
public spaces, 113–14
role of, Dr. John Watson, 76
sacralization, 99
as site of optimism, 19, 88–89, 110, 162
subjectification, 111
state fantasy, 3–7, 8, 13, 14, 15, 16, 17, 18, 19, 21, 23, 24, 26, 87–89, 96, 107, 108, 131, 159, 161–62, 164
state subjectivity, 88, 89, 161
The Story of an African Farm (Schreiner), 21–22, 24, 26
  administrative rationality, 37
  antagonisms among groups, 32
  anti-romance method, 27
  Bonaparte, 34, 35–39, 40
  British colonization, 29
  characters, 28–29, 33–34, 37–38, 41, 43
  colonial life, 27
  dedication, 32–33
  fragmentary nature of colonial world, 30
  high imperialism, era of, 29
  inscription, 33
  knowledge and material wealth, 31
  landscape depictions, 30
  liberal governance, 28
  melodramas and, 36
  military state of farm, 38
  mirrors, 32
  moonlight, 30–31
  opening paragraph, 30
  Otto, Bonaparte and, 35–36
  photograph obsession, 31–32
  Ralph Iron, 32–33
  realism over melodrama, 39
  reality-effect of, 27
  recent scholarship on, 26
  Scramble for Africa, 29
  state, 27, 29
  stranger, belief in nothing, 40–41
  themes, 32
  violence, 34
  Waldo, 39–40, 41–43
Stowe, Harriet Beecher, *Uncle Tom's Cabin*, 106–7
structure of feeling, 122, 168
A Study in Scarlet (Doyle), 22, 48, 71–84
subjection, external forces of power, 134–35
sympathy, 23, 39–40, 80, 88, 95, 105–7, 136, 153

Taussig, Michael, 43, 163
Tennyson, Alfred, 111–12
Tess of the D'Urbervilles (Hardy), 94
The Theory of Moral Sentiments (Smith), 106
Thomas, Paul, 9, 133–34
Tory government, 52
Trafalgar Square, 115, 118–20
The Transmission of Affect (Brennan), 168
Trollope, Anthony, 82
Tucker, Irene, 18
Two Treatises on Government (Locke), 4

Uncle Tom's Cabin (Stowe), 106–7

Victorian Afghanistan, 22, 48, 72
Victorian Literary Studies website, 168
Victorian literature, 3, 161
Victorian period, 9–10, 46, 80
Victorian state subjectivity, psychic split, 161
violence, 34, 38
voting, 94
vulnerability, women, *The Odd Women* (Gissing), 109

The Warden (Trollope), 82
Waverley (Scott), 57
Webb, Beatrice, *English Local Government: The Story of the King's Highway*, 92–93, 166
Webb, Sidney, 5, 11, 12–14, 27, 92–93, 94, 114, 166

Williams, Raymond, 8, 18, 168
Windscheffel, Ruth Clayton, Gladstone's Midlothian speeches, 55–56
womanhood, identity and, 137
women, 33, 136, 137–38
The Woodlanders (Hardy), 22–23, 85
   Beaucock, divorce and, 99–100
   Bristol, 90
   desire between Giles and Grace, 104
   divorce, news of, 99–100
   Edred Fitzpiers, 96–98, 99
   fantasies, 87–88
   Felice Charmond, 97, 102–3
   George Melbury, 100–1, 102
   Giles Winterborne, 86, 87–88, 103
   Grace Melbury, 86, 87–88, 96–97, 102, 104, 105–7
   imperial law, 86
   law, idea of reshaping subjects, 102
   liberal theories of personhood, 95
   Little Hintock, 94–95
   local as backbone of nation, 94–95
   marriage, 96, 97, 98
   Matrimonial Causes Act of 1857, 86, 87, 103, 104, 107–8
   meridional line, 90–91
   opening sentences, 91–92
   political illiteracy of characters, 87
   political knowledge, acquisition, 100
   rambler, 90, 93–94
   road, 89–90, 91, 92, 95, 96, 166
   secularization of society and sacralization of state, 99
   setting, 89–91, 95
   state, 88–89, 92, 107
   state intervention, 88
   state subjectivity, 88, 89
   sympathy, 88
world-historical epistemic project, 57

Young, Arlene, Gissing's realism, 114

Žižek, Slavoj, 20